CLOUD BY DAY

Photo Courtesy of U. S. Steel Corporation

END OF THE DAY'S WORK—Work in the mine is ended and these miners are alighting from the cage at the top of the shaft. Miners greet each other by first names, and all follow the friendly custom of painting names on hats

CLOUD BY DAY

THE STORY OF COAL AND COKE AND PEOPLE

MURIEL EARLEY SHEPPARD

Heritage
202 Lexington Place
Uniontown, Pennsylvania 15401

To my parents

CRAYTON and FLORENCE EARLEY
and my sister LOUISE

With appreciation and affection

FOREWORD

WHAT I HAVE TO SAY IN THIS BOOK REFERS TO THE Coke Region that is my home, to our miners, our operators, our living conditions, our misunderstandings, our peculiar problems. This is a territory important enough to affect national life, a sort of economic Medicine Hat where labor weather brews; but it is also small enough for one to see the pattern of things and be more or less acquainted with those who make up the opposing factions.

If the question arises: Who is she *for?* Is she pro-labor or pro-management? the answer is: I am not pro-anybody, only pro-people. The miners needed a union; they have it and it is a good thing—but only so long as the leaders remember that it is made up of people who are first of all American citizens, whether by birth or by adoption. When the individual shrinks to a pawn in big-time politics, that is something else.

When I talk about management I am thinking about men, many of whom I know as fathers and husbands, carrying heavy responsibilities under trying conditions, often working longer hours than the men they employ, who let me go underground in their mines, loaned me guides and paraphernalia over and over again, and helped me with technical questions.

When I talk about labor I am thinking of individual people taken together; of the mechanic who explained the intricacies of the shining machines in a hoist-house and how proud he was of them; of the friendly foreman in a carbarn who showed me how the electric motors which haul

vii

the mine-trips are designed to prevent short circuits that might set off an explosion; of the machine-boss underground who ran coal-loading and -cutting machines up into a lighted heading where I could see what was going on when they were in operation. I think of the coal miners dressed in their Sunday clothes, singing in the colored light heavy with incense in the white brick church with the lily-bulb turrets under the hill at New Salem; and I remember the old miner from the county home who used to wait by the road for my husband to drive past on his way to work to ask for a ride to church on Saints' days, and how, when he got out of the car, he would stand bareheaded in any weather while he said politely, "I thank you and I thank Mister God for this so great kindness."

In writing this book I have tried to explain the present in the Coke Region by what has gone before; to explain why certain abuses of the past came to be, and where they are no longer a factor to be reckoned with in our district, I have indicated when they ended. Both sides have trespasses to be forgiven as well as to forgive. When we are able to do that and start anew, there is a chance for peace in the Coke Region.

MURIEL EARLEY SHEPPARD

Uniontown, Pennsylvania
December 9, 1946

ACKNOWLEDGMENTS

I am happy to have this opportunity to express my gratitude to my husband, Mark Sheppard, for his constant encouragement and valuable advice during my work on *Cloud by Day:* to Frank Meléga for permission to reproduce three of his paintings as illustrations for the text and book jacket, as well as for invaluable assistance with research material; to Mr. J. H. Lowrey of Augusta, Georgia, for criticism and counsel; to Mrs. H. D. Hutchinson and the staff of the Uniontown Library for their assistance and cooperation; to Miss Rose Demorest, Librarian of the Pennsylvania Room, Carnegie Institute, Pittsburgh; to Donald Maust for suggestions and introductions as well as for the loan of photographs and research material; to Ann Kulamer Shoun of Alexandria, Virginia; to Mr. William Gladden, Fayette County Probation Officer; to Canon Bernard C. Newman and Emil Burgess of the Fayette County Delinquency Clinics; to Mr. B. T. Silman and Mr. F. H. Shimshock of the Fayette County Prothonotary's Office; to Mr. Harry Gould of the U. S. Immigration and Naturalization Service; to Mr. and Mrs. David Day of the American Friends Service Committee's Penncraft Housing Project; and to Mrs. Fred Perkins of the Fayette County Red Cross.

I am deeply indebted to the Reverend George Yankovich of Holy Trinity Russian Orthodox Church in New Salem for making it possible for me to familiarize myself with the customs of the Eastern Orthodox Church, for invitations to special services, and for loaning me research material in translation; to Reverend Mother Macrina of the Order of the Sisters of

St. Basil at Mount St. Macrina in Uniontown, and to Sister Augustine, Sister Agnes, Sister Deria, Sister Sylvestre, Sister Alexandria, and Sister Evangelista for their many kindnesses, as well as to Father Bernadini of St. John's Greek Catholic Church; to Mr. J. G. Carroll, Sr., Miss Edna Evans, Miss Ella Roselle, Mr. Rodney D. Mosier, principal of the Uniontown Senior High School, Chief of Police Alfred Davis, Mr. Wiley Byers, Mr. Buell Whitehill, Mr. Chester M. Lingle, Mrs. Jasper Cope, Mr. and Mrs. Donald Dowlin of Crucible, Miss Elizabeth O'Bryon, Miss Angela Gigliotti, Evelyn Abraham Benson, Miss Margaret Lewis, Mr. Louis Kamensky, Mr. George Swetnam of the *Pittsburgh Press,* and Miss Ruth Love of the *Morning Herald.* I want to thank Hurford Crosman of the Philadelphia Office of the American Friends Service Committee, Mrs. James Carroll, the Pittsburgh Station of the U. S. Bureau of Mines, and Mr. W. Everett McLaine, Eric Ferguson, and Robert W. Evans of the United States Steel Corporation for the loan of photographs.

Miss Virginia Reynolds of the University of North Carolina Press has been of great assistance to me in the preparation of *Cloud by Day* for publication. I am especially grateful to Miss Ida Grove for taking the responsibility of my house during the several years while this work was in process so that I might be free to do the research and writing.

MURIEL EARLEY SHEPPARD

CONTENTS

xi

ILLUSTRATIONS

Between pages 238-239

CLOUD BY DAY

"The pillar of cloud by day, and the pillar of fire by night, departed not from before the people."—EXODUS 13:22

CHAPTER I

SMOKE OVER THE VALLEY

NEAR THE TOP OF CHESTNUT RIDGE A PROMONTORY looks out over the tops of second-growth saplings to a broad dim country like a cloudy lake washing the lower slopes of the mountain barrier. This is the Coke Region, the land of silver cinders: a strip of undulating valley in southern Pennsylvania, lying between the Allegheny Mountains and the Monongahela River and extending a little beyond, whose mines provide the coal that makes the coke for the great steel mills of Pittsburgh and the Ohio Valley.

It is a country of extremes, ugly by day with banks of coke ovens, tipples, sidings, and fields gnawed to the rock with strip-coal operations; luridly beautiful by night when the glare of the ovens paints the sky and works magic with headframes and sooty buildings; a place of great wealth and great poverty, with too much smoke, too much violence, and far too many people. The new men, dumped on the district in recurring waves from the eighties until 1920 as labor wars brought trainloads of strikebreakers and expanding operations called for additional workers, have filled the country to overflowing.

Thus far, coming over the mountains from Cumberland, Maryland, the road has looped easily through thickets of scrub interspersed with tilled fields, past brick and timber farmhouses, summer cabins, and the restored stockade of Fort Necessity; past the Washington Inn Museum that used to be a famous stagecoach stop in the days of the Cumberland Road, General Braddock's grave in which he may or may not be buried, and on to the Summit Hotel where the road starts down the mountain.

It depends on the wind and weather, the season, the time of day, and the coke market how much there is to see from the Chestnut Ridge lookout. Early on an autumn morning with a damp wind blowing from the Monongahela and the long strings of coke ovens sending up plumes of smoke ravelling sideways, a violet curtain full of moving particles of soot blots out the valley. The spring smoke is apt to be whitish-blue, that of winter brown or gray, and any time of year it ranges from pinkish-lavender to gun-metal tinged with purple at evening.

It takes a fine summer morning to see what the valley is like, with Uniontown sprawled in the flat in the foreground, Leith ovens smoking busily in the fields to the right near the smooth slopes of the Country Club, and the long ranks of Continental No. 1 ovens far away in the middle. The distance across the coke country to the Monongahela River is only about twelve miles but the industry has travelled lengthwise, beginning up the valley beyond the far blue distance in the Youghiogheny Valley around Connellsville, Broad Ford, and the Mount Pleasant hills.

Some of the best coking* coal in the world once lay in these valleys—the Nine-foot Pittsburgh Seam*—but business kept moving toward the Monongahela and the vast reserves of Greene County as the coal was mined out, leaving behind it a trail of dismantled mine buildings with the windows knocked out, abandoned tipples, and long rusty banks of coke ovens with little trees growing out of their caved-in roofs.

Uniontown, the county seat of Fayette, until recently the center of active production in the Coke Region but now on the edge of it, is a rich, smoky little city with one tall building on the sky line, the narrow Main Street, shaped like an elbow with the gray stone county courthouse in the angle, bisected at its busiest corner by a freight railroad that paralyzes traffic on five streets every time a coal-drag inches through, and the business section cut on the bias with blocks shaped like a wedge of pie. It can look forward to remaining the executive center of the district as long as it holds on to the offices of the Frick Coke Company and the Coal Mining Division of Republic Steel. Quaker Henry Beeson laid it out and disposed of the building sites by lottery on July 20, 1776, but it long ago outgrew its colonial boundaries without changing them, a fact which makes for an enormous saving in taxes to urban residents theoretically living in the country. The end of its dominance was already in sight when World War II increased the rate of depletion of its coal lands.

---

* Practically every grade of bituminous coal is found in the Pittsburgh district but the Pittsburgh Seam is the most volatile, 33 percent to 41 percent. In the Coke Region the only other coal mined to any extent is the Sewickley vein which lies above the Pittsburgh, although the Waynesburg and Redstone seams are mined in a few places.

Beyond the city limits of Uniontown, West Main Street becomes Route 40 again, running smoothly over rolling country past the iron gates and stone walls of the convent of the Sisters of St. Basil in the old home of J. V. Thompson, western Pennsylvania's most famous coal baron. From here, going straight across the Region to Brownsville, the road passes through only one company "patch," Brier Hill, with its blackened houses and brackish pond, red brick school and little church. Many of the big brick and stone farmhouses antedating the coal era once served as inns for stagecoach passengers.

If one really wants to see the coke country it is worth while to make the thirteen-mile detour through the teeming patches of the Klondike, where the boom of the first decade of this century developed mines and ovens so close together that after the underground headings had been extensively worked it was sometimes practical to take the coal out of one mine through another. Most of the coal has been mined out now because so many companies worked it so fast, but the people still live in the plant houses and go to work at active operations by car or trolley.

A turn to the left leaving the main road by the county home leads through farming country for the first four miles, then past the abandoned Shamrock Mine with a crumbling bank of ovens running around the base of a hill, into New Salem and out by the big burning dump of Buffington on the edge of town fronting a row of company houses in the path of its sulphurous fumes. About a mile farther on, a turn right and then left brings you through Fairbanks and Filbert, which saw so much disorder in the strike of 1933, past Cardale and the Orient patch. Then the road winds between old Tower Hill No. 1 and Republic Mine into the village of Republic where it cuts back through the big Allison patch on the ridge, overlooking the ovens in the valley, to join Route 40 by the water tower above Brownsville. You may lose your way in the network of small roads of the Klondike but, if you do, there are plenty of people to ask for directions.

Beyond the bend where Route 40 starts down to the valley there is a first view of the Monongahela River, sliding smooth and blue down to the white line of foam that marks dam No. 5, with an old whiskey warehouse on the wooded slope of the far side above an iron suspension bridge. Brownsville, the center of Fayette County's river traffic, crowds the narrow flat by the water and climbs the steep slopes to march out in the country in detached squads of closely packed houses of brick and stone, composition siding and clapboard, with here and there a colonial doorway or a graceful iron stair rail that belongs to the days when people used to say that Pittsburgh might make quite a city if it were not so close to Brownsville.

In the heyday of the National Pike, before the B. & O. put the horse-drawn stage and freight lines out of business, Brownsville was the junction point where passengers for Pittsburgh left the stagecoaches for the river packets.

Today, with the beehive ovens outmoded* and working only part time, an ever increasing tonnage of coal goes down the river to the by-product plants of Pittsburgh and Ohio in long lines of barges—about six thousand tons to the tow—oblong flatboats, heavily burdened, two feet above the water, with a nine-foot draft, slipping quietly in pairs through the brown water that brims the locks. They are always pushed, never pulled, and usually a blunt-nosed stern-wheeler does the job, churning along with cascades of water streaming down its paddles, looking like a holdover from the fifties.

Some of the new tugs are screw boats, beautifully streamlined, but they push the same as the others, using a blunt framework extending beyond the prow. The barges loaded with parallel rows of conical piles of coal have come from tipples that discharge simultaneously from a number of bins, one pile for each chute. Those filled with a solid bed of coal have been moved back and forth under a tipple with a single chute. It is no easy task to maneuver an unwieldly tow down-river, dodging shoals, keeping to the channel under bridges, avoiding the rough water at dams, keeping from getting entangled with other fleets, getting safely into locks and out again, and negotiating sharp curves without piling up.

Turning up the river road on the Fayette County side, one comes on Frick's Bridgeport Mine with its long black conveyorway that straddles the red and green company houses from the headframe of the shaft to the river tipple. Just beyond are the marine-ways of the Hillman Barge and Construction Company, and then more company villages, lining both sides of the river: Alicia with red fire licking out of the trunnel holes of its "pusher" ovens; Denbo and Vesta No. 7 of Jones and Laughlin Steel Company on the Washington County side of the river edging up to a black mountain of dump with a row of empty barges tied up below the tipple. Farther on, Maxwell lies on a flat by the water, a double row of well-kept, identical two-family, two-story houses, alternating red and green, the sashes painted white, with poplar trees, green lawns, and an alley running between the dahlias, cabbages, and neatly painted double privies of the fenced back-gardens. A sunny brick school stands a little apart on the bank of the river with jack-o'-lanterns in the windows. Where the village road leaves the highway, an old sign left over from the days when the coal and iron police kept the patches closed announces, PRIVATE PROPERTY: ALL PERSONS WARNED AGAINST TRESPASSING UNDER PENALTIES.

The company towns have been open to the public just as any other

---

* In 1920, twenty-four million tons of coal were used to make sixteen million tons of beehive coke, thereby wasting 216 gallons of tar, 600 million pounds of ammonium sulphate, and 120 billion cubic feet of gas that might have been used as manufactured gas in homes and industries. See "Report of the Smithsonian Institute" as quoted in Richard T. Wiley, *Monongahela: The River and Its Region* (Butler, Pennsylvania: The Ziegler Co.), p. 191.

villages since 1933. One wonders that they remained shut off so long, considering the slight benefit that came from restriction compared with the ill will it caused. Now that the system no longer exists, the companies are as glad as anybody to be rid of their coal police, who often got them into trouble.

The older patches are pretty much alike, springing out of the fields, creeping up to slate dumps, climbing hilltops in rows of identical double houses with narrow frame porches divided in half, fenced back yards, and outdoor toilets. Usually a company store goes with each patch, as does a church, a union hall, and a bar; often there is a consolidated school, incongruously large until one discovers how many children there are to use it.

Some of the company towns lately built up the river in Greene County are quite different. Nemacolin, Mather, and the Emerald Mine's housing developments look like pleasant rural villages anywhere. It is not worth while to rebuild the old patches because the Nine-foot coal of central Fayette is nearly exhausted. Greene and Washington Counties, with hundreds of thousands of acres of undeveloped coal land, expect to be producing for at least a hundred years yet.

Most of the coal on the upper river is owned by steel companies and most of the big operations are "captive" mines—that is, owned by steel and utility companies who use the output in their own plants. Thus the Frick mines, the largest chain in the district, ship their coal to the United States Steel Corporation; Nemacolin to the Youngstown Sheet and Tube; Vesta No. 7 and Vestaburg to Jones and Laughlin Steel; the Clyde mines to Republic Steel; Crucible Mine to Crucible Steel; etc.

When the coal is gone in Fayette County there will probably be no major exodus. Connellsville and Scottdale in the eastern part of the Region went through their reconversion period without losing too much population. Meanwhile, central Fayette turns out coal in lessening quantities and plans to meet the need for a change in economic set-up when it gets here with a solution not yet figured out.

Newcomers to the Coke Region are apt to complain bitterly because a good deal of the year they fight a losing battle with smoke and cinders. Window curtains have to be washed continually; bureau drawers must have their contents covered; silver and brass tarnish overnight and each spring ushers in an orgy of cleaning wallpaper, rugs, and upholstery. Even the daisies in the fields have dirty faces.

The old residents complain about the dirt, too, but they get a good deal of satisfaction out of being able to cope with it. A lot of things keep them from moving away: owning property, not wanting to leave their friends, dread of a new environment, even little things like wanting to stay where one can be lavish with coal in the winter because it is plentiful and cheap.

Whatever the Coke Region may look like to strangers, it has a beauty of its own for those who know it well: the thick sweet mists of spring absorbing sunlight; smoky twilight blending fields and orchards, mines and patches; slate dumps at night glittering with wrinkled seams of blue flame and patches of vermilion; strings of beehives like jolly fireplaces blazing through the fields; a row of poplars against fiery clouds; smoke piled up at the end of a street like a blanket of violet wool tossed in a heap. Life has always been violent and unpredictable here, sometimes sordid, but never monotonous. After a while one gets a taste for it.

Coke Region people think about these things when they hear outsiders saying they don't see why anybody stays here who doesn't have to, but they don't say much. It's hard to explain things like that to somebody fuming about a cinder in his eye.

CHAPTER II

THE MAN WITH THE LAMP

STEVE KUPCA AND HIS WIFE SOPHIE* LIVE IN HOUSE NO. 104 at Luna Mine. Steve is a short man with wide shoulders and a bent back, blue-eyed, square-faced, his mouth wide and tobacco-stained under a sandy handle-bar mustache. It is a trouble to keep clean but Steve is proud of its luxuriance. His hair used to be thick too, but thirty years under a hard hat have sweated most of it off.

Sophie is built wide without a waist-line—a motherly woman with a broad, plain face, shiny and pink, her light brown hair brushed straight back to a stony bun. There is no nonsense about Sophie. She likes to do the way she always has done and she has a poor opinion of Margaret Babusca, two doors down the street, whose hair looks like a lot of angleworms since she went to Americanization school. The school was fine—Sophie went herself—but, as she has told Margaret, what she learned was how to read and write and not to copy the teacher's fancy hair-do. Sophie manages Steve's money for him and does a good job of it. One of these days, when he can't work in the mines any more, they are going to get a little place down the road and sell groceries and beer.

The company patch where the Kupcas live is an old one, built about 1912, with three long rows of identical double houses recently covered with asbestos shingles—four rooms and a shed to a side, the first row facing the highway and the smoldering mine dump beyond that looks as if the earth

* Names of persons and places in this chapter are not intended to indicate any actual persons and places.

is still folding and cooling in the dawn of creation. At night, thin lines of blue fire trickle along its sides and run into glowing red lakes. Behind Kupca's house runs an alley lined with privies and hen coops with here and there a garage. The other two rows of houses face an upper street with the back yards of the lower side running down to the alley.

The Old Country people like to crowd their strips of yard with grape arbors, outdoor ovens, and pens for pigs and chickens, leaving only enough room for the wash line and a few tomato plants, but the younger ones go in more for gardens and garages. Each house has a poplar tree by its side window. On the upper street they are big and handsome, but down where the Kupcas live the leaves grow only on one side because of the smoke from the dump.

Steve has been living at Luna for thirty-two years, ever since he came to America from Slovakia in 1913, only then it was part of the Austrian Empire. In Europe it was always fight-fight over something. A man could get rich in America and not have the army always breaking in, or that was the way he thought it would be. Steve hasn't gotten rich and, the way it worked out, five of his boys had to go off to be soldiers in Europe after all. They're home now, married and gone for themselves, all but one who isn't coming back—Johnny, the youngest, buried somewhere in Germany. Mike, the second boy, learned to fly an airplane when he was in the army and came back a first lieutenant and married to an English girl. He's got a fine job now at the airport in Philadelphia, but the other boys went back to their old jobs in the mines on the river.

Now that there is nobody at home but Steve and Sophie, it's nice to have the children settled close by. Anna, the eldest girl—Mrs. Nick Gorowski— lives up the hill in the second row; Mary, the other one—Mrs. John Turik— went over to the new company town at Annice No. 2 that has single houses all painted white and set around the hill from the works so it is almost as clean as a farm.

Mary tried to get her father and mother to come too, but Steve has no mind to move anywhere till he gets his store, and neither has Sophie. She likes her oven in the back yard. It is a good baker and she wouldn't trade it for Mary's electric stove in her fine house over at Annice. She likes her neighbors. Mrs. Durich, on the other side of the house, is Hungarian, from the Old Country like herself, a Greek Catholic of the Byzantine Rite, but they are under the Pope too. Mrs. Orlov, on the other side, is "Hard Russian" (Russian Orthodox) so she goes to church in New Salem, but she's a fine neighbor.

Sophie gets up about four o'clock every week-day morning, builds a coal fire in the range, and calls Steve. His bucket stands ready on the handsome white kitchen cabinet that Louis bought her when he was working at Luna before the army got him. She "loaded the bucket" last night with big slabs of her homemade bread, an apple, a wedge of pie, and a chunk of raw bacon. Steve likes to slice it as he eats it. He doesn't care much for sweets unless it's pie or *makovnik*, the good horseshoe roll she makes for holidays out of yeast dough, butter, milk, honey, and raisins, dusted over the top with poppy seeds. The bottom of the bucket holds two or three quarts of water; that is why it has to be so big. None of those thermos bottles in a tin box for Steve. He knows that if he got penned up in the mine somewhere, so that he couldn't get out for a few days, the water might save his life.

Sophie has never gone down in a mine and doesn't expect to. The men think that if a woman goes in the pit, pretty quick there will be a slate fall or an explosion. They are such bad luck that some of the miners wouldn't go to work if a woman had been below ground and they found out about it. Sophie doesn't know why anybody would want to go down if he didn't have to. It is a dirty place, dark and wet, but the men seem to like it.

By the time Steve comes downstairs in his pit clothes carrying his mine boots that are a cross between shoes and galoshes, Sophie has his coffee poured, a stack of bread cut, and a piece of smoking blood sausage on his plate. A man needs a hearty breakfast when he is going to work hard all day, but he can't spend much time at it because if he were to miss the man-trip,* he'd have to lose the day.

When Steve puts on his hard hat and leather jacket, Sophie goes back to bed for a while, unless it is Monday when she will go at the washing and try to have it on the line before the other neighbors are ready to hang theirs out. All over the patch lights are winking out as the men leave. Nick Gorowski, Steve's tall, black-eyed son-in-law, is waiting by the car in the alley as he comes out of his back yard.

Luna Mine is worked out, so for the past few months they have been going over the river to Liberty No. 3. It is a quarter of five as Steve eases the Chevrolet out of the grainy black slush of the lane and picks up speed down the state road past the ruined brick powerhouse of old Apple Gate No. 7 and along the glowing ranks of the Fanny ovens with their long plumes of smoke blown sideways in the sharp morning wind.

As the car skims down the steep hill to the river, the valley is choking with smoke-filled fog so heavy that a boat blowing insistently at the bend below the rosy smudge of the Clermont ovens sounds like a worn-out penny whistle. A low yellow light, intermittently visible as the mist billows in ribbons, marks the ferry against the Greene County shore. Steve flashes the headlights of the car and toots the horn. Nothing happens for three or four minutes, and then a searchlight picks them out. The ferry has come across,

---

* A train of mine cars is called a "trip"; the train that carries the miners from the portal along the haulageways to the sections where they work is the "man-trip."

invisible in the murk, and is already pulling up for them. It lies so low to the water it looks like a segment of floating roadway with a little shed clinging to each side. They drive on board; the chain clanks behind them, closing the end of the boat; the tiny motor goes into action, propelling it along the guiding cables, and presently a series of parallel dots of light on top of the bank ahead lift themselves out of the dark, marking the Liberty patch.

The plant lies on a narrow flat down the river from the ferry-crossing and below the highway, a thick sprinkle of electric bulbs with halos of moving particles dotting the black mass of the headframe and powerhouse. High up in the coal-washer building is a square of bright-blue phosphorescent light. The plant policeman looks briefly out of his little booth as they turn down the lane to the parking lot.

The one-story brick building at the far end of the yard, with men coming and going black against the light streaming out of the open door, is the lamphouse. Outside Nick and Steve separate, the younger man to splash across the black puddles of the yard to the coal washer on the far side of the tracks, while the other goes in for his lamp. When Steve was younger he used to be a loader, but now he is operator's helper on the coal-cutting machine.

Inside, a round-faced, middle-aged man stands behind a counter next to a tall rack where lamp batteries are charging. When he sees Steve coming he takes down his lamp and pushes it across to him, ready with juice enough in it to last eight hours. Most of the shift have already gone in, so Steve snaps the oblong battery on his belt in a hurry and slides the lamp with its long rubber cord into the fixture on his hat; then he hangs his identification disk on the board and puts the other in his pocket. The lamp has been locked shut and cannot be opened again until an electric mechanism releases it after he comes out of the mine, lest opening it for adjustment let out an electric arc. It takes only one spark in the right place to set off an explosion.

In the old days they weren't so fussy about sparks, but they didn't have so much electrical equipment, either. Steve used to work by the speck of light from a safety lamp hung up somewhere. Now the company is very particular that nobody has them but the fire bosses who make an inspection for gas before each shift.

The safety lamp is a kind of dim lantern with a tiny flame burning in a glassed-in chamber beneath two fine wire gauzes. If the air filtering into the lamp is of normal composition the light burns low, but if there is a dangerous accumulation of gas it brightens and a tiny explosion takes place under the screen. As long as the flame is not allowed to run up over a long enough time for the gauze to become heated, the lamp will not ignite the gas accumulation it has detected. Accidents have occurred because no one happened to be looking at it as the flame grew taller. If the warning of gas accumulation goes unheeded long enough, the gauze becomes incandescent and sets off an explosion.

When Steve gets to the mine early, sometimes he likes to walk down to the bottom by the easy concrete stairs of the new "slope" (inclined tunnel) where the coal rides up a thick rubber belt to the storage bins on the way to the coal washer. When they were building it the grade looked so steep he thought the coal would surely slide back, but it doesn't. Paul, his eldest son, worked on the excavation for the tunnel and it was a nasty job. The ground was bad till they got to the rock, liable to come down any minute; if they got ten feet a day that would hold they thought they were lucky. It looks fine now, like a big concrete pipe boring into the ground, light and quiet inside, with a strong draft because it is the air-intake for the mine.

Today Steve is in a hurry so he crosses quickly to the headframe and joins the little group of miners waiting to go down the shaft. When the cage comes noiselessly to the surface, Steve steps aboard and takes hold of one of the straps dangling from the ceiling; the last man to get on rings the bell to tell the engineer in the powerhouse that they are ready and the car plumps to the bottom like a stone dropping. It is designed for men or horses, as well as coal cars, with two solid sides and two open ones closed by a chain hooked between rings.

The "trip" is waiting just ahead on the No. 2 "empty" track,* a long line of gray steel cars, twenty or more of them, each seventeen feet long. Over to the left in the main haulage, the rotary dump roars rhythmically, tipping loaded eight-ton cars bottom-side-up to empty into the bin that feeds the belt in the slope as easily as Steve would knock out his pipe.

There is plenty of light in No. 2 "empty" track where the man-trip starts, at the dispatcher's office, around the dump and in the checkweighman's office that looks out on it, but back where the men are going it is dark except for an occasional bulb where light is necessary.

The tracks run through a tunnel carved out of a nine-foot vein of coal, iridescent and shiny, running off into the shadow in wavy layers. Many things in America have disappointed Steve but not its richness. Where else would there be thousands of acres of coal nine feet thick, all in one piece so big they can run car tracks through it and cut rooms in it? A man can break it out with his fingers, dig it out with a pick and shovel, cut it out with machines—get it out any way he wants to and burn it just as it is. This particular coal will get extra washing and grading in the coal washer, but thousands of tons just like it will be used exactly as it comes from the mine.

It is a forty-five minute ride back to the "face" where the coal is being cut, shot down, and loaded to come back to the rotary-dump in cars like the

* The "empty" track is where the trip wagons are stored after being dumped before they go back to the "face."

one Steve is riding in. An eighteen-ton electric locomotive, with a brake that looks like a steering wheel and no very comfortable place to sit, pulls the trip. The motor is behind the driver under a cover to keep slate and dirt from dropping into it and to guard against the possibility of an electric arc.

Liberty No. 3 was short about two hundred men during the war, but after it had been mechanized it turned out as much coal as before. The use of electrical machinery in the mining industry has enormously increased efficiency, but the death rate has climbed with it. The minimum of electric wiring is dangerous enough. Of the six major disasters in 1940, four were caused by electric arcs.

And yet it is not the spectacular explosions that account for the high death rate among miners; it is the slate falls that steadily and unobtrusively swell the total. Men used to working underground are always listening for "the top talking," by which they mean the faint warning creaks that precede a slate fall. Sometimes they can see or hear the "squeeze" coming and have time to get out from under, sometimes not.

A mile from the main entry the trip passes the stable lights. There are only twenty horses in it now, although Steve can remember when there were nearly a hundred. Some mines use mules but there are only horses here, fine big ones like those that used to haul the brewery wagons. They bring them to the surface if they get too badly galled, but so long as a horse is all right it may stay in the mine several years before coming up.

Steve's crew gets out of the trip at No. 27 "butt," * a fifteen-foot heading stretching away to the left, pitch-black and so still that the men's footfalls grinding the coal underfoot sound loud and measured. A man coming up a few feet away is only a low moving light and a blacker blackness, then a set of shoulders, an illuminated pair of eyebrows, a nose and a mouth. Eight hundred men work at the mine but they are so spread out in the miles of headings a man forgets they are there. Liberty No. 3 used to be very wet but is now dry because they "grouted" the water off, that is, pumped water and cement into the cracks in the sandstone above the coal and let it harden in there to stop the drainage into the mine. One crack took up 2,700 bags of cement.

The coal is cut according to an orderly plan, leaving pillars to support the roof, the work being laid out by a mine survey party and the progress recorded on the map that fills one end of the pit boss's office above ground. In opening up a new sector, a mine crew cuts a fifteen-foot entry running back into the coal deposit. When they have gone as far back as the bosses tell them, they begin cutting rooms into the sidewalls of the heading, leaving

---

* The "rooms" or entries where the men work are usually classed as "flat entries," or "butt entries," according to which way the coal breaks.

pillars about thirty-five feet wide between. The next heading off the main haulage will be several hundred feet farther down, leaving the coal between as a supporting pillar. Then another series of rooms begins, each supposed to be fifteen feet wide but more apt to be twenty feet because mechanical mining requires a little more space. Brattices—curtains of wood and cloth—cut off the headings from the main haulageways and deflect the air driven into the mine by the fan so that it is distributed evenly through the workings.

Steve and Dominic Caso, from the Liberty patch, run the cutting-machine; Dominic as operator, with Steve to help move it and run water on the cutter bar, when it is working, to keep the dust down. It is the face boss's business to tell them where to cut.

In the dark heading the machine looks like one of the prehistoric monsters which walked the earth when the coal measures were laid down. When Dominic turns on the power it cocks its big drum-like head slowly, takes a good look at the wall of coal, and darts a ladder-like tongue into it inch by inch with a noise like the chattering of dry bones. Chips fly and dust sifts down in spite of the water Steve is sluicing on the cutter bar; then as Dominic pulls another lever the head majestically removes the tongue, leaving a clean, straight gash to show where it has been.

When they have cut six or seven feet deep on three sides of a block of coal, the shot-firer comes in, bores a row of holes at the bottom and fills them with dynamite while Steve and Dominic start cutting somewhere else. When a blast is about to go off, the men nearest go into the next heading or around the corner to be out of the way.

After the explosion, the mechanical loader takes over. It is a curious animal-like machine with a neck like a giraffe, a long back suggestive of a dachshund, and the powerful tail of kangaroo. A double line of vertebrae with a movable track between runs up the tail and on to the spinal column. When the operator pulls a lever, the vertebrae travel upward coaxing coal between them; he pulls another handle, the contraption shakes itself, arches its back a little, and a second track goes into motion carrying the coal the length of the body and out the long flexible neck that will place it anywhere. A loader like this can fill as many wagons in an hour as a man could fill in three days, hand loading. When a trip is loaded it rattles back to the dump, usually twenty-five wagons in a string carrying eight tons apiece.

In the old days Steve cut coal with a pick, bored his own holes, and shot it down with black powder brought from home in a pouch that he filled every day out of the keg in the cellar. He used his own tools and set off the charge when he got ready, using short fuses he carried in his pocket. Until the industrial upheaval in the summer of 1933 he and his buddy loaded the coal they shot down in wagons, smaller than the ones they use now, and put a hump on it so high that if the boss leaned his elbow on top of the box with his hand straight up a man on the opposite side couldn't see his fingers.

They got their pay by the wagon with nothing extra for the fifteen to eighteen bushels or so in the hump, but they had to put it on anyway. After 1933 the companies put in scales and paid by weight with two check-weighmen keeping the records, one for the men and one for the company. All the men are on straight time now at the mine where Steve works.

It takes considerable figuring to arrive at the total that Steve may expect in his pay envelope because if he works on Saturday and Sunday, that is, sixth. and seventh shifts, the rate goes up fast. For the first five days, according to the 1946 government-negotiated contract, he gets $1.328 an hour for seven hours, plus $1.9915 for the eighth hour, plus $1.7775 "portal-to-portal," the time he spent riding to and from work in the mine. That adds up to $13.06 a day. But Saturday, the sixth shift, he gets time-and-a-half hourly which gives him $1.9915 an hour or $15.932 for eight hours, plus $1.7775 riding time, which makes $17.71. On Sunday, or the seventh shift, the hourly rate goes up to twice what it was for the first five days so he gets $21.248 for eight hours, plus portal-to-portal, or $23.12. Steve knows that it works out to a $65.30 total for a five-day week, $83.01 total for a six-day week, $106.13 total for a seven-day week, and he won't miss a day if he can help it as long as he has a prospect of getting in a six- or seven-day week. If, however, something happens so he knows he cannot get in more than five shifts, he is apt to figure that the week's work isn't going to amount to very much anyway, and he may work only four days. He looks forward to running the coal-cutting machine himself as soon as he gets a chance, and then he will make $71.40 for a five-day week, $90.83 with a sixth shift, and $116.24 for seven shifts.

Nick, who works on the picking-belt, is counted outside labor so he gets no portal-to-portal pay, but he receives a flat bonus (equalization rate) of $1.07 a day to make up for it. A slate picker never has the opportunity to work the seventh shift in any one week. His wages figure out

7 hours a day for 5 days @ $1.07 per hour or		$7.49
1¼ hours a day for 5 days @ 1½ time per hour		1.97
Equalization rate		1.07
	Wage per day for 5 shifts	$10.53
	6th Shift	
8¼ hours @ $1.60		$13.19
Equalization rate		1.07
	Wage for 6th shift	$14.26
Total for 5-day week		$52.65
Total for 6-day week		$66.91

Trackmen and timbermen will receive $59.25 for a five-day week, $75.25 for six shifts and $96.08 for seven shifts.

At eleven o'clock the men have a half-hour for lunch. When Steve and Dominic come out into the main haulage with their buckets, heading for the face boss's office a little way down the track where they can eat in the light, a haulage crew is unloading pit-posts to shore up the ceiling, and bags of rock dust. They blow it all over the workings every two weeks, using powdered limestone, which is inert and makes coal dust nonexplosive when mixed with it in high enough percentage. The men have to breathe quantities of it, but it does not give them silicosis as some other kinds of rock dust would.

When Steve finishes his dinner, he cuts a fresh plug of tobacco. No one is allowed to smoke below ground. The fire boss has pronounced his section safe to work in, but that was hours ago. There is no knowing how much "firedamp" may have seeped out of the rock since. Liberty No. 3 is naturally a gassy mine but is exceptionally well ventilated to reduce the hazard. Steve and Dominic don't know the fancy names of the gasses, but they know which ones to look out for and what they will do to a man.

If there is firedamp (carbureted hydrogen with methane) in the heading they wouldn't know it because there is no smell to it. The thing in it that kills is marsh gas (methane). Sometimes they can hear it hissing out of a coal cleavage, but it doesn't do any harm as long as there is a current of air to dilute it. If it were to collect and explode it could start a whole train of trouble, one blast setting off another in the flying coal dust that is explosive when mixed with air in the right quantities.

Then is when a fellow has to look out for afterdamp or it may put him to sleep. That is mostly marsh gas too, but there is a little odor to it, something like the sweet smell in a greenhouse. White damp (carbon monoxide) is about the most dangerous. It comes when there has been an explosion without enough oxygen present to burn up all the gasses and it gives no warning. A man's lamp goes on burning and there is no taste or smell to it, but he gets weak and it snuffs him out before he knows what has happened. And when the air seems bad and his head aches and he is sick to his stomach, probably there is some blackdamp (carbon dioxide and nitrogen without enough oxygen in proportion). In the old days the miners used to know that they needed to look out for it when their lamps burned dim. There is liable to be some in any close, unventilated place where most of the oxygen has been breathed out of the air; but it also escapes from the coal and rock strata. It seems to come extra thick along the ground where there is dampness and rotting timber. Then there is stinkdamp (hydrogen sulphide) that comes after an explosion of black powder or where water is being drained from a flooded part of a mine. It smells like rotten eggs so anybody would not need to know about gasses to run away from that. A little of it makes a man's eyes smart, but if it is strong enough it paralyzes his breathing apparatus.

If Steve gets caught in an explosion it won't be the first time. He'll cover his face with a wet handkerchief and try for the main entry; if he can't make it, he'll take his bucket of water and brattice himself in near an airshaft somewhere, hoping the rock dust will keep the fire down until a rescue party comes for him.

The men start back to the surface at 2:30, their faces black with light rims around the eyes, cheeks bulging with tobacco, trouser bottoms wet and flapping.

Up in the building back of the headframe, Nick Gorowski, with four others, has been snatching pieces of slate out of the coal all day as it slid past on a picking table before tumbling into the storage bin. The powerhouse and the lamp house with the pit boss's office in one end lie to the right; the brick machine shop, the fan house, the surface stables, and office spread out fanwise to the left. Behind, on the river bank, is the tipple where the barges are loading. The room in the bin building where the pickers work is noisy with machinery and clouded with coal dust. It opens on to the conveyor-way which is a continuation of the slope running from the bottom of the mine.

In the six-story coal-washer building next door, coal that has been fed across from the bin passes through sluices where the remaining slate separates itself out by gravity. Everywhere there are screens, black water running in troughs, and rivers of fine coal like thick gravy that slither down trays and separate into jumping pancakes. The same water goes round and round, but before it starts the circuit over again, it passes through slow turning filter disks that recover the coal pulp too fine to be gathered in any other way and shear it off into "filter-cake" to go back with the other coal.

Then the wet coal gets another belt-ride, writhing like an endless snake across to the river tipple, showers over a last screen, and disappears into boats being moved back and forth underneath to be taken to the by-product plant down river.

When Steve comes out of the pit mouth, Nick is waiting to ride home with him. There is no washhouse at Liberty so they start away just as they are. Nick would like to stop for a beer at Lulich's on the river bank, but Steve is not interested in anything right now but getting washed. Sophie will have good hot water waiting when he gets home and he can drink some of his homemade berry wine while she sets supper on.

After some of Sophie's *halusky s'kapustu* (sauer kraut and dumplings), he may walk down the road to Pete Falla's Place for a couple of hours where he talks with his neighbors over a few glasses of beer; or perhaps he goes up the hill to play *burika* a while with his friend Paul Buvelsco—who came from his home village—and a couple of the neighbors, and they split a bottle of prune brandy. On paydays, the thirteenth and twenty-eighth, he plans to stay up later and get some good of the money he earned. If he goes in to town he will drop around at the Slovak Club and later, maybe, patronize the *Krczma* on Penn Street. But it is more likely he will go to Pete Falla's where he can see the people he knows.

Pete's bar sits back from the main road by the trolley stop, the center of a wheel whose spokes are paths leading in every direction: to the mine, the patch, the company store, the Fanny ovens. Pete's Place is a one-story frame building with the bar in front and living quarters in an ell at the back, the whole covered with imitation red brick siding. When Steve pushes open the door the room is full of men, the juke box going full blast. The big bar is a fine sight—stacked with bottles, the mirror ringed with electric lights with a clock on top edged in red neon tubes and the little shelves along the sides filled with knick-knacks—two googoo dolls with their skirts tilted naughtily, a plaster cast of a white horse advertising whiskey, a pottery mule with a plant growing out of his back.

Over the heads of the men leaning on the counter, Steve can see that Emma, Pete's wife, is tending bar. That means that Tajic, the bartender, is drunk again, and she is giving Pete a chance to eat his supper. Emma has enough to do making sandwiches in the kitchen without having to worry with the drinks, but she has to spell Pete when Tajic lays off. She is a fine big woman, fair-haired and blue-eyed, with a ready tongue able to give the men as good as they send. Nick, Steve's son-in-law, is sitting in the front booth with Tony Di Cuzzo, the fat little blacksmith from over at Fanny.

"A beer," calls Steve, and then as he joins Nick and Tony, "make it three." He is a rich man tonight with his pay in his pocket—that is, all that Sophie didn't make him turn over to her—and before he is through he wants to sample a little of all there is: St. Monica, so rich and good it climbs the glass, sweet with herbs and fiery without a headache; peppermint schnapps; and lots of good whiskey for the backbone of the evening.

Pete comes through the curtained doorway at the back, a big man but not fat, 250 pounds of bone and muscle in a pair of pants and an undershirt. His face is handsome, if heavy, with square white teeth and ruddy brown skin shadowed a little with black beard that grows so fast he can't keep up with it. When she sees Pete coming to take over, Emma starts for the kitchen.

As she goes by, a man at the end of the bar calls, "Hey, Emma! How about a fried-egg sandwich?"

"A pity you couldn't eat home once in a while," she answers tartly.

"I ain't been home yet."

"That's what I mean. Leona might like to see you." But she gives him a friendly push when she says it.

"Put in an egg for me," calls Tony di Cuzzo from the front booth. "And some ham with it."

"What else you got?" calls a one-armed man, putting nickels in the juke box.

"I haven't eaten myself, yet," retorts Emma from the kitchen door.

"Do I get my egg?" asks the man by the end of the bar.

"What do you think?" she says and disappears through the doorway.

A party of strangers comes in—two of the American engineers from the construction gang putting in the coal washer down the river at Glass's Ferry showing their wives what a river bar is like on pay night. The men in the booth behind Steve get up and join the crowd at the bar, leaving their table free for the newcomers. Pete comes around the counter to take the orders.

"Let me have something I couldn't get in an American bar," says the younger of the two women, a pretty redhead in a fur coat and a green beret.

"I'll fix you something," says Pete. "A lady's drink."

"Will you tell me what its name is?" she asks to prolong the conversation. Pete is worth looking at.

"It hasn't any."

"I think I'll take *polinkivak,*" she says brightly. "I've heard about it."

"She won't like it," calls Nick in Polish over the partition. "It's too bitter. Show her the bottle so she can see what it's made of."

"You can try a little and see if you like it," Pete tells her and brings the bottle and a liquor glass.

She pours a swallow and makes a face. Then she reads the label. "Ugh!" she says. "Listen to this: colombo root, gentian root, calamus root, juniper berries, laurel berries, calanzal root, star anisett, caraway seed, cinchona, licorice, cinnamon, cloves, orange flowers, palmetto berries, elicamponi, mace, angelica root, bloodroot, bleached cardamon, chamomile flowers. No wonder it tastes terrible! I'll let you make me up something."

The older woman doesn't think she wants anything but settles on sherry; the men order whiskey. Emma comes back from the kitchen with the sandwich orders and looks the sight-seers over appraisingly. When Pete brings the strangers' drinks he sets a small glass of peppermint schnapps in front of the girl in the beret.

"The drinks are on the house," he says.

Three of the men by the bar know the engineers. They each order another schnapps for the redhead and more wine for the older woman, speaking in Slovak. Emma carries the drinks over this time and points out the men who sent them. The women nod thanks, looking embarrassed.

"I can't drink four of these, one right after another," the girl says doubtfully, looking at the glasses in front of her.

"You can if you take it slow," Emma tells her in an undertone. "It'll hurt their feelings if you don't."

Tim O'Shea, the little old watchman from Fanny in the back booth, gives a handful of nickels to the man opposite him and tells him to prime the box. When Frank Sinatra comes on he sings with him in a quavering voice. Tim has been at Pete's since five o'clock and is too unsteady to stand. He throws a ten-dollar bill and a handful of change down on the table in front of him and calls to Pete to tell the boys at the bar that the drinks are on him.

Pete comes over to Tim's table. "Can you get him home, Johnny?" he asks his companion. "Put his money in his pocket."

Tim is showing signs of going to sleep. The man called Johnny rolls a quarter across to Nick. "Give him a drink in the morning," he says. "He'll be needing it." Then he stuffs the rest of the money in the old man's pocket and taps him on the shoulder. "Got to get going, Tim!"

Steve watches Pete chaperoning the old man out of the door. He is in a mood to see all the good points of his friends. Where is there a better-run bar than Pete's? If the boys get loud, all Pete has to do is to come over and tell them to pipe down and they know he means business. Now take the time when Joe Sconza got to drinking when he was supposed to be working on his house so it stood half done all summer. Pete shut off his liquor till he straightened up and then loaned him the money to go on with it. There are plenty of women and kids around Luna who would have pretty slim pickings if it weren't for Pete.

A short red-faced man in a miner's raincoat comes in, the president of the local U.M.W. Union. Seeing Steve he greets him with "Going to make a speech tonight?" Nick and Tony laugh and Tony slaps Steve on the back so hard that he spills his whiskey.

Steve is a man of a few words; a drink loosens his tongue but he never gets noisy. The only speech he ever made was at a union meeting at Luna. Tired of a series of walkouts that keep scaling down his pay check, he rose in the midst of deliberation for a fresh strike and shouted: "Strike? Strike! No strike? NO STRIKE! LET'S GO TO WORK!" The men like to kid him about it. He pulls his mustache in embarrassment and tries to think of a reply in English. None comes.

"*Idite svoej doroho*" (Go your own road), he says. "*Ostavte, meňjá v pokoji!*" (Leave me in peace).

Nick and Di Cuzzo are playing the finger game, loser pay for the drinks, counting in Italian because "It's no fun unless you play it in Dago." Each holds up a clenched fist and then flings one, two, three, four or five fingers forward, shouting simultaneously the number he thinks the total his fingers will make added to the number the other fellow throws out.

"*Tres!*" shouts Nick, holding out one finger, but Tony has played all five, calling *ocho* so the total was six and neither has won. They clench their fists again.

"*Cinco!*" calls Nick, holding up two fingers. Tony shouts *siete*, holding up three fingers, and loses because the total was five, the number Nick guessed. So Tony sends for three whiskeys while Nick as winner plays Steve for the next round.

It is nearly eleven by the illuminated clock over the bar. Four o'clock comes just as early the day after "the gravy train" as any other day. Too bad it doesn't always come on Saturday. Steve rises regretfully to leave and Nick goes with him. As they pick their way along the path across the lot, Steve can see a light in his daughter's house; down below, in the cloud of smoke from the dump, his own is dark. Sophie has gone up to sit with Anna while Nick is out, but she'll be coming home directly when he turns on the kitchen light.

"*Dobra noč,*" he tells Nick as they separate at the alley. "See you in the morning."

CHAPTER III

SILVER CINDERS

THE STEEL MILLS MUST HAVE PIG IRON TO MAKE STEEL and the blast furnaces must have coke to make pig iron, so that if anything happens to shut off the coke supply it is a case of "Stick won't beat dog, dog won't bite pig, pig won't jump over the stile," and the steel mills have to bank their fires until the iron makers get more coke.

The problem is this: iron ore in its raw form is iron oxide (iron rust). In order to make it useful commercially it must be converted into a metal by taking the oxygen out of it. Oxygen will unite with white-hot glowing carbon but, unless the carbon is relatively pure, certain unwelcome properties, such as sulphur, may be carried over into the pig iron. So the iron makers have always been in the market for a source of nearly pure carbon—first charcoal, later anthracite, and finally coke.

Charcoal is the ideal fuel but it cannot be had in sufficient quantities. The little cold-blast furnaces of the early 1800's produced only about two tons of iron a day but they consumed about four hundred bushels of charcoal per ton in the process. Considering that in the early days of the industry the charcoal-fired Warwick furnace used the product of about 240 acres of woodland each year,* and that a modern blast furnace makes as much iron in twenty-four hours as the old cold-blast furnace working *twenty-four hours a day for two years,* the number of acres of woodland that would have to be stripped to fuel a blast furnace with charcoal would be fantastic.

---

* A. C. Binning, *Iron Manufacture in the Eighteenth Century,* Pennsylvania Historical Commission (Harrisburg, 1938), IV, 75.

Anthracite can be used as a source of carbon but its texture is too dense; it has too much ash and must be used in larger quantities than coke made from high-grade bituminous coal.

Coke is coal from which the volatile matter—the tar, oils, and gas—has been burned out, leaving mainly fixed carbon. However, some of the bituminous coals will not melt together to form coke; some that will make coke are too weak to support the great weight of the blast furnace burden; some have too much sulphur, phosphorous, or ash.

Luckily, when the iron masters of Pittsburgh began casting about for something to replace charcoal, they found just what they wanted in the coke from the rich Nine-foot coal of the Connellsville field, porous but strong, low in ash and sulphur. There were hundreds of thousands of acres of it and it was easily available by rail and river. So Connellsville coke made Pittsburgh rich, and Pittsburgh steel and iron made millionaires in the coal country up the Youghiogheny and Monongahela Rivers.

The coke-making process is designed to drive off the volatile matter from the coal without letting combustion go far enough to burn the carbon. This matter will combust with the addition of very little oxygen; the fixed carbon requires a large amount of oxygen so the coal is burned with very little air in order to leave the fixed carbon or coke. The process used to be carried on exclusively in beehive ovens that wasted the gas and oils cooked out by the heat. Modern by-product plants that save the valuable gas, ammonia, and tar make most of the coke nowadays, but the very primitiveness of the beehive coke process keeps it alive because whenever the market warrants extra production it can resume without too great an outlay.

With the beginning of World War II, coke operators began ordering fire brick to refurbish their idle beehives, cleaning up the yards, and calling the old men back to work. Every week Coke Region papers announced new batteries of ovens going under fire. Bank ovens, block ovens, pusher ovens, hand-drawn and mechanized, went to work to fill the orders that were more than the by-product plants could fill.

A beehive coke oven looks like an igloo with a hole in the roof.* Coal is poured inside the hole or "trunnel-head" from lorries which run along a track on top; the gases ignite from the stored heat of the last burning, consume the volatile matter, and leave the carbon or coke. Before this has time to burn, it is quenched with water and drawn out of the door in silvery metallic cinders. The yield of coke from coal is generally figured as 66 percent, although some ovens do better than that.

Sometimes beehives are built into a bank or hillside in a long single line following the contour of the slope. They are cheaper to build that way because the hill into which they nestle helps to hold the heat in and adjusts

* See Appendix A, page 261.

itself nicely to the wall expansion during burning, and the dirt taken out in construction can be worked into the grading necessary for the tracks in front. Also, ovens facing the fresh air are supposed to make brighter coke than block ovens facing each other; but in the early days of the coke business, when bank ovens were most popular, operators had to be careful about getting too many in a string or it made too long a haul for the teams and lorries bringing coal from the tipple.

Block ovens are easier to load from, because cars standing on a railroad siding running between two ranks of ovens can be filled from both sides at once and the lorries running along the top have access to two parallel strings of ovens with their backs to each other, when they come to fill them.

In the heyday of the coke industry about three hundred ovens were considered the most profitable number for a plant. If there were more the plant became unwieldy; if there were less it was uneconomical because the fixed charges were too high. A man could manage two three-hundred oven plants located close together with more ease than one of six hundred ovens; thus the country became dotted with small operations, and companies designated their works as No. 1, No. 2, No. 3, etc. The size of a plant depended on a nice balance between blast furnace demand and coal supply. Furnace men didn't like to mix different sources of carbon so one coke plant needed to produce enough coke to take care of the needs of at least one blast furnace, or, better, two. Counting that a blast furnace would use about 2,100 tons of coke to run seven days, and each coke oven would produce about two tons of coke a day but only ran six days a week, the coke plant had to figure on producing 350 tons a day to keep up with the blast furnace, and that meant 175 ovens for one customer, or 350 ovens for two.

In the eighties, teams drew coal to the ovens in the wagons that came out of the mine and dumped it through the trunnel-head in the top without further handling. When it was carbonized, coke-drawers raked it out of the little door facing the siding, wheeled it in barrows across the wharf in front and tipped it into the railroad car spotted below. In order to give the loader a straight wheel, the whole block of ovens and wharf were built up off the ground on a dry wall. Now, when mechanical loaders are largely in use, the expensive foundation is no longer necessary and the newer plants sit at track level.

Designing a mechanical coke-drawer for the circular interior of a beehive presented a nice problem, like making a gun that would shoot around a corner; but the machine was invented. The modern "pusher ovens," while working on the beehive principle, are built in a series of rectangular corridors which may be emptied by the simple process of ramming the contents out the far end.

A visitor to a modern beehive coke plant in Fayette County finds a large installation functioning in two parts, below-ground mining and above-ground processing. The above-ground layout consists of an office on a green lawn, a brick boilerhouse that looks like a Victorian church with a smoke-stack for a steeple, a headframe and tipple with a loaded car flashing up at intervals, a hoist house, washhouse, lamp house, machinery sheds, and car-barn. Ranks of shadowy block ovens lie below on a flat blurred with grainy blue smoke which fronts a short row of blank ovens burrowing into the knoll on which the boilerhouse stands. No smoke issues from the bank ovens because there are heavy iron lids over their trunnel-holes to divert the gases to the boilers.

Inside the power house four great boilers, bricked into square towers, rise to the roof radiating heat. The fires are just coming up, brilliant orange flame billowing in the fireboxes like a veil blown down a wind, but already the heated stone floor over the channel where the gases enter is uncomforta-bly hot to stand on. There would be gas enough for the city of Uniontown if all 350 ovens were capped, but only that from the 58 ovens in front of the building is being used. The procedure of diverting the gas is simple and does not hinder the coke-making process. By putting an iron lid over the trunnel-hole the gases can be forced to burn wherever an outlet is supplied; in this case it is under the boilers that run the steam hoist.

In the brick washhouse across the cinder yard, where a warm moist breath rushes out of the opening door, there are showers and a big dressing room where the men hang their wet work clothes up to dry in wire baskets that swing up to the ceiling on pulleys. The yard boss's office occupies the rest of the building.

Going down the path to the ovens, one passes from the sunshine into a dim brightness without shadows and moving with tiny cinders; a few steps farther and a dusty gray cloud blots out the sky. In the murk between the first and second blocks of ovens two conveyors hang suspended over two coke cars on the railroad track, but the smoke is so heavy in there that he goes on to where the wind has drawn it away a little. In a few minutes he learns to keep his eyes narrowed to slits but even then cinders prick the eye-balls and float about in smarting tears. It is a surprise to find that once one is thoroughly immersed in coal smoke the sensation is rather pleasant. On the green lawn by the office the morning scent of green things and newly plowed ground give one kind of pleasure, the pungent medicinal aroma of the burning gases gives another, but they are both good in their way, just as one may like the smell of perfume as well as that of broiling steak, although they give different satisfactions. The distaste for coal smoke is partly the thought of the black particles sifting down, but the dirt does not matter when one is already dirty, just as a warm rain is not unpleasant to somebody sopping wet.

The coke machine works from a little shanty that settles down over the track while a man inside directs a powerful hoe, jointed to work in any direction, into the packed mass of hot coke filling the oven door. On its return stroke, a shower of coke comes with it and tumbles on to a belt conveyor, which also serves the door of the oven just drawn where a man with a "duck-bill" is busy scraping out the coke the machine missed. The coke travels along the conveyor to a screen by the oven wall, climbs up an inclined conveyor, is screened again, and rattles into a coal car. The fine coke—the "breeze"—that sifts through the screens will later be carted away by a horse and wagon to be sold as fuel.

It is important that the drawing and cleaning be gotten over with quickly so that the lorries can charge the ovens while they are hot so as to start the gases by spontaneous combustion. It takes the coke machine only twelve to fifteen minutes to draw an oven. Then it moves on to the next, pulling its coal car behind it by a cable. The little shanty with man and machine in it looks so permanent on the track that it is a surprise to see it majestically move off to set up business farther along. It runs on a trolley as does the lorry coming along the top of the ovens a little way behind, pouring coal into two trunnel-heads at once. The men seem to be charging by guess but from long experience they know how much they are getting in; six and one-half tons on Monday and Tuesday, seven on Wednesday and Thursday, and eight on Friday when they charge for seventy-two-hour coke. The latter used to go to the foundries while the forty-eight-hour, made the rest of the week, went to the furnaces, but now the steel mills take all of it.

After the lorries have poured in the coal, the piles are levelled into a bed that reaches somewhere near the point where the roof begins to taper toward the trunnel-head. The door is bricked up and daubed with mud, leaving a narrow air fissure at the top. The coking process depends on the burner's judgment of where and when to daub the mud that regulates the draft. After the gases ignite and the ovens "catch-up" he has to consider the height, luminosity, and color of the flame that licks out of the trunnel-holes to know how much air to let in. If too much flame is coming out, there is not enough air inside; if there is little or no flame visible, too much air is getting in. If the temperature is too low, the coke structure will be soft and poor; if it is too high, some of the coke will burn up, making the ash content higher than it ought to be and the yield less.

During the recent boom period, blast-furnace men have run into difficulties causing a reduction in iron output because some of the beehive coke they have been getting is not as good as it used to be. Part of this is the result of coke plants having to use poor coal because the Connellsville deposit is practically mined out and, although there is plenty of Nine-foot left in near-by territory, it runs higher in sulphur unless it is washed. A good many of the skilled operators are gone and some of the ovens that have been idle for twenty years are poorly insulated.

The Bureau of Mines ran a series of coking tests at local plants in 1943 to determine what an oven might be expected to do in efficient practice. Taking a sample burn, suppose that the oven is quenched at 4:30; it can be drawn and filled again by a little after five o'clock. By that time the temperature of the walls, whose stored heat will ignite the gases, will be down to about 660° F. After the door is daubed, about 5:30, it starts going up. Between then and 6:00 it will reach 1180° F. and the gases begin to burn. White smoke comes out first, then black smoke and dull red flame. The whole process of quenching, drawing out the finished coke, charging with new coal and igniting for a new forty-eight-hour or seventy-two-hour burn can take place in a little more than an hour and a half.

In the carbarn at the other end of the ovens, the Slovak machine boss, burly, sandy-haired, and friendly, is tinkering one of the long flat electric locomotives of gray steel used in the mine. Three women worked in the shop during World War I but one of them was killed when she got in the way of a lorry so since then there have been no more women employees.

In modern practice every effort is made to reduce the hazard by strictly enforced regulations and education, but still accidents happen. There are so many things one must remember not to do. On the wall in the narrow hallway of the lamp house where the miners check in before going down the shaft, there is an honor roll for departments with no accidents. Beside it is the rack of identification disks that tell whether a man is in or out of the mine. If he is in the mine he is somebody's responsibility until he is out again. In case of an explosion the rescue crew knows whom to look for, and if a man cannot be identified in any other way, the disk he carries, duplicating the one on the check-board, tells who he is.

At the back of the lamp room a first-aid room, complete with pulmotor, oxygen machine, sterile cabinet for instruments, cots, and well-stocked supply cupboards, acts as a combination doctor's office and emergency receiving room. The company doctor is on call twenty-four hours a day, his services paid for by the company for any accident incurred by an employee at work. The man's family will also call for the company doctor when they need him, but in that case a charge is made.

At this particular plant it is only a matter of weeks until the glittering machines in the hoist house will be idle and the torrent of coal rattling down the tipple like a black Niagara stops for good. The ovens will keep burning while the demand for coke is good but they will be charged with coal trucked in from other mines on the company's holdings.

The experts have been saying the beehive coke business was doomed since 1895 but its best year came thirteen years later. Certain by-products could be saved from beehive ovens to make the process more profitable but, except for occasionally diverting the gas for plant uses, American producers have not found it worth while to make the necessary installations.

In England, as early as 1891, the Thorncliffe Collieries worked out a process of saving the gas, ammonia, and tar products from the burning coal in beehive ovens by putting outlets in the floor of the ovens so that the liquids could be drawn off. The gas went through a series of pipes to eight big boilers that had been consuming two hundred gross tons of coal a week until the new process supplied free fuel from the waste gas.

The Latrobe Coal and Coke Company installed an experimental plant after the English model in 1895 that worked successfully, but not long. The process seems to have been all right but it didn't take hold in the district. The market for by-products was weak and there didn't seem to be much to do with the gas after it was saved. It would fire the boilers and cut down coal consumption, but there was not much point to that when so many royalty contracts only called for payment on the actual coke produced, *not on the coal burned.* Then its introduction coincided too closely with the sensation caused by a much better by-product oven, the Semet-Solvay, that would do a lot of other things besides save ammonia, tar, and gas.

It consisted of a narrow chamber or retort six feet high, eighteen inches wide, and about thirty feet long, with heating flues running lengthwise. When the coking coal swelled during the burning it could not expand because the sidewalls squeezed it in and the weight of the charge pressed it down, so that it became extra hard and dense. In a beehive oven when the burning coal swelled, the gases released made vertical passages in the coke like those in a cornstalk. With the Connellsville coal this open-work texture did not matter because it was naturally strong, but there were large deposits of coal in the neighborhood not considered fit for the beehives because the coke made from them was so weak it would not stand the weight in a blast furnace. A Semet-Solvay * oven made coke from this coal hard enough to satisfy the furnace men and thus created a market for coal acreage not considered valuable before. In addition it decreased the objectionable sulphur and ash in the coke, increased the yield, was much faster, and still saved the by-products. On the other hand it was more expensive to install—$3100 as opposed to $325 for a beehive oven; and the by-products distilled by the early ovens were not first class. When the Dunbar Furnace Company installed one in 1895, the ammonia recovered was seven to nine pounds of sulphate per ton of coal, but the oils produced were useless for lubricating,

---

* There were other types of by-product ovens coming into use at this time but I have mentioned only the Semet-Solvay because it was the only one tried out in the Region and the early tests from Connellsville coal were made in the Semet-Solvay Company's experimental plant at Syracuse, N. Y.

the tar and paraffine of inferior quality, and they had no market for the phenol.

The beehive operators reasonably concluded that inasmuch as the experts were saying that the Connellsville coal would not last more than a few years longer anyway, they might as well go on using the plants they had and not put any more money into equipment. By the time their coal was exhausted, their plants would be worn out, and when new ones were built they would probably be by-product. They have been patching up old ovens ever since, and when they built new batteries they did it cautiously, figuring the expenditure to meet a demand that would soon be over.

The beehive industry struck its peak in 1909 with 579 plants and 103,982 ovens. There were then only three by-product plants with 754 ovens in all of western Pennsylvania. Twenty-seven years later the beehive plants had decreased to 71 with 13,012 ovens working mostly in periods of unusual demand. The by-product industry meanwhile had advanced so rapidly that, in 1915, nineteen plants in the Pittsburgh coal area carbonized nearly 40 percent of the total coal in the country coked in by-product ovens. There was no point in building by-product plants in the Coke Region and piping the gas to Pittsburgh open hearths when it was so much simpler to send the coal to ovens built at the steel mills where the gas and tar could be used as fuel, so, except for the plant of fifty ovens at Dunbar operated about fifty years ago by the Dunbar Furnace Company in connection with their blast furnace, the new plants went elsewhere.

Nowadays sometimes the beehive plants work; sometimes they do not, according to the market. Industrial life in the Coke Region is like a long roll of drums with abrupt intervals of silence. When the smoke hangs low there is money in circulation and the Region feels good; when the smoke goes away and there is not dirt enough to notice, money is hard to come by, but nobody seems greatly cast down, assuming that another miracle is on its way. Thus far it has always come.

CHAPTER IV

BONANZA

AS FAR BACK AS 1759 PEOPLE KNEW THAT THERE WAS coal in the Virginia country along the Monongahela and the Youghiogheny Rivers. Colonel James Burd, who came from the East over Braddock's Road with two hundred men to trim the brush out of the path from Christopher Gist's Settlement (Mount Braddock) to the Monongahela, noted in his diary for September twenty-second of that year that he had found a creek bottomed with good stone coal and "the hill on the south of it is a rock of the finest coal I ever saw." He put a bushel of it on his fire to try it out and it burned well. The occurrence of coal was noted as a curious fact, not as a commercial discovery liable to amount to anything. The fuel of the day was wood and its by-product charcoal.

During the Revolution the garrison at Pittsburgh kept warm with coal from Coal Hill, owned by the Penn heirs, on the south side of the Monongahela. The seams were twelve to eighteen feet wide and lay close to the surface so it was easy to cut out the lumps and roll them down a trench in the hillside to boats moored below. The townspeople used it too and carried away all they wanted for a penny a bushel. When a hole had been worked so deep that the overburden seemed likely to cave in, they started another until the face of the hill was pocked with openings. European travelers to western Pennsylvania marveled at the great deposits of "stone-coal" that stretched for sixty miles around Pittsburgh.* Wagon wheels cut into it; it

---

* Howard N. Eavenson, *The First Century and a Quarter of American Coal Industry* (Pittsburgh, 1942), Chapter XII, "Western Pennsylvania, 1783–1800."

was "discoverable in the gullies of the road and among the roots of the trees that have been overturned by the wind." The drinking water was bitter with it and, where rivers had eroded their banks, there appeared seams of coal five or six feet wide that probably extended far below the water-line. People of the western settlements used as many as two fires to a house and kept their grates going late in the spring and early in the fall. Probably that was why they were so free from the low fevers that plagued eastern cities in damp weather. They preferred wood for cooking just as easterners did, but they used coal for everything else and saved the wood for the mechanics and shipbuilders. Coal was only two cents a bushel at the pit, four to six cents delivered. Up the Youghiogheny River in Connellsville it cost nothing at all because when Zachariah Connell laid out the town he offered free coal from neighboring deposits to prospective lot purchasers.

People began complaining of the Pittsburgh dirt even before 1800. In that year an Englishman named John Bernard wrote that it reminded him of London the way "a cloud of smoke hung over it in an exceeding clear sky." As the city grew bigger and attracted more industries, the black haze above it was visible for two or three miles. When they painted the steeple on the courthouse white, it promptly turned slate-gray. People couldn't keep their clothes clean, or their faces, either, and visitors wondered if their complexions might be permanently affected. An article in the Pittsburgh *Mercury* of December 7, 1814, when the low ground between the rivers was particularly murky, philosophized that "initiated here in infernal habits and familiarized to blazes, heat, smoke, soot and the blackness of darkness in this life, the transition to that which is to come will be easy and Hell thus stripped of half its terrors."

Pittsburgh became the coal capital of the country with a lively export trade down the Ohio and Mississippi. Coal had been moving on the Monongahela since 1788, punted along in barges of rough planks that would be broken up and sold for wood at the end of the journey. In 1811 a Mr. Roosevelt put a 450-ton steamboat on the river and increased the range of the coal trade until before long New Orleans and St. Louis became Pittsburgh's best customers. At first the coal came from the hills immediately surrounding the city, then from high up the reaches of the Monongahela and the Youghiogheny. At the mines only the lump coal was shipped or paid for. The slack that might have been turned into coke went on the dump or was left to choke the mine.

The little iron furnaces that painted the night sky red over the neighboring woods could have fueled more cheaply with coke but it meant learning a new process and they were used to using charcoal. That had been all right back in the 1790's when ironmasters could afford thousands of acres of woodland, but people were beginning to realize that not even our vast

American forests could keep them going long. It took 840 bushels of charcoal every twenty-four hours for a furnace with a daily capacity of two tons. That meant twenty-one or twenty-two cords of wood and, figuring one acre of land to produce twenty-five cords of wood of twenty- to twenty-five-year growth, or nearly an acre a day, the number of acres stripped yearly was enormous. It was always hard to keep enough charcoal ahead because it had to be kept under cover or it deteriorated, and the bulk for even a week's running was large. Pretty often the furnaces had to shut down while the whole crew helped the wood choppers and colliers make a supply of charcoal so they could go on running.

England had already gone through the same thing * and solved the problem nicely with coke, made at first very much in the same way as charcoal in long or conical ground-ricks. The pile of coal was covered with earth, leaving just enough air holes to allow the gases to burn off without being consumed. Rick coke was not very uniform but it was being used in making iron pots and small molds as early as 1709 or 1713. Then the furnace men began using it for pig iron and after 1760 they went into large-scale production of coke using ovens instead of ricks. For some reason American ironmasters were slow in trying out the process already well established in England, and when they finally experimented with coke in eastern Pennsylvania in 1811 and 1819, instead of taking advantage of the English experience they began back at the beginning using ricks.

When John Beal, an iron founder lately from England, announced in the Pittsburgh *Mercury* of 1813 that he was ready to offer his services to ironmasters to "instruct them in the method of converting stone-coal into *coak*," which was so much superior to charcoal that they would use it regularly after they tried it out, nobody seems to have paid any attention.

Colonel Isaac Meason had used coal at his Union Furnace on Dunbar Creek, probably in connection with his "bloomery," as far back as 1801. In 1817 he tried out rick coke successfully at his Plumsock Forge on Redstone Creek that was to become famous as the place where the first rolled iron in America was puddled.† According to one story, it was a Welsh immigrant named Samuel Lewis who interested Meason in the new iron-making process and supervised the building of the puddling furnaces; quite possibly he also brought with him the knowledge of how to use coke successfully. Another tradition gives an Englishman named Nichols the credit for introducing coke as fuel at Plumsock. After five months of operation,

---

* In England laws were passed against the deforesting by furnaces in Sussex, Surrey, and Kent in 1584 and prohibited the charcoaling of beech, oak, and ash trees. Henry C. Mercer, *The Bible in Iron* (Doylestown, Bucks County Historical Society, 1914), p. 149.

† Alton G. Campbell, "The Iron Industry in Fayette County: The Earliest Furnaces," in *Ft. Necessity and Historic Shrines of the Redstone Country* (Uniontown, Pa., 1932), p. 109.

just when the little plant was getting well established, Colonel Meason died and the work stopped.

A little later Meason's son-in-law inserted in the Uniontown *Genius of Liberty* an advertisement for "the Plumsock Iron Works, the most valuable property on the western side of the mountains...five miles northwest of Uniontown and thirty-nine miles from the city of Pittsburgh. Bar iron of a superior quality is made on this forge by rolling instead of hammering. An inexhaustible pit of coal, within one hundred yards of the forge, supplies *the only fuel used in making the iron.** Three men with a horse and cart are sufficient to raise, coke and haul to the forge all the coal necessary for keeping the works in full operation."

It took as many as twelve colliers to provide charcoal for one little cold-blast furnace.

After the settlement of the Meason estate, Plumsock operated under new management until 1824 when a flood on the Redstone partly wrecked it. After that it faded into oblivion. The settlers of the valley between the Youghiogheny and the Monongahela had something more than coal and iron to think about, now that the newly built Cumberland Road gave them an outlet east and west. Iron and coal were too heavy to transport. What they wanted was more cleared land to raise oats and hay for the teams that drew the Conestoga wagons and stagecoaches that streamed past their doors. Then there were all the travellers to be fed.

Uniontown was built over a bed of coal, but without water transportation her prosperity depended on the Pike. In addition to being the county seat and getting the court trade, she had a big stage yard, the headquarters for Lucius Stockton's stagecoach line, and a coach factory. Famous personages stopped at the new inns that sprang up on both sides of Main Street and her citizens spoke intimately of LaFayette, President Monroe, Henry Clay, and General Jackson. Brownsville was doing a double-barreled business as transfer point for stage passengers going West by the river packets. It looked as though it would outstrip Pittsburgh.

Connellsville watched the traffic hungrily from twelve miles away but, although her farmers could sell all the whiskey and provisions they hauled to the Pike, she wasn't in on the boom. Her only means of transportation was the shallow Youghiogheny River, but the only time it was navigable for more than a rowboat was in the spring and autumn freshets, and then if the cargo shifted somebody was likely to be drowned. Apparently the village fathers would have to get one of the new-fangled railroads if she were to share the general prosperity.

They began trying to coax one their way but the prospect was not promising. In 1835 it looked as though if a railroad came it would go through

* Author's italics.

Uniontown, who didn't want it for fear of hurting the Pike traffic, but the Connellsville promoters worked on doggedly. Two years later they got a franchise for a line to Pittsburgh but it remained a railroad on paper until the fifties. Even with the promise of a year-round outlet to the West there was not much to ship but a little bar iron. The Youghiogheny Valley had plenty of coal but it was too soft to transport well. Pittsburgh preferred the harder variety on the lower reaches of the river that could be boated out easily.

The only way to use the Connellsville coal seemed to be to make coke out of it and then try to create a market for it. Nichols, the Englishman who seems to have been associated with Colonel Meason, was still in the neighborhood, and when he took charge of Lester L. Norton's iron furnace in Connellsville in the early thirties he persuaded his employer to let him fuel it with coke. Isaac Meason's Plumsock mill had used rick coke, but Nichols proposed to burn coal for the Norton furnace in a twelve-foot coke oven similar to the ones used today. In 1833 he hired John Taylor, a local stone-mason, to build what seems to have been the first coke oven in America on Connell Run, in what is now the city of Connellsville, and charged it with coal from the Plummer Mine close by on the east bank of the Youghiogheny. Apparently the Norton furnace operated successfully on the new fuel because the next year John Coates, another Englishman, supervised the building of several more ovens, probably to supply Nathaniel Gibson's furnace near by. In 1836 F. H. Oliphant was burning coal in ricks to fuel the Fairchance furnace and, where Isaac Meason had used the Four-foot Redstone deposit, he carried the industry a step farther by delving into the Nine-foot vein lying a few feet above the Blue Lump iron ore that he was using. Thus he was able to mine the ore and the fuel to burn it with by the same operation. An advertisement of the same year lists a coke oven being offered for sale along with a ball furnace, finishing-rolls, a puddling furnace, etc., in Brownsville, across the county, but most of the interest in coke remained centered in the Connellsville area.

Thus far all the coke produced had been used locally. In the autumn of 1841 two carpenters, Provance McCormick and James Campbell, got John Taylor, who had built the coke oven for Nichols, to build two for them on his own farm. Then while Taylor burned the coke, they set about building two boats to carry it down the Youghiogheny. As soon as the spring freshets raised the water they floated down to Cincinnati to call on the iron manufacturers with nearly two thousand bushels of coke. But when they got there, the furnacemen looked at the porous gray cinders that had been coal and would have nothing to do with them. The Yough men finally peddled part of it off for groceries and the rest for a patent iron gristmill that would not work when they got it home. Later some of the coke they had sold went to a foundry in Dayton owned by a Fayette County man who knew how to use it. He liked it so well that he came up the Yough looking for McCormick and Campbell to get some more, but they were too discouraged to take the order.

The Cochrans, James and Sample, and their uncle, Mordecai, were the first men from the Coke Region to make money from coke manufacturing it for the public market. The next fall after the McCormick-Campbell expedition to Cincinnati they rented the ovens on the Taylor farm and built two boats that would hold six thousand bushels apiece. In the spring they set out with no money and thirteen thousand bushels of coke, bought provisions in Pittsburgh on credit, and sold their cargo in Cincinnati for seven cents a bushel. Then they went home to build more boats to carry more coke. The Cochrans were lucky in that they started to produce just when the furnacemen were getting their process worked out to use it advantageously.

A good many furnaces had tried it in the thirties, some built especially for coke but, although several made experimental runs with good results, they soon abandoned it.* Even F. H. Oliphant, who made such satisfactory iron at his Fairchance furnace using coke that he sent samples to Philadelphia to the Franklin Institute, seems not to have followed it up commercially. For one thing, it was hard to control with a cold blast. Anthracite could be used but it was not entirely satisfactory on account of its dense texture and it was available only in a limited area in the East. Up to now the furnaces had fired very well on charcoal but as ironmasters built bigger furnaces to supply a swelling demand for their product, the charcoal was too weak structurally to bear the increased weight of the burden; it cost too much; and the time had come when, with the forests exhausted, it could no longer be had in sufficient quantities.

In 1840 the Great Western Iron Company at Brady's Bend above Pittsburgh began making coke iron as a regular product. The Graff-Bennet Company of Pittsburgh followed in 1859 with their Clinton furnace using Connellsville coke just four years after the long awaited railroad began running into the Yough region. When the Civil War increased the demand for pig iron, Pittsburgh built some of the new hot-blast furnaces and fueled them with Connellsville coke, easily available over the new railroad. After that, if Pittsburgh made the Coke Region, the Coke Region no less made Pittsburgh because it was her coal fields that gave Pittsburgh a running start.

The Connellsville coke basin had twenty-six ovens when the railroad was completed in 1855. Five years later, there were more than double the number. Coal land that cost $37 an acre jumped to $100.

* The Mary Ann furnace in Huntington County made gray forge iron with coke in 1835 but continued only one month. In 1837 the Lonaconing furnace in Maryland got up to seventy tons a week on coke and in 1840 the two blast furnaces of the Mount Savage Company used it with mild success.

Uniontown, jealous of the Pike traffic, had fought giving a right of way to the B. & O. when it wanted to go to Pittsburgh by way of Fayette County, but the railroad got through by routing through West Virginia. As soon as the trains began running, the freight traffic on the Pike slowed to a trickle and Uniontown realized too late that when it turned away the B. & O. it lost not only the Pike freight that was bound to go anyway, but the main line of the railroad. If the coal deposits in the center of the county were going to be moved, there had to be rail transportation. The citizens finally got a connection with Pittsburgh by building a branch line of their own the twelve miles to Connellsville, but they had to finance it themselves at a cost of about $400,000.

Ten years after the Civil War there were almost sixty-four times as many ovens as there had been in 1860; in the next five years the number doubled again. On the Monongahela side of the district the mine shipments down river increased from 1845 to 1880 at the rate of two million bushels a year, and coal land prices climbed steadily.

In the early days the coal from the Monongahela mines was poled down the river to Pittsburgh in flatboats hastily thrown together to be torn up and sold for lumber when they were unloaded. Then as the Ohio River traffic grew busier, coal went farther west, first as ballast, then in regular coal boats, poled like the rafts but of stouter construction, lashed together in pairs with a cabin built over the load that served as bunkhouse, mess hall and storeroom. The crew for a pair of boats consisted of from eight to a dozen men, a cook, relief pilot, and captain.

Up the Monongahela, river men began using tows before 1840, cautiously descending as far as Pittsburgh, but they did not attempt the Ohio to any extent until the middle sixties. For a long time coal going to the Gulf travelled in coal boats, poled and steered by the crew, and, when the cargo was discharged, the men walked home or took passage on a ship for Philadelphia or Baltimore to return cross-country over the mountains. When steamers began to make the up-river trip, the crews came back as passengers, bringing as much of their gear as they wanted to salvage.

The heavier coal boats that began to appear on the river as the southern demand increased were designed to make more than one trip, but they were hard to steer and their larger loads called for deeper draft, so they could travel only at flood tide with its swift water and dangerous currents. The river men depended on luck and the pressure of the water to keep their heavily laden craft from bursting at the seams; if the loaded boats collided with anything they cracked like egg shells, and they rode so low in the water that waves of any size would swamp them. The traffic during the Civil War was particularly hazardous because the Confederates were eager for coal and whenever possible they seized or sank the cargoes. If a boat got through the profit was enormous. Tugs, boats and barges swarmed on the spring and fall tides.

In 1869 the *Ajax* was making three trips a year to New Orleans. On its fall trip in 1868 it piloted down twenty thousand bushels of coal and every time it went it took the product of four acres of coal four feet thick. Cincinnati was taking as much coal as St. Louis and New Orleans combined. She paid only ten cents a bushel afloat in the barge compared to New Orleans' fourteen, but the difference in haul made up for it.

Thomas Mellon, cannily consolidating the fortune that would be the nucleus of his sons' immense holdings, went into the down-river coal trade. He liked land and money manipulation, and what was coal but a kind of land, salable as soon as portable? In 1863 he wrote to his son James, who had not yet made up his mind what he wanted to do:

"Learn the *modus operandi* of the coal business and merchandising ... it may be useful to us hereafter.... As to the coal business, I consider it one of the best and highly respectable."

The newly developed manufactured gas business was enlarging the tonnage nearer home. A bushel of small-lump river coal that cost two cents could be coked to produce 336 cubic feet of gas, or nearly 8,000 cubic feet a ton. The Pittsburgh gas company sold it to private customers for two dollars a thousand and had the coke left as an additional profit. The project was so successful that before long Coke Region coal shipped by water and rail illuminated Chicago, Detroit, Port Huron, Milwaukee, and three cities in Ontario, Canada. When natural gas was piped into Pittsburgh about 1875 it spoiled the manufactured gas business in that district, but by that time other industries were taking so much coal the loss of tonnage in that field made little difference.

From 1870 to 1884 coal production increased 300 percent, but the price went down until it was out of proportion to the cost of the labor that produced it. That meant hard times. Operators tried to cut costs in a hurry and had strikes on their hands. The unstable transportation system always kept the business in confusion. Boats sank, rammed each other, got stuck on shoals or bumped into piers; sometimes they ran all the way to New Orleans only to find the market glutted. When the demand was good their antiquated production methods were not able to keep up with it.

When the industry was beginning, the coal easiest to move was stripped and quarried, cut and pried out by hand, packed in a hide sewed into a bag, and rolled down to a boat or wagon. Sometimes, as at Coal Hill * near Pittsburgh, the miners tumbled it down a convenient fissure in the hillside

---

* Across the Monongahela from the down-town section of modern Pittsburgh, Coal Hill is now known as Mt. Washington.

to boats waiting in the water below. Where it was necessary to cut a drift into the hill they dug only a little distance. As soon as the going was hard they started another. When the demand became greater, and drifts went deeper, the men used barrows or dragged the coal to the pit mouth in boxes. Naturally, the next step was to put wheels on the box and make a pit wagon. Usually a miner and a dog pulled it, hitched tandem, the dog in front. Itinerant miners brought their dogs with them and wherever they went they worked as a team. Horses and mules began hauling coal in mines with openings tall enough for them to stand up after Michael Dravo started using them around McKeesport in the late thirties. The haulageways underground were so bumpy for pit wagons that mine owners laid wooden rails for the wheels to run on. Later they extended the rude tracks outside to the "coal-drop," making some of the first railroads in the country.

There was little system to the underground work. By 1869 some of the deep mines were being worked in "rooms" with six-foot barriers running parallel between. Generally there was no ventilation, although sometimes a stove put at the bottom of a shaft set the air to circulating by making the heated column of air above it rise, creating a draft below. The miners fumbled their way in the dark with only a speck of flame to work by for fear of the gases that might have accumulated without their knowing it.

The hours they worked depended on the state of the rivers. Except for gas purposes it was not profitable to ship coal by rail over fifty miles. The year-round coke trade served by the railroad supplied steady work for part of the Youghiogheny miners but the others on both rivers worked only when the boats could run. In the summer there was not enough water; in the winter it froze up. That left only seven months to get out coal to satisfy a year-round demand. In season, miners made good wages when compared with those of other skilled workers—four to six dollars a day, but they went into the pits at one o'clock in the morning and sometimes they did not come out until eight o'clock at night.*

The rate of payment was by the bushel, but when the mine owners found expenses mounting they made the bushel weigh more. During the Civil War mining costs went up sharply from two cents a bushel in 1860 to seven cents in 1865. The men were supposed to load only the lump coal and heap the bushel, but they got in so much slack that operators installed scales and paid only for what went over the screen. When prices steadied after the war the rate for mining was four cents for a ninety-six-pound (heaped) bushel of round coal, run over a screen, with the slack handled for nothing. In good

* Howard N. Eavenson, *The First Century and a Quarter of American Coal Industry,* p. 201, quoting James M. Killap, a Scotch professor who visited America in 1869 and wrote his impressions of the coal trade.

coal a miner could get out from three and one-half to four tons a day, in an extra thick seam, five or six.*

In the early days of the industry mine owners worked in the mines themselves. Little Jim Cochran, the pioneer operator in the Connellsville Basin, used to dig coal with a lard lamp in his cap, and when the wick burned out he would tear a piece out of his sleeve to make another. And he hauled out the coal in twelve-bushel cartloads by the aid of a strap around his neck. He had no mules, and when he had to get men to help he paid them fifty cents a day in provisions. He kept on boating to Cincinnati, good years and bad, until the blast furnaces began to congregate in Pittsburgh. Then he gave up the river and shipped by rail. When he needed a tramway to run the coal down to the cars he bought lumber for it from Henry Clay Frick, who was clerking in his Grandfather Overholt's saw- and gristmill over at Broad Ford near Connellsville. Outside capital was coming to the region to build banks of thirty, forty, finally one hundred ovens in a string. The panic of 1873 slowed things up some but he was able to keep his fires burning and even help some of the new operators to tide over. Now they were calling him "The King of Coke," but the time was not far off when the title would pass to Rainey and to Frick.

The new overlords did not keep in touch with their men the way Little Jim did. They hardly knew what the men looked like. W. J. Rainey,† who came to be sole owner of thousands of acres of coal property and plants that totalled three thousand ovens, lived in Cleveland, and the big show place he built on Euclid Avenue, with its black walnut-panelling and crystal chandeliers, was only something to read about in the Coke Region, where the money to pay for it came from. His brother-in-law, T. J. Mitchell, managed the mines and ovens for him.

Rainey's rival, Henry Clay Frick, actually operated larger properties but he represented a company allied with Carnegie Steel Company. Frick was a Westmoreland County boy of Swiss-German extraction, a grandson in the prominent whiskey-distilling Overholt family. It is hard to understand why, considering his frandfather's prosperity, he was given so little chance

---

* In that same period other workers' wages ran as follows:

mining boss or manager	$3.50 to $4.00 a day
river boss or pilot	$3.00
weigh boss or banksmen	$2.75
blacksmith	$2.75 to $3.00
carpenter	$2.50 to $3.00
engineman	$2.50
laborer on coal banks	$2.00
coke-oven worker	$1.00 for filling and drawing each oven
farm laborer	$20.00 to $25.00 per month with board

† "W. J. Rainey," by S. J. Kelly. A reminiscence in manuscript form loaned by Mrs. H. D. Hutchinson of the Uniontown Public Library.

to go to school. His whole education amounted to five terms in primary schools and three terms in those of higher grades. Then after a brief period of clerking in Mt. Pleasant, with the privilege of sleeping on the counter at night, he was promoted to a thousand dollars a year clerking in the family distillery.

But although young Henry dutifully undertook the job, he had no intention of staying in it any longer than he had to. By the time he was twenty-one he was running a few coke ovens on the side, financed mostly by a ten-thousand-dollar loan wangled from Judge Thomas Mellon, the Pittsburgh banker. When he made his first borrowing trip to T. Mellon & Sons in 1871 he had nothing for security but ambitious plans and a little coal land, but the impression he made on the old financier was so good he let him have the money anyway.

Before the first bank of ovens was finished Frick was back in Mellon's office again asking for another ten thousand dollars to build fifty more ovens. This time Mellon sent an investigator to Broad Ford to see what kind of use the young operator had made of loan number one. According to the report he received it appeared that, although the young man had built well as far as he went, the operation was small; also, he was not giving all his time to the coke business. That is, he was keeping the Overholt distillery accounts, and the living room-office that he occupied in a frame shack was littered with books and pictures unrelated to either the coke plant or the whiskey business. The prudent investigator sent by Mellon recommended that the loan be refused. So Thomas Mellon temporized and sent his mining partner, James B. Corey, to Broad Ford.

"Land's good; ovens well built"; reported Corey, "manager on job all day, keeps books evenings, may be a little too enthusiastic about pictures but not enough to hurt; knows his business down to the ground; advise making loan." *

So Frick built fifty more ovens and began to manufacture coke for the market just in time to be caught in the Panic of 1873. He applied desperately to Thomas Mellon for credit but the banker was too harried by the perilous times to have any money to spare. Frick did however help Mellon to engineer the sale of the little railroad line that connected Broad Ford with the B. & O. at Mt. Pleasant. The fifty-thousand-dollar commission that fell to Frick from the deal shored up his tottering company but it could not hold out for long without orders. He set out to get them, spending five hours a day on trains to and from Pittsburgh, canvassing from office to office to build up his tonnage, calling on Fayette County farmers nights in a buggy trying to exchange notes for cash, and somehow running the plant along with everything else.

* George Harvey, *Henry Clay Frick—The Man*. New York: Scribner's, 1928.

The little general store he ran in connection with the coke works helped to solve his problem. He could get goods for it on credit, although he could hardly tell where the cash for his pay roll was coming from. Why not make his own currency, redeemable in goods at the company store, and thus tide over both the plant and the men who depended on it?

The scrip bills that presently issued from Broad Ford looked very much like government greenbacks except the face was ornamented with an appropriate group of miners with picks and the announcement that Frick and Company's mines were due the bearer in merchandise one dollar at Broad Ford, Pennsylvania, 1874. It was a splendid idea for the emergency but it proved too profitable to abandon when the necessity for it no longer existed, and its misuse as it became widely adopted by operators all over the Coke Region became a continual irritant in labor relations.

The strain of '73 and '74 began to tell on Frick and a severe illness brought on by overwork nearly killed him in February of 1875. In March he was up again, trying to work out a stock company that would include the interests of his principal rival, the Morgan Mines. The proposed consolidation did not come off, but in 1877, when the pall of depression was at its blackest, the Morgans fell into distress so serious that he was able to take them over. The next year he sold to E. M. Ferguson of Pittsburgh an interest in his company and with the added capital completed the Morgan investment. Then, with his most serious competition disposed of, he announced the formal organization of H. C. Frick and Company on March 9, 1878. The solid groundwork of his fortune was laid.

The Mellons had stood by him handsomely through the bad years. After the successful termination of the railroad deal, Thomas Mellon managed a mortgage loan for him in spite of the tightness of money, followed by others until the credit secured from the Mellons in the difficult period amounted to $100,000 with security of only 471 acres of land, (143 of it coal-bearing) and two town lots in Broad Ford.

Frick met Andrew Mellon, the banker's son, in 1876 when he was twenty-six and the latter twenty-two, a diffident, lonely young man who felt at home only in the office world of ledgers.* The friendship that sprang out of the meeting, founded on two powerful dissimilar personalities inspired by the single aim of making money, was to make financial history for forty years. Frick supplied the daring and far-reaching perspective, Andrew the caution; both could be equally ruthless.

When times began to pick up in 1879, the H. C. Frick Company was ready for them. The railroad lines of the country had taken a severe beating in the three years just past. As reorganization mergers launched reconstruc-

---

* Harvey O'Connor, *Mellon's Millions: The Life and Times of Andrew W. Mellon* (New York: The John Day Co.), p. 44.

tion programs, orders for rails began pouring into Pittsburgh and steel mills called for coke shipments in a hurry. Prices jumped from ninety cents a ton to two dollars, three dollars, four dollars, and finally five dollars, of which three-fifths was net profit. Purchasing agents found Henry Clay Frick producing about 80 percent of the entire supply. By the end of the year his ovens were shipping a hundred cars a day and he had a thousand men on the pay roll.

On the night of December 19, 1879, Frick spent the evening playing chess with his cousins, bought a nickel cigar, and walked around the corner to the village hotel. It was his thirtieth birthday and he was a millionaire.

So far the new Coke King's life had been all work and no play. Now he felt he could get away for a trip to Europe with his friend, Andrew Mellon, and it was time he began to think of setting up a home for himself. In 1881 he married Miss Adelaide Childs and Mellon acted as his best man. It was while the couple were on their wedding trip that Frick first met Andrew Carnegie and out of the meeting came the announcement that the Carnegie group was entering into a partnership with Frick. The reorganization that followed under the name of the H. C. Frick Coke Company meant a reduction of Frick's interest in the company from 33⅓ percent to 29½ percent, but he received $325,000 cash and became allied with his best customer. Also the immensely stronger new corporation assumed the indebtedness of the old one.

Business continued to improve but the labor situation in the Coke Region was always in a ferment. As the plants multiplied Frick manned them with gangs of Slavs fresh off the boats. Theoretically they were supplied by labor brokers, but Coke Region people believed that Frick agents did their own recruiting in southern Europe. How else did the groups of Hungarians come already ticketed for Frick Coke Company?

The native population of the Region watched the influx with alarm and resentment. They had assimilated the English, Irish, Welsh, and Germans who came earlier, a few at a time, but this wholesale dumping of aliens was another matter. The strange foreign women who came to town with knee boots and short, flared skirts, their hair tied up in kerchiefs, were just as apt to walk down the middle of the street as on the sidewalks. The bosses could hardly keep them out of the coke-yards they were so eager to help their men. Even when they were six or seven months pregnant they would snatch a coke fork and start shovelling. It made it hard for the Americans when the foreigners were so crazy to work. No matter what the bosses asked they would do it, if he could make them understand what he wanted. They would go into the worst wet holes in the mine, live in any kind of a shanty, get along on half what it took to keep an American family. When bosses could get men who could be driven like sheep, of course they would want to hire them instead of the home folks—and pretty soon where would the home folks be?

Disorders between the newcomers and the English-speaking laborers occurred with increasing frequency. New violence developed when labor leaders undertook to organize the Coke Region. There had been strikes before, one in 1848 over wages and another in 1859 when the miners wanted scales to replace bushel measurement, but they had been nothing like these mine wars stirred up from outside. The foreigners followed the agitators as blindly as they did the bosses, depending on who won their allegiance. There was always trouble of one kind or another, either between the English-speaking miners and the foreigners or between the companies and the men.

Frick took no nonsense from his help; but, although he disciplined small rebellions from time to time, the trouble wouldn't stay settled. As time went on Frick was to find that in matters of labor management his ideas differed widely from those of his partner. Carnegie was fond of quoting as a fundamental principal: "Thou shalt not take thy neighbor's job." As later expressed in a private note to Frick: "My idea of beating in a dispute with men is always to shut down and suffer; let them decide when they desire to go to work—say kindly, 'All right, gentlemen, let's hear from you . . . when a majority vote to start, start it is.' "

Carnegie believed that the operators ought to confer with the workmen's organizations and "wait patiently until they decide to return to work, never thinking of trying new men, never. . . . Workmen can always be relied upon to resent the employment of new men. *Who can blame them?*"

Mr. Frick's idea was that when there was work to be done, if one man didn't want to do it, he'd find another who would. While an operator might confer with his workmen if he wanted to, he was not compelled to do so. He had a right to run his own business in his own way and it was the duty of the state government to see that the rights of property were not interfered with.

To complicate matters further, some of the dreaded Molly McGuires moved into the district after they were run out of the anthracite fields. Their presence was first realized in June, 1881, when presumably some of them killed Maurice Healey, the superintendent at Dunbar Furnace. The county offered two thousand dollars for the murderers, the furnace company one thousand dollars and hired Captain Linden of the Pinkerton Bureau to direct the search. He tracked down his quarry but sprang the trap too soon, so that the state's case was weak and, of the seven members originally indicted, only two went to trial. Of these the jury acquitted one and the second got off with only a second-degree murder sentence. Apparently the Molly McGuires did not find the Coke Region fertile ground in spite of the leniency of the court, because, after dealing out death warnings to the prosecuting attorneys,

William Playford and C. E. Boyle, they ceased their activities in the Youghiogheny Valley.

The bad blood between the English-speaking and foreign laborers continued however, and fomented a growing resentment in the Yankee population against the outside capitalists who were investing money in the district.

"One of the most degrading influences brought to bear upon our community is the indiscriminate portion of Hungarian serfs and their employment in public works in preference to good located citizens who are willing and can perform more and better labor for the same pay," stated a placard called "An Appeal to the Christian Public" tacked up at one of the Mt. Pleasant mines. "It has been the custom of certain coke operators not living among us to import and forward these serfs and give them employment in preference to good citizens.... Little do they care for our working men or our business men. They are ruining both and well they know it.... Go to any of the coke works where these serfs are employed and you will find women and children at work fit only for the stoutest of men, women at work with infants lying promiscuously on the cold ground; girls under ten years of age working and drawing coke;... extreme promiscuity in their marital relations; carrying on an illicit whiskey traffic.... If it really takes men, women and children at hard labor to keep a family which lives on the cheapest and filthiest of wares, what will other American citizens do for a living? ..."

In spite of all its troubles the Coke Region had a good deal to be complacent about in 1882. There were 8,400 ovens producing coke now where there had been only 3,000 six years before. By the end of the year the operators expected to have turned out well over four million tons. Besides the steady demand from Pittsburgh and the Ohio Valley, Youghiogheny coke was going to the gold and silver states out West to be used in the refinement of precious metals; and Mr. Frick had just installed a new screening and grading process that was going to put coke in hundreds of homes all over the East that had heretofore used anthracite.

If all the output for 1882 were put on one freight-haul travelling at the usual speed of fourteen miles an hour, said the new *History of Fayette County,* a man watching the train pull out at a given hour one morning would see coke cars passing in unbroken succession without a moment's pause or slackening for nine days and nights before he saw the tail light on the last car. By that time the engine would be 2,800 miles away.

According to the local papers, everything would be fine if the Region could just get rid of the foreigners and labor troubles.

CHAPTER V

IF THEY GET HUNGRY ENOUGH—1894

A CROWD OF MINERS MILLED AROUND A FIRE ON THE
hill above Wheeler coke plant getting noisier as they fortified themselves against the raw April wind with *polinkivak* and Monongahela rye.*
Toward morning somebody got hold of a box of dynamite and they let off
a few charges to wake up the mine bosses and let them know they meant
business. Tomorrow nobody would hitch up mine mules or dig coal or draw
coke; if W. J. Rainey and Cochran and the McClure and the Cambria Iron
Companies wanted to run their ovens, they'd have to dig coal themselves.
It was the night of Sunday, April 1, 1894, and nobody was going to work till
the operators came to terms with the scale committee. The days of canvassing and negotiating were over. After a month of uncertainty the miners and
coke-drawers of the Coke Basin knew what they were going to do.

"Better to starve idle than starve working!" they said and made the tipple
rattle with another explosion.

The women in the company houses up and down the valley stood on their
porches listening to their men having a good time. Maybe everything was
going to be better as the men said, but they remembered sons and husbands
gathering another first of April night just four years ago, armed with stones

---

* The Region has always considered the industrial conflicts that shake it from time
to time as private fights and discouraged news coverage. Thus while nearly everyone
knows about the Homestead Steel strike, the coke strike of 1894 which involved more
operations, lasted longer, and cost the lives of more people is hardly known outside
the district. In this chapter therefore I have used eye-witness accounts as far as possible,
supplemented by local newspaper articles of the period.

and clubs to go up against guards with Winchesters back of the barricades at Morewood plant. When the shooting was over seven strikers lay dead and twenty wounded, some of them later to die. That night had started off just like this one, only better, with marching and band-playing, but it cost thirteen lives and the governor sent soldiers afterward so the men couldn't fight back.

There were eight thousand people jammed in the square at Scottdale when the train came bringing the bodies for burial; four thousand walked the mile to the cemetery, and men took the coffins out of the wagons to carry them on their shoulders; but all the honor and the fine preaching with two priests and decorating their graves every year wouldn't bring the men back to life again. They were brave all right, but what did it get them?

Every five or six years there was the same thing to go through again. The men asked for more pay; they didn't get it and so they quit work. People were hungry and some got killed, and then they worked again for just the same pay they got in the first place. But if you didn't keep trying how would you ever get more money? That's what the men said and there was no stopping them from going out now. They *were* out.

Trouble had been brewing in the Coke Region all the lean winter of 1893–94. Some of the men around Fayette City hadn't had more than two months' work in a year and a half and there were patches where commissaries had to be set up to feed the people. The coal trade had developed more rapidly than the necessities of the country required. There were too many mines, too many men to work them, and not enough orders. The result was a price war that drove coke down to a dollar a ton, and in order to produce it the companies had to take it out of the men.

The Connellsville Basin was running full but plenty of operators weren't meeting their pay rolls. Men complained that they hadn't been paid in eight months. When a miner wanted to promise something at a far-off date that might never come he'd say: "I'll do it on Rainey's payday!" Only the men who worked for Rainey didn't think the wry joke was funny.

Miners and coke-drawers with empty pockets had to buy at the company's "pluck-me" stores where two dollars' worth of work didn't seem to buy more than a dollar's worth of goods. They had to live in the company houses, too, or the job went to somebody who would; and it wasn't easy to find another job with so many men scrambling for them that they'd pay good money to a labor boss to get preference for a place on a gang. English-speaking workmen complained that the Slavs and Italians would give the bosses as high as ten dollars to get on. And when you got the job what did the operators give you for blasting out coal and loading it, maybe in water to your waist in holes so low you couldn't stand straight? Just about a dollar a day, with the deductions to come out of that. Suppose you made $1.12—

and that was a good average—in a five-day week you got $5.25, in a four-week month, $21.00. Out of that the company took $6.50 for house rent, $1.00 for coal in summer, $2.00 in winter, leaving $13.50 to live on and raise your family. The wages, based on piecework at so much a wagon, varied according to the coal you were in. You might be able to dig as high as seven wagonloads one day, but maybe the next day you wouldn't get more than two; and the company demanded heaped wagons with seven to ten bushels in the hump a man got no pay for.

There was no uniform rate for the same work, either. The Frick miners had a contract that gave them enough to live on, with provision for an orderly advance, and they got their money on time. If Frick could do it, why couldn't Rainey and Cochran and Cambria Iron, McClure and the bosses at Oliver?

On Sunday, March fourth, the men at Oliver met and delivered an ultimatum. They had had no pay for eleven weeks and they wouldn't wait any longer. If it was not forthcoming, along with a promise of semi-monthly wages after that, they would lay down their picks and coke forks. That same day a secret meeting of a thousand miners from the vicinity of Uniontown took place at the foot of the mountain near Hopwood and planned a campaign for a uniform wage scale, level wagons, and cash pay instead of credit slips. A good many men sympathetic to the movement were afraid to attend, so the meeting gave six organizers authority to admit members without their making public appearances until the Big Push was under way.

The Uniontown *News Standard* got wind of the undercover gathering and announced that the miners were organizing but the operators scoffed at the idea. The men had been so thoroughly beaten when they struck in '91 that they wouldn't want to try it again so soon, and anyway they couldn't afford to go out now just when the coke business was beginning to pick up. If there were an organization, it didn't represent the rank and file of the coke workers. There would be no strike.

Presently the miners came out in the open with a meeting at Scottdale, organized a branch of the United Mine Workers Union under the direction of Patrick McBride of the National Committee, and elected L. R. Davis of Uniontown president and Daniel Darby secretary. Then they invited the operators to meet with a scale committee at a general conference of coke workers the next week to draw up a uniform wage rate for the district. Now that they were part of a nationwide labor organization already mapping strategy for a nationwide strike, perhaps the operators would be willing to talk over the problems peculiar to the Region.

None of the operators answered the letter or came to the meeting. There were more miners there, however, than the leaders expected. Rainey's men, who hadn't played with the strike idea in ten years, turned out, and there

SLATE DUMPS—Wherever there are mines there are slate dumps—gray, smouldering mountains by day and veined with blue fire by night

A COMPANY PATCH—In the shadow of the slate dumps the older patches climb hilltops in rows of identical houses, fenced back yards, and outdoor toilets

HEADFRAME AND TIPPLE

FIRE BOSS—The fire boss taps the roof to test the possibilities of a slate fall. He carries a safety lamp with which he tests the workings for gas before the miners enter

Photo courtesy of Pittsburgh Coal Company

MECHANIZED COAL MINING—This universal cutting machine slices nine feet deep into a thick deposit. It is operated by two men, machine runner and helper. Here the helper wears U. S. Bureau of Mines approved cap lamp with battery attached to his belt

BORING HOLES—The machine is boring holes for dynamite charge to shoot down a block of coal

UNDERGROUND WAITING STATION—At the end of the day's work, miners await their turn to enter the cage that will hoist them to top of the shaft

PICKING BELT—Here the slate is sorted from the coal on its way to the storage bin

COKE PLANT AT NIGHT—The plant is luridly beautiful by night when the glare of the ovens paints the sky and works magic with headframes and sooty buildings

COKE OVENS—These long blocks of ovens are loaded with coal from lorries which run along a track on top and have access to two parallel strings of ovens with their backs to each other

Photo courtesy of U. S. Steel Corporation

DAUBING—After the coke oven has been charged with coal the door is bricked up and daubed with mud, leaving a narrow air fissure at the top

END OF A BURN—The flames coming out of trunnel tops have died down but the doors will not be opened till the "quenching"

Photo courtesy of U. S. Steel Corporation

QUENCHING—After the volatile matter is consumed, the coke is watered to prevent its burning

DRAWING—When the coke is drawn it comes out in silvery metallic cinders

Photo courtesy of U. S. Steel Corporation

"ANOTHER DAY"—An oil painting by Frank L. Meléga shows a common scene in older patch houses where modern bathing facilities are lacking

"PIT BUDDIES"—This is another oil by Frank L. Meléga. Note the large, round dinner buckets which hold water in case of accident

were men from all the other plants from Fairchance to Latrobe. The hot-heads wanted to strike at once if the operators weren't going to recognize that they had any demands. The more conservative element set the date for April first to allow time to hold meetings and give the operators a chance to arbitrate if they wanted to. The most the men hoped for was a uniform scale as good as the Frick men had, although for trading purposes it might be well to ask for more. The rate finally settled on called for ninety cents per hundred bushels for mining coal; all other inside and outside labor asked for an increase over the Frick scale of 12 percent.

For a week the opposing parties jockeyed for position through the newspapers. The independent operators proclaimed that they paid as much as if not more than the Frick scale. U.M.W. Secretary Darby replied that independents like McClure, the Oliver mines, and the Stewart Iron Company theoretically paid fifty-eight cents per hundred bushels, but actually the men did not get that much. The operators insisted that they could not pay more wages with coke selling for a dollar. If the men struck now, western Pennsylvania would lose the business recently coaxed away from West Virginia. Would the men rather have cold ovens and no money at all?

One producer suggested reasonably that the operators ought to organize as well as the men. Business had been good between 1886 and 1891 when both sides had a union of sorts. If the coke producers would get together again and restrain the operators who wanted more than their share of the business, they could put coke up to $1.50 and pay the men a living wage.

"The foreigners are to blame for the cheap coke that is degrading American Labor," shouted the Region press, choosing an angle that would offend neither capital nor English-speaking labor, who were all they needed to worry about because the Hungarians naturally did not read the American papers. "If the operators will raise the price of coke and hire only Americans to make it, everything will be all right."

Nothing came of the talk. The operators refused to admit until the last day that there was a union in the Coke Region. Who was Davis anyhow? A Uniontown bartender, head of a claque of blowhards. Let him set dead lines and give ultimatums! The men wouldn't go out.

The first of April fell on Sunday and was quiet until the whiskey and dynamite got to circulating at the Wheeler works. In the morning the nucleus of strikers who had spent the night celebrating marched to Humphrey where the men were working and drove them away, went on to Anchor and closed that, adding to their ranks as they swept along. At Hill Farm there was a little fighting and the strikers tried to burn the shanties but thought better of it. No need of getting tough the first day.

The men at Oliver had promised to notify the superintendent when they would strike so they could have the coke all out of the ovens, but they didn't do it. The company tried to take it out with other workmen but the strikers chased them away. By night the labor leaders estimated that about four thousand men had laid down their tools. Oliver, Anchor, Humphrey, and Hill Farm were out, as well as Lemont I and II, Leisenring II, and the foreigners at Moyer. The English-speaking men stayed at their posts. On the whole the strike was a success in the southern part of the Region but the Frick works from Connellsville north were going the same as usual; so were those of McClure, Rainey, and Cochran.

The thing that worried the strike leaders was the cleavage in the strikers' ranks between native and foreign workmen. The English-speaking men weren't standing by like the Hungarians. If they didn't come out and the operators filled up the places vacated by the foreign strikers with Americans, they would turn the whole thing into a race war instead of a struggle to better living conditions.

The second day of the strike there was a mob of five hundred on the prowl, closing plants as fast as they came to them. At Leith and Brownfield the men in the pits wouldn't come out. The strikers sent word down to them that if they had not come above ground by the time they came back they would stop the fan and suffocate them. Then they went to the next plant leaving guards at the pit mouths.

The Frick men were not joining the strikers. They had a better wage scale than the other miners and regular paydays. When they had struck before, they had taken a lot of punishment but it hadn't gotten them much. In 1887 it looked as if Mr. Carnegie were going to do something for them. He had a quarrel with Frick about his hired deputies, but the next time there was trouble Frick had his way. They didn't want another Morewood.

So when the mob came they stopped work only long enough to see them out of sight; then they went on as usual. But when Rainey's men went out on the fourth they were really out, and their joining the strikers affected 1,422 ovens. It was the first time in ten years that they had suspended operations and the strikers were jubilant; the operators were not too sorry about it either, remembering the other times when Rainey had shipped coke as fast as he could load because his men worked when their men wouldn't, leaving them tied up with cold ovens unable to take advantage of coke prices rising as supply dwindled.

That third day of the strike the shooting began. At Donnelly and Mayfield some of the English-speaking miners wanted to go to work; the Hungarians called them "blacklegs" and surrounded the plants so they couldn't get in. Bosses, guards, and superintendents gave battle, and in the melee a striker was shot but whether fatally or not the paper failed to report, because that day there was bigger news than a minor riot.

The Frick Company's Davidson works on the Youghiogheny River a little below Connellsville was running, but the men had mostly finished work for the day and gone home when a call came into the company office that a mob of strikers was marching from Broad Ford down the B. & O. tracks. W. O. Kennedy, assistant to the general manager, took the message and passed it on to Hugh Coll, machinery engineer, who happened to be in the office. They started for the shaft, running part of the way, and met the men as they came in the road. They were playing for time until help came, since they could not hope to hold the men back for long.

Kennedy asked who the leader of the mob was and at first received no answer. Then an American named Sam Mason stepped out of the crowd and said the strikers wanted to talk to the Davidson workmen. Kennedy asked if Mason could control his men, and Mason said he thought he could. There was a brief parley in which Kennedy warned the strikers against damaging company property, and the mob withdrew after throwing a few stones at the tipple. A little later they came back by way of the old steelworks and halted at the glass plant.

Kennedy saw them move toward the tipple and sent Hugh Coll for the deputies. After that, part of the mob went up the hill to the company houses while the rest of them milled around in the road. Coll was on his way to the shaft when he ran into Joseph Paddock, chief engineer of the Frick Company.

"Hadn't we better go up and order them off the company property?" asked Paddock. So they went up the hill after the strikers and followed them from house to house, warning them to leave the men alone. In about the fourth block the strikers wavered and it looked as though they were going to leave peaceably. Coll said later that he and Paddock had turned to go back down the hill when they realized that the mob was coming toward them. Paddock said to Coll, "Don't shoot!" but Coll, seeing a man pick up a stone, emptied his gun in the face of the mob. They were only fifteen feet away when he fired. Stones flew in earnest then, and the two company officials ran backward, firing as they went. Coll got down the hill first and went over a bank to safety. According to his story, when he last saw Paddock the mob had caught up with him and he was trying to protect his head with his hands.

It is hard to know just what happened then. One version is that Paddock ran or was chased into the tipple and jumped out of the window to the lorry track forty feet below. The company witnesses said that Paddock was beaten and stoned to death when the crowd caught up with him, but that did not explain the bullet hole in the back of Paddock's neck. It could hardly have come from the strikers who were in front of him as he and Coll ran backwards, firing. However he may have died, his bruised body was picked up later on the lorry track and carried to the Union Supply Company store while the mob retreated to Broad Ford.

Trouble let loose in earnest after that. Joseph Paddock was highly thought of in Connellsville, a member of the city council, and a vestryman of the New Haven Episcopal Church, with important church connections in Philadelphia. Connellsville citizens scoured the country under deputies arresting any hapless foreigner who fell into their clutches. They picked up thirty at Dawson, eleven around Connellsville, and when a Hungarian ran instead of halting at Broad Ford, a deputy shot him dead. His body lay uncared for all night by the tracks until somebody turned it over to the undertaker the next day.

That night President L. R. Davis was arrested in Scottdale and brought to Connellsville by horse and buggy on a charge of murder, although he had not been at Davidson. Darby and two prominent organizers, McSloy and Simkoski, were rounded up too, as soon as they could find them. The wildest rumors ran like quicksilver. Connellsville heard that eight hundred strikers were due to pass through town on their way north, and excited citizens flew to the armory for guns to disperse them, but Captain George Munson, company commander, stationed guards around the building and kept them out.

The next day fifteen hundred bewildered strikers camped at Everson, twin town of Scottdale. Their leaders were either in jail or on the run; almost a hundred strikers had been arrested and the anti-Hungarian fury that turned public opinion against the strike had driven the wedge deeper between the foreign and English-speaking miners. Some of them began drifting back to work and the papers announced that the death of Paddock had doomed the strike. Now let the operators "drive from their employ the ignorant and vicious foreigners that have degraded American labor and set the Coke Region in incalculable disorder and turmoil." Now, urged the press, if only Frick would refuse to employ foreign labor, the hordes of Slavs that had been dumped on the Coke Region would get hungry enough to leave.

But when Mr. Frick was consulted on the subject just as he was leaving the Pittsburgh Station for New York, he announced flatly that he was going to go right on hiring Slavs or Italians or anybody else who was a good worker. The foreigners were not so bad as represented. They were credulous and easily misled, but if they were given fair treatment they would conduct themselves properly.

The Region papers announced the interview regretfully. The great Mr. Frick operated more than half the ovens, so it didn't look as though the foreign element would be banished after all. Whether people liked Mr. Frick's pronouncements or not they quoted them with respect these days.

He was a big man in Pennsylvania, chairman of the board of the Carnegie Steel Company, in control of the biggest steel company and the biggest coke company in the world. Mr. Carnegie was theoretically the chief but it was Frick who ran the combine. The two did not agree about labor policy, but ever since the time when Carnegie stepped in and ordered Frick to settle with the men in the coke strike of 1887 and found himself saddled with a 12½ percent increase in costs, while the other operators held out for the old price and got it, he had given his manager a free hand. Frick had resigned from the coke company in June, 1887, following the overriding of his policy but by January he was back in the saddle again, and when he fought it out with labor at Morewood and Homestead, Carnegie preferred not to inquire too much into how he accomplished results. The winning of the Homestead Strike in 1892, climaxed by the publicity attendant on the abortive attempt on Frick's life by Alexander Berkman, had enormously increased his prestige.

Through all the fury of recrimination the Hungarian strikers held firm. A miners' convention at Scottdale on April tenth elected Michael Barrett president in place of the imprisoned Mr. Davis and passed resolutions deploring violence.

"There is no nationality in this," urged Barrett in a circular to the strikers aimed to heal the breach in their ranks. "No Hun, no Slav, no Italian, no other thing than an effort to improve the condition of the coke workers. ...Do not break the Law; if you strike, stay at home, and don't forget that you are citizens (in fact, or in prospect) and let your acts prove that you can be both and still be a striker."

Sixty men at Frick's Youngstown plant, taking it that the strikers were going to be orderly, went to work hauling and drawing and some went into the pit. Suddenly at a signal four hundred strikers—some from the woods, some from Mt. Braddock and the Leisenrings—swooped on the plant armed with clubs and stones. The workmen ran leaving coats and tools, some of them to the protection of the company store where deputies stood armed with rifles. The strikers swarmed up and demanded the workmen who had taken refuge on the second floor of the building. For a while the deputies held off the mob but when it looked as though their own skins were in danger they gave up the workmen. The strikers beat a colored man so the blows could be heard two hundred feet and knocked some of the white men around a bit. Then they went off to Leisenring.

Barrett didn't have his men in hand yet. The next few days were like a crazy circus with all the actors trooping into the ring out of turn. Deputies flew from plant to plant by train trying to keep up with the roving bands of strikers; the jails were full and the tax payers worried about the cost of feeding so many prisoners. The Polish, Hungarian, Austrian, and German priests complained to Washington that their imprisoned countrymen were being treated badly. Father Orback of Mount Braddock had called on some of the Slavs held at the Uniontown jail and reported shocking conditions. The men were only half fed and forced to sleep on the floor without mattresses or covering, huddled like cattle in a pen.

"Did you expect to find these prisoners sleeping on sofas and eating chicken-pie and ice cream?" asked the Uniontown *News Standard*.

The Austrian Embassy sent emissaries to look into the matter but they found nothing amiss when the sheriff took them around. He admitted that for a couple of nights sleeping conditions were not ideal but since then all had had mattresses. The Washington visitors wanted to know what was being done about the Slav shot at Broad Ford but he had already joined the anonymous dead.

There had been talk for weeks of a National Coal Strike. All the early part of April the Region press announced that even if it came off on the twenty-first as the National Committee promised, it would not affect Fayette and Westmoreland Counties because the coke strike would be settled by then; and anyway, the National Mine Workers' rulings did not apply to coke workers even if they did mine coal. A strikers' meeting at Scottdale on April twenty-third ruled differently.

As soon as the local strike was officially part of the national one, the workmen in Frick's Valley and Standard plants laid down their tools. The Monongahela River mines had already gone out on the twenty-first, shutting down everything from Brownsville to the Fourth Pool (Lock No. 4), affecting some thirty mines and five thousand men. They cleaned up their rooms, carried home their tools, washed their faces and started marching; the lukewarm faction of English-speaking strikers whipped into line. Meanwhile the operators ordered more deputies from Pittsburgh and more Winchesters to be ready for a long siege. It was the first time coal miners had worked in unison over the whole country, 180,000 of them.

The new deputies were professional hard-guys used to labor war. When they went to arrest Michael Fetzo for throwing stones at Oliver ovens they knocked his wife down for trying to prevent their dragging him from the house. She got to her feet and, reinforced by neighbor women who gathered at her screams, came at them again. They knocked her unconscious that time and dispersed the others with bayonets.

There was a disgraceful scene at Kyle works near Fairchance when a drunken deputy in a buggy leading a party of eighteen guards broke into a file of 150 Hungarian strikers marching peaceably from camp on Mrs. Mickey's farm. The party of deputies came upon the column from the rear. The men opened ranks and let them go through. When the chief deputy's buggy reached the front he jumped from the seat, snatched a cane from the nearest striker and beat him with it while the other occupant of the buggy held a Winchester on him. Unexpectedly there was no riot. The strikers marched away while the drunken officer struck furiously with his cane at every man within reach, and a boy deputy, too young for his badge, fired into the retreating column.

Suddenly the public began to realize that Michael Barrett was turning the guerilla bands of strikers into a disciplined army. On May third, a hundred strikers' families were ordered out of the company houses at Oliver and the neighborhood looked for trouble such as they had in 1891, but when the eviction crew arrived with their wagons they found thirty-seven of the houses empty. The only resistance they encountered was from one Hungarian woman who had built such a hot fire in her stove they couldn't touch it.

The trouble, when it came, happened in another quarter. Early in the morning of the fourth a crowd of two hundred men called at the McClure Company's Painter works to persuade the morning shift not to go to work. The deputies fired at them and a woman fell with a bullet through her ankle. When the strikers saw her go down, they came at the deputies with so much fury that, as the officers complained later, they had to fight in such close quarters that they had no room to use their Winchesters. Still, they must have used them because when the fray was over there were three strikers dead. The paper estimated that at least fifteen were shot, some of whom would probably die, but it was impossible to get accurate figures because they carried away their wounded. Afterward the forty deputies arrested thirty-five Hungarians for riot and sent them to the packed Uniontown jail.

The march of the strikers to Painter that ended so disastrously was part of Michael Barrett's campaign within the law. The men were to take advantage of their right to peaceable assembly, to march in the public road, and to persuade without violence. When they camped near a plant to advertise the strike, they leased the ground they camped on. There were now about 125,000 miners out in the country, and coal was soaring. The railroads worried how they were going to run their engines, and furnacemen clamored for coke. Hill Farm was the only plant running full in the Coke Region on May eighth and that was mining boiler coal for the local furnace. Where any effort was being made to mine coal, the bosses and clerks had to do it, and when they were lucky enough to get hold of a few men, they set them to loading from the stock piles. All up and down the Region the sun shone baldly down on the sooty houses; and the winding rivers, swept clean of their shrouds of smoke, mirrored the blue spring sky.

If the operators were to take advantage of the market they would have to run their plants with new men. Rainey applied to Judge Acheson for an injunction to make the strikers refrain from gathering about his works and got it. There was, however, some question as to whether the injunction would apply to the 1,200 strikers camped on the eleven acres Barrett had leased by Rainey's Moyer works. Rainey claimed a prior lease but Barrett's lease held and the men continued to camp. They had no tents but they stuck it out through wind and rain and remained quiet under continual provocation from the deputies. One day only two men turned up for work at Moyer, and the company induced the deputies to lay down their guns for coke forks.

Meanwhile, Rainey sent for strikebreakers from West Virginia, a portable Gatling gun that would shoot a thousand balls a minute, repeating carbines, and twenty-five horses to mount his deputies so that they could reach any of his plants in an hour. Frick's Valley plant began running with new men under the protection of armed guards, and McClure Coke Company brought in a carload of strikebreakers from Pittsburgh, unprofitable, expensive labor who would learn their jobs under the protection of Winchesters, if they didn't run away.

The dismal business of evictions went forward in earnest to make room for the families of the new men. At Everson ten families of strikers slept in the public road. When Sheriff McCann evicted twenty-five families at Tarr he set their goods along the highway for half a mile. The township constable received complaints that the traffic was blocked and turned the matter over to the superintendent of roads, who ruled that it was up to the sheriff to clear the highway of the stoves, beds, and chairs. Meanwhile the strikers' women and children slept in sheds and fence corners while the men marched and took turns keeping camp at Moyer, Kyle, and Hill Farm.

The good behavior of the strikers began to pay dividends in public favor. Sheriff McCann of Westmoreland County complimented them on their orderliness and told them they might meet and march all they wanted to as long as they were not violent. The farmers around the strikers' camp at Kyle were giving provisions to help out and some of the storekeepers in Connellsville sent a wagonload of food to the hungry army at Hill Farm. The strikers were watching company movements there closely because, although theoretically they were making boiler coal, they might be tempted to start shipping to the booming market. The company, afraid that the presence of so large a body of strikers near by would intimidate their men, put up a lighthouse with reflectors to command a view of their boundaries night and day, sent their men to work on flatcars, and complained to the governor. The appeal to Harrisburg was the outgrowth of a squabble with Sheriff Wilhelm over who was going to pay for the Hill Farm deputies. Sheriff Wilhelm said that the other companies paid for their own and Hill Farm could do the same. So the company officials played with the idea of state troops, but when they approached Governor Pattison he intimated that he saw no necessity for so drastic a move unless Sheriff Wilhelm asked for them. He would, however, send Colonel Thomas Hudson to the Coke Region to have a look around.

The colonel reported that in his opinion the sheriff would not have exceeded his authority in arresting the armed strikers on ground leased near the plants for the purpose of intimidation, but that he seemed to have the situation under control. The strike leaders denied vehemently that their men were armed; "If they were there would not be a deputy left in the county!"

Nevertheless the rumors that the strikers were getting guns continued. People said that maybe the Yough miners did not have any but the Monongahela men did. They were on their way to the Connellsville district then, warned the *News Standard,* and trouble might be expected. The operators ordered another thousand rifles from the Marlin Arms Company in Connecticut, the fourth order of its kind within a month. A meeting of priests and ministers in Connellsville begged them to arbitrate, to hire as peace officers respected men, and to import no more cheap labor; but the carloads of Negroes and Italians kept on coming.

On May twenty-third Michael Barrett launched another appeal:

"TO THE MEN OF THE COKE REGION:

"Keep on as you have been doing; march and meet frequently, but be sure you do not violate the law. The operators are now making a desperate effort to get you to riot and the man who does anything to cause a riot or a breach of the peace is a traitor and a scoundrel....

"We do not want their plants nor do we care what profit they earn from their capital, but we maintain that we should get living wages for our labor."

That same day about four hundred strikers from the river district visited the works at Stickle Hollow to try to get the workmen to join them. They sent a committee to talk to the bosses without result and camped for the night near by. In the morning they proposed to hold a meeting at the schoolhouse and, if possible, dissuade the early shift from going in. Reinforcements gathered as the night wore on until, when the men from the Yough River district joined those from the river mines at the crossroads in front of the Stickle Hollow store at five o'clock in the morning, the combined bodies numbered about two thousand. The river men had brought a band along from Fayette City and while it played a tune or two in the dismal smoke-laden fog, the hungry marchers tried to buy cheese and crackers in the store. The storekeeper would not let them in so they went to the boardinghouse. Later a girl who lived there admitted they were orderly but after they left some pies were missing.

The shift was late in starting for work. Finally the men began coming out of the houses by fives and tens but they were afraid to go to the coke works. When the deputies rushed out to escort them the strikers warned them to go back. The workmen retreated. At that 'a great shout went up from the strikers and simultaneously the deputies began firing, some from the shelter of railroad cars. The strikers ran and the guards chased them, shooting as they went. One deputy pursued his quarry almost a mile; they shot at men huddled in ditches and drains, making no effort to defend themselves. Later one of the guards testified to shooting a striker because he saw he was eating a piece of pie and he knew it must have been some of that stolen from the boardinghouse.

When the strikers who had taken refuge back of the mill put out a white rag on a stick, the deputies started rounding up the prisoners, some of whom had been at the schoolhouse and had not seen the riot. They picked up others when they came back to carry away the dead. There were four of them: one lay in the wheat field five hundred yards away, shot in the back; one near the brick house; one at the sawmill; and one in the meadow by the mill. This time one of the dead was an American and there were Americans among the hundred prisoners huddled in the freight cars waiting to go to Uniontown. Part of the band was there, with horns and drums, and some unfortunate onlookers who had nothing to do with the fight. For the first time after a shooting there were English-speaking wounded who told the public their version of what happened.

"I was trying to save myself by crawling into a ditch when I was shot," said John Troy. "The deputy who wounded me shot at me three times before a bullet took effect. Another striker was shot through the head and instantly killed while standing in front of me. I lay in the field for three hours and a half when some deputies took me to the sawmill and from there to a barn." One deputy asked another what to do with him. The second said he would not need care for long because he was going to die anyway, so they let him lie without medical attention for twelve hours.

The same day of the Stickle Hollow fray a Perry Township squire impanelled a jury and heard witnesses, mostly deputies, to determine the cause of the morning's unpleasantness. There was no one to represent those shot down, no coroner and no district attorney, so he arrived at a speedy verdict. The four men had met their death from bullets fired by deputies acting in self-defense. Therefore the deputies were justified and the case might be considered closed. Only it wouldn't be hushed up so easily. Coroner Echard of Connellsville opened the matter and it looked as if this time some of the deputies would be called to account. When they came into town people hooted at them in the streets; queues followed them so that they had to take refuge in stores and slip out the back door; sometimes they were not fed in restaurants if they were recognized.

The public kept asking questions. If the guards had only fired in self-defense against armed men the way they said, how was it that the strikers had not used their guns if they had them? None of the deputies was hurt. And was it in self-defense that they had to shoot a man in the back when he was running away? Why did they need to chase the men at all? One of the dead strikers was a third of a mile from the plant. And how about the law-enforcement officers stopping the walking speak-easies who were keeping the deputies supplied with liquor until they were so quarrelsome some of the operators could hardly handle them themselves?

Sympathy for the strikers took concrete form as Connellsville businessmen opened a commissary and sent eight wagonloads of provisions to the camps. The Dunkards of Meyersdale donated five thousand loaves of bread, two thousand sandwiches, and two thousand pies, and help was to come from the National Committee of the U.M.W. who had heretofore been too busy with other parts of the country. The operators had temporarily lost face, but they were increasing production every week as trainloads of strikebreakers poured into the district.

June was a month of lawing. The Paddock cases came up and were polished off with a good deal of fanfare. The case against President Davis and the strike leaders flattened out so he was let go along with McSloy, Simkoski, and Mason. The matter of the bullet in Paddock's neck that could only have been fired from the rear might reasonably have cleared the strikers but it got lost in a mass of confusing testimony. Somebody had to be punished, so two Hungarians, John Husar and Mike Furin, got twelve years apiece.

Looking through the brittle yellow pages that record the trial one has the feeling that grave injustice was done, the evidence against them was so slight. Husar was variously identified as carrying a smooth stick, a rough limb of a tree, and a pole eight or ten feet long and somebody testified that he had said: "Throw the lorry off the track and the mules into the ovens!" Anyway he had been on Nigger Hill and was as good as anybody to punish. Nobody knew very much about him except that he had been in this country a couple of years and had a wife and five children. The conduct of the case was complicated by the prisoners' not being able to speak English and the defense's repeated objection that the Commonwealth interpreter was not repeating what the witnesses said, but the court ruled that the defense might use its own interpreter for cross-examination.

The twenty-eight Hungarians tried en masse for murder went free, to the annoyance of the judge who discharged the jury without thanking it. Outside in the corridors there were demonstrations of joy when the men who had been in jail since April joined their families.

The Stickle Hollow strikers went home too, absolved of the charge of riot. As yet nothing had happened to the deputies who did the shooting. Nothing ever seemed to catch up with the deputies.

There were more killings by guards early in June. A deputy sheriff, attacked by strikers on the street in Connellsville, shot and killed a Hungarian named Comisky and very nearly got lynched for it. More trouble grew out of a week-end kidnapping.

One Saturday night a party of strikers seized four workmen employed at Frick's Valley works at the New Haven depot as they were on their way home to one of the Leisenring patches. The sheriff sent deputies to find them but although they trailed the workmen through the Leisenrings, Morrell, and Youngstown they could not catch up with them. Sunday morning one of the deputies got the idea that the men were being held at the mine patch at Lemont. He surrounded the settlement with guards so the kidnapped men could not be spirited somewhere else and set men to searching the houses. The party had no warrants but when they encountered resistance they broke in the doors. They found nothing.

There was no clear report of what happened to start the trouble but in one of the houses the women began making a great outcry. Men ran into the street and the officers used their Winchesters. John Mokaff, who was getting ready to go to town to the laying of the cornerstone of the new Roman Catholic Church, was killed by a bullet in his back as he came up the walk from the privy at the end of his yard. Steve Cornack, a sixteen-year-old boy on crutches with a broken leg, toppled to the ground with a bullet wound. George Restorshick (Richarchick), who was shot as he lay on the grass, went with him to the hospital where both of them died. The missing men had never been at Lemont at all. The next morning about ten o'clock they were found unharmed at Kyle camp.

The priests and ministers with foreign congregations had been almost the only spokesmen of the Hungarians, Italians, Austrians, and Slavs in the press and before the law. When Mrs. Demeter said that a Rainey superintendent forced six men out of her boardinghouse to go to work in the pit at the point of a gun, it was Father Orback, Father Zubay, and the Reverend Lambardin who came with her to Uniontown to give information against the company for forced labor. The men thus shanghaied had told Mrs. Demeter as they left to notify their union headquarters if they were not back in an hour. She did and called the priest as well. He tried to talk to the superintendent, but the superintendent would not discuss the matter and the men did not get out until the work was done.

In Uniontown when the clergymen laid the case before an attorney he did not want to have anything to do with it unless the men themselves gave the information. So the six miners appeared to affix their unpronounceable names to the charges, one more piece of unfinished business for the court.

The more the priests saw of the treatment of their parishioners the more they despaired of the future of the foreign colony in the coke region. A hundred foreigners arrested for murder in the Paddock case, twenty-eight of them tried after being imprisoned without bail; but the two deputies, tardily arrested for shooting the Broad Ford Hungarian, got a release pending trial without any trouble. The district attorney said he could not make a first-degree charge stand and yet there were ten men to swear that one of the deputies took deliberate aim and shot the Slav dead. But the Broad Ford Hungarian's death only came to the public notice because Washington was interested in it. As far as the Region was concerned the nameless ones who died at Painter and Stickle Hollow did not seem like people. The priests knew them as men with names who had to have funerals and who had left behind wives and children. If these foreign people were ever to make a place for themselves in America, maybe they would have to go elsewhere.

The English-speaking public received the news of a movement on foot to transplant the foreign colony with rejoicing. Then the Americans would have all the jobs and get fine wages. Officials appeared from the Canadian government and it looked in July as though there would be a mass migration to the Northwest. Some twenty thousand were to go on foot to Niagara Falls under the leadership of Prince Michael Zapolya, the current descendant of the last independent King of Hungary, and pass thence into the British Dominion. The only thing that stood in the way of the hegira was the lateness of the season. There would be no time for a crop until next year and the settlers would have to depend upon the government for supplies until they could find work or feed themselves from the land. While the Resettlement Committee negotiated with the Canadians, delegates of the Slovak community looked into another project in Arkansas that was being fostered by the Slavic Colonization Company.

The National Strike had petered out after eight weeks but the coke workers fought on stubbornly, even though the Region plants were running full now with practically the entire foreign population evicted to make room for the strikebreakers' families. In July a thousand people in Fayette and Westmoreland Counties were sleeping in the fields. Nineteen families were camped in the park at Uniontown and a hundred miners with women and children were herded into the school grounds at Standard near Mt. Pleasant. Most of the English-speaking miners had been left undisturbed and an alarming number were going back to work.

Michael Barrett valiantly tried to hold his forces together. Now was the time to stand firm, he urged, when the new men were about to be put on piecework. When they didn't get $1.50 a day and board any more and had to take the same rate the miners could not live on, they would leave or join the strikers. Suppose the operators *were* running their plants. It was ruining them to do it with five dollars a day for each deputy and having to board and pay high wages to men who didn't know their jobs.

An observer at Lemont plant noted that in a day, seventeen of the strike-breakers got out only one wagon apiece and they were not heaped, whereas an experienced digger would have gotten five with humps at thirty cents each. The seventy-two men working that day got only 168 wagons, 2⅓ wagons per man, which at $1.50 a day flat wage made the coal cost a little over sixty-two cents per wagon. The two thousand new men brought into the Region cost three dollars a head from the employment agents. That was $6,000 right there, and with carfare added to that, the total immediate outlay for the "blacklegs" was at least $20,000 before they started work. There had been about 12,000 ovens in blast when the strike became general containing about 50,000 tons of coke, 25,000 tons of which went to ashes—a dead loss at eighty-five cents a ton or $21,250 plus the cost of cleaning out the ashes. There had been about twelve hundred families evicted at $11 apiece. That made $13,200 more, and the three months' rent the companies had lost amounted to over $23,000. Then the companies were maintaining from eight hundred to a thousand deputies at $5.00 a day for those from Pittsburgh and other cities, $2.50 for the local men, to which the overhead costs for bosses, clerks, day-men doing repair work, and the maintenance of livestock must be added. It all amounted to several hundred thousands of dollars, but the demands of the workmen would have meant an added cost of only about $37,500 a month, if they could have gotten it. The loss of wages to the strikers totalled nearly $600,000.

The strikers still assembled and marched in July and August. Governor Pattison had decreed against it but they did it anyway, and after armed strikebreakers fired into a peaceful column passing the Summit works on their way to a meeting in Scottdale, a good many paraders had revolvers with the handles sticking out of their pockets so as not to be liable for carrying concealed weapons. Thirty armed men headed a parade of 4,000 in Connellsville on July twenty-first even though Barrett urged them to march without guns lest they lose the hard-won approval of the public. When a party of five hundred headed by a column of sixty armed men went through New Haven on the way to a strike meeting in Scottdale, McSloy and Davis disarmed them and entrusted their guns to the burgess, but almost a hundred went home angry. They couldn't see why they shouldn't have weapons when the "blacklegs" had them.

Sporadic violence of a kind particularly hard to deal with broke out. Forty Hungarian women armed with sticks and stones ran off the company men at Leith and chased them through the fields to the highway. Then they gathered up the worker's coke forks and dinner buckets and threw them into the ovens. That afternoon deputies arrested thirteen of them and took them to jail, accompanied by thirteen babies. Most of the trouble however, was anonymous. A charge of dynamite by an abuttment of the P. & L. E. bridge over the Youghiogheny; company houses fired at Valley works; a bomb with a smoking fuse by a tipple; box cars destroyed; a gas pipe full of dynamite flung into an engine house because the strike was going to be lost anyway and it was a satisfying gesture to destroy walls and machines grown alien and hateful.

Some of the Negroes were leaving just as Barrett had predicted they would. Things had gone wrong from the first day they set foot in the Coke Region. They came supposing that the company was paying the car-fare. Then they found that they had to pay it themselves. The bosses promised that the deductions would be spread over a long period so they wouldn't feel it, but it all came out the first thing so if the strikers frightened them out they would not leave owing the company. Even with paying back the transportation, there was plenty of money at first but they could not get much fun out of it. The little groups of colored people already settled in the towns had their own life and connections. The white strikebreakers with experience were unwilling to work with them because they did not know how to use their lamps and lighted cigarettes in places that they didn't know were dangerous; and the old men whose jobs they had taken kept them in a panic hanging around the plants in the daytime and marching with torches at night. They didn't like the work but they hung on while the pay was good, fortified with gin and armed with razors and pistols. Then the companies announced that they were going to pay by the wagon, and after that the cruel drive of piecework was worse than a boss with a whip. They couldn't make more than seventy-five cents a day at it, either. The men who travelled light left first. It took the family men longer but they started south as soon as they could.

Now was the time when a rally of the crumbling labor forces could have won the strike, but the men had been hungry too long. The companies who had sworn never to hire foreigners again remembered that after all they used to be good help if only they didn't get ideas about more pay. Bosses offered to let bygones be bygones if the strikers wanted to come back at the old rate.

A company man at Brownfield remembers those days when the strike was breaking. The operators had the plant running with a police organization so strong that the strikers couldn't do a thing. That was after the first batch of colored men they brought in had taken to their heels and hid in the mountains, afraid of the strikers. The management never did find them, so they protected the next lot better.

"We had 112 deputies," he says, "and 35 special police. When the men went to work eight guards took each 12 men to the pit mouth and brought them back the same way. When we evicted the old men we carted their goods up the hill and dumped them under the trees. They'd rigged up some stoves to cook on but they didn't have much to cook. We were feeding the Negroes on a big scale with some of the double houses made into kitchens. When the storekeeper would load up a wagon of food for the colored people maybe there'd be three hundred hungry strikers standing by, watching. They'd call out: 'We'll get you for this!' but there wasn't much fight left in them. We had a guard at each corner of the building and all the clerks sworn in as deputies. When they got starved out they were ready to come back. Their tools were mostly stolen so they had to start all over and they were pretty meek."

As fast as the operators could make up a labor crew of old hands they hustled the Negroes out. There was a good deal of bitterness as the Slavs saw their solid front crumble. When two Polish miners returned to work at the Summit mines, the company sent two uniformed deputies to get their goods, stored with those of other evicted miners in the Polish school building. An angry crowd of strikers tried to prevent the loading but Father Smigiel persuaded them to allow the officers and teamsters to do their work. When the wagons started the crowd broke loose with two hundred men, women, and children screaming in pursuit. There was a running fight for half a mile, and when it was over the furniture lay strung along the road, smashed to pieces, and the wagon-beds were riddled with bullets.

The Canadian settlement scheme had fallen through. Prince Michael had an American job and declined to lead his people anywhere, but there was still Father Lamberdin. He had discovered an alternative in the offer of a lumber company of Superior, Wisconsin, who wanted strong Slav workmen for their timber lands. The citizens of Superior would send $6,000 for their transportation, and the B. & O. offered special rates. The lumber company was willing to build a school for the new settlement, assign forty-acre plots to each homesteader at a nominal price, and erect houses to be paid for over a convenient period of years. On September 4 the Reverend Lamberdin left for the West with a band of three hundred and the newspaper account of the withdrawal noted that, although many had not realized it, this man who had worked so tirelessly for his alien parishioners was a polished and learned gentleman who spoke four languages.

On September 1 the United Mine Workers local declared the strike off in the north from Summit to Broad Ford. It lasted three or four days longer in the south where a convulsive action shut down the Kyle plant for a day or two. Then it died out. The strike was over, except for some legal mopping up and a few private grudges to settle.

The Mariettas were an influential Connellsville family who had persisted in seeing the strikers' point of view. Marcus Marietta, the flagstone contractor, had been on Nigger Hill the day Paddock met his death and the story he told of the performance made the prosecution a good deal of trouble when they tried to prove that Paddock was unarmed. Marietta had to tell his story over and over for the successive hearings and trials in the Paddock case but he could not be shaken, even though Attorney Playford flayed him unmercifully.

Then on the day when the deputy shot Comisky in Connellsville and angry citizens surrounded the building that housed the lockup and post office, Harry Marietta, the postmaster, came out and ordered a crowd of deputies to get off the sidewalk in front of the building. Early in September an officer arrested the young postmaster along with three others for inciting to riot the day of the Comisky affair. Connellsville raged at the arrest on what the townspeople considered a trumped-up charge, but the case went to trial in spite of a petition of six hundred names for leniency. Out of it Marietta got a five-hundred-dollar fine and a reprimand for defying the forces of law and order, but the threatened demotion from office did not come off.

The court dropped the action against the deputy for shooting the Slav at Broad Ford on a technicality and dismissed the slayer of Comisky and the officer responsible for the goings-on at Lemont. The Grand Jury ignored the bills against the rest of the deputies. As for the five foreigners convicted of riot at Lemont, the judge announced that they might go home too, on payment of the costs; but they did not have the money so they went to jail for thirty days.

The strike was lost but some things were different. The company stores had a new policy now. They were going to have experienced managers, buy in large quantities so they would be able to undersell and take on more lines—furniture, hardware and clothing—to compete with the town merchants who had been making a bid for the labor trade. It looked as though the foreigners were in the Coke Region for good; company economics would see to that. If they were ever to be driven out, mourned the old guard, this should have been the time, only it didn't work out. A few English-speaking miners had gone to the anthracite fields but the few who left were more than made up for by the new men who stayed; so the Coke Region was as crowded as ever.

Maybe next time when the operators sent south for strikebreakers the colored men wouldn't come, after their last experience in the Region; and maybe the operators would give the old employees a hearing when they asked for a raise, remembering the cost of deputies and greenhorns.

Next time—

CHAPTER VI

THE GOLDEN DAYS

JOSIAH THOMPSON, JASPER THOMPSON'S BOY, WAS GOING to marry Miss Mary Anderson, Minnie Redburn's cousin, who was visiting her in the red brick double house with the big chimneys on Main Street by Jacob's Run. Uniontown was pleased with Josiah and with the match. He was an up-and-coming young fellow, as smart in figures as his father. If you just looked back a few years and compared the amount of business the bank did in the fifties with what it did in the sixties and seventies after the Thompsons were at the helm, you could see what a pair of business men they were. In the days when John T. Hogg ran it, it was just a little private bank in a chain that included Brownsville, Connellsville, Mt. Pleasant, Bedford, and Somerset, and most of the business went to Brownsville.

The elder Thompson hadn't started out as a banker. Up to 1862 he was a cattle buyer and farmer, a good one, too, with a comfortable place a couple of miles out of Uniontown on the McClellandtown Road. Probably he didn't know how good he was at handling money until he got the job being internal revenue collector of the twenty-first district of Pennsylvania. After that he was weaned away from farming for good. In 1864 he helped start the First National Bank and pretty soon he was president. Besides the work at the bank he collected a lot of other responsibilities, among them the presidency of the new Uniontown and West Virginia Railroad that was going to open up the coal deposits in the southern part of the district. Even though he was a Republican, Fayette County sent him to the legislature.

When Jasper Thompson's sons, William and Josiah, graduated from Washington and Jefferson College in 1871 he had a stool ready for Josiah in the bank. That summer the boy farmed forty acres on his own and did the plowing in his bare feet. Then he got a haircut and a clean collar, put on his best clothes, and went to Uniontown. When he started at the First National he was seventeen years old, a serious-faced, fat young man who could go up a column of figures like a streak. He was teller the next year and cashier by the time he was twenty-two. That was in 1877 after James T. Redburn died, the old cashier who had been with the bank ever since the days when Hogg owned it. On Sundays Josiah sat with his brother William and his sisters Ruth and Lenora in the family pew at the First Presbyterian Church; and when the young bloods of the town got noisy on Overholt and Monongahela Rye on Saturday nights, Josiah wasn't among them.

He'd picked a wife who was a nice, sensible girl with good family connections. She was a little older than Josiah but not enough to amount to much, and it was a lot better than as if he'd married some pretty young flibbertigibbet. The Thompson children were building up a solid phalanx of prosperity. Lenora had married John Nicolls, a merchant; Ruth was the wife of Dr. J. T. Sheplar; and the William Thompsons were managing the 650-acre farm.

Josiah and Mary Anderson were married in December, 1879, and set up housekeeping in the old cashier's house where Mary had been visiting when he met her. It was a pleasant old-fashioned place with rambling additions, a pillared portico at the front and a narrow stoop on the side looking into the garden shaded by a giant honey locust. Old residents remember that little George Marshall, later to become Chief of Staff of the U. S. Army, nearly impaled himself on the fence when he fell off a limb there one morning. The yard was apt to be under water whenever Jacob's Run overflowed its shallow margin but all the village traffic went past the door; George Marshall, little George's father, lived across the road in a two-story brick house on the lot where four years later Josiah was to promote the building of the Opera House block; the White Swan Hotel was just up the hill, and so was the abnk. Her husband spent most of his time there, so Mary came to be glad that it was no farther away than the end of the block.

When Jasper Thompson died in 1889 he left Josiah a hundred and one thousand dollars and the presidency of the First National. Josiah talked a little of buying the imposing Boyle place on the edge of town after that but Mary wanted to stay where she was. Josiah was so busy she could hardly get him home to eat, and if home were all the way to the other end of town on the Pike, he'd never get there.

Josiah grew middle-aged and portly, his round face sobered by a fringe of whiskers; Mary was prim in her dolman and bonnet at service on Sundays, a pillar of the missionary society and the Ladies Aid. They were a hard-working pair—Josiah at the bank, Mary busy with her housekeeping and gardening. Her tulips were finer, her lawn greener than anybody else's in town. The big yard was a riot of fuchsias, freezias, cinnamon pinks, gloxinias, and geraniums. Even in the winter she raised flowers in a little conservatory heated by a stove. There were two Thompson sons now—Andrew, handsome and precocious; John, quiet and heavy like his father. The yard was always filled with children who played jacks on the cellar door and knocked the back gate off its hinges sled-riding, but instead of scolding Mary only called them in the house and gave them cocoa and cookies.

In 1896 she fell ill, and Josiah, all attention when her well-being was threatened, sent her to New York for treatment. When she came back it was with the knowledge that she had only a month to live. It would take that long for the growth in her throat to cut off her breathing. There was never any nonsense about Mary. She announced her approaching death quietly to Josiah and the boys.

"Let's make this the happiest possible month," she said, "and later on, don't forget my tulips. Next year I hope you'll plant them just the same."

So Mary died, and after that there was nobody to tell Josiah to shave and cut his fingernails. Work became for him what whiskey is to some men. He was president of the Borough Council for eight consecutive years; a member of the school board, president of the News Publishing Company and of the Union Cemetery Company, and secretary and treasurer of the Fayette County Railroad. In 1900 he and J. D. Ruby put up the Thompson-Ruby building with a silver-painted dome at the corner of Main and Morgantown Streets. He induced the National Steel Company and the American Steel and Wire Company to invest millions to develop the Klondike coal fields in Southern Fayette. Most important of all, he was making plans to build a new bank, this bearded man in a baggy suit, slouch hat, and fine boots, half the time without a necktie, his shoulders stooped from leaning over a desk, absent-mindedly living in the old brick house while he dreamed of a million-dollar building. It was going to be a skyscraper that would be as well equipped as any Pittsburgh bank. Sometimes he stayed at the office for a week on less sleep than an ordinary man would get in a night. When the clerks came in the morning they would find him working just as they left him the night before. He was branching into coal now, buying coal land from the farmers around the district, consolidating it into blocks for resale at three or four times the purchase price, but he was generous in sharing the profits by letting business men of the community participate.

The First National was the nucleus of everything. There was no bank in the country like it; employees were better paid than those in other banks but they were not allowed to drink or use tobacco. When Mr. Thompson dedicated the Uniontown drinking fountain he drank a glass of the water saying: "Nothing stronger has ever passed my lips. Not even coffee." His employees were not bonded but none of them ever went wrong. J. V. figured that if you had any doubt of a man so that he needed a bond he ought not to be in a bank. The "Honor Bank" never asked more than 6 percent for its loans and paid no interest on deposits. It became a kindly arbiter of credit in a rapidly expanding community. The accounts were kept the old-fashioned way without using machinery, each check carefully listed in long hand. If a man wanted money for a legitimate need, the president would let him have it without security. He repaid bank employees for faithful service by allowing them to share in coal deals that made them rich. If a widow was in straitened circumstances, he made some money for her. People flocked to the First National begging him to invest their savings in coal, and when the miracle happened they built fine houses along the National Pike, down Gallatin Avenue, and out Fayette Street.

Ever since 1891 coal production between the Youghiogheny and Monongahela had expanded steadily at the rate of 25 percent a year. The Spanish-American War gave it an extra push in the right direction, and as Pittsburgh boomed the Coke Region boomed with it. Andrew Mellon of the great Union Trust Company and his friend George I. Whitney had gotten control of the Monongahela River Consolidated Coal and Coke Company and made a river monopoly of it. The amalgamation comprised 96 of the 102 working mines along the lower river backed by 40,000 acres of coal lands and 50 river tipples to load into their own barges, 3,000 of them. River coal went to the monopoly's own docks in Cincinnati, Louisville, Memphis, and New Orleans in mighty tows 350 feet long and 150 feet wide; and the whole operation was underlaid by a mortgage owned by the Mellon interests.

Other outside capital, represented by Judge Moore, also working through the Union Trust Company, had gotten hold of Rail Coal and welded it into the Pittsburgh Coal Company, a $64,000,000 corporation with Andrew Mellon and Senator Oliver on the board of directors. Coal was getting to be Big Business, very dramatic and complicated, but Fayette County people proposed to run their finances without benefit of Pittsburgh.

The skyscraper was to stand on the Round Corner on Main Street, the most valuable bit of real estate in the county with a long frontage on Main and Pittsburgh Streets. While the building was under construction Mr. Thompson transferred the bank funds across the street to temporary quarters and hired "a man with an axe" to guard them. The construction was finished on August 18, 1902, an eleven-story building that cost $1,100,000 and towered 152 feet to the top of the cornice with a 40-foot flagpole on top of that. It contained 750 rooms, 94 baths, and 45 lavatories with marble corridors and mosaic all over. There were four high-speed elevators, one reserved especially to carry occupants to the private apartments on the four floors at the top of the building. The middle stories were given over to offices, each with a small fireproof vault, which presently became the quarters of a swarm of independent coal operators. The bank itself was housed in a circular room 52 feet in diameter, finished with Italian marble, Spanish mahogany, and bronze, with a heavy ornamental ceiling 29 feet high. People talked proudly of its impregnable vault. Four time locks guarded its giant door weighing 16 tons, which when unlocked could be opened by a light touch of the hand. Now that the village had been honored with all this magnificence, it began building to live up to it.

J. V. Thompson had become the big man of the Coke Region, but he was just the same friendly, abstracted, not very tidy farmer-boy-come-to-town that he had always been. He found time to go to the First Presbyterian Church and acquiesced in the ordinance that church-goers were forbidden to buy ice cream on their way home from service.

The Region was proud of Henry Clay Frick, too, but he didn't seem to belong to it the way Thompson did. When you thought of Frick you thought of Pittsburgh and the big men he worked with—Mellon, Phipps, and Carnegie, and how Mellon banks served Frick's steel towns. Thompson stood for coal and the home folks, and the First National was the Coke Region's own.

Then Honey Hawes came to town from New York for a visit. She had been born Blanche Gardner of Smithfield, ten miles or so down the road to West Virginia, and she had gone barefoot to church, riding pillion behind her mother on horseback. Then she moved from the Coke Region and her fortune improved. People came to know her as Honey Hawes in sporting circles and on the race tracks all over the East. When she came back to Uniontown around 1901 she was the dashing widow of a Johnstown sportsman with $75,000 that she wanted to invest in coal land. She was even more interested in marrying Uniontown's coal baron, who had now been a widower more than five years.

"Show me your millionaire and I'll marry him," she said, and she approached Mr. Thompson with the pious suggestion that if he would help her to increase her fortune, she would use it to found an orphanage. The idea appealed to the Presbyterian banker and he obligingly ran her stake up to a quarter of a million.

There was a coal operator in Uniontown named James Barnes who often worked with him when a big coal sale was to be managed. He could supply the finesse that J. V. lacked, and, what was particularly important, he knew how to handle the big New York capitalists. Part of his technique was to establish fine quarters in the Waldorf and entertain on a magnificent scale. Mr. Thompson would complain that the wining and dining cost too much and wasn't necessary, but Barnes undeniably produced results, so he let him have his way. After J. V. undertook business negotiations for Honey Hawes he began really to enjoy the New York sales trips that gave him a chance to see her. Her pointed little nose and chin were audaciously pretty; she was always available, always gay, and when they were together he had fun spending the money he had been accumulating and hadn't thought much about before.

On August 10, 1903, they were married at the Waldorf-Astoria. Mr. Thompson was nearly fifty, and up to now he had never had a real vacation. The day after the wedding, the eleventh—his lucky number—he embarked with his thirty-one-year-old bride on the most tremendous honeymoon he could think of. Business was slack all over the country and it was a good time to get away. They were already on the Atlantic when Uniontown heard about the match, and if the home folks were disappointed in his choice they assumed that old J. V. probably knew what he was doing. Anything he took hold of turned out all right.

During the next fifteen months the Coke Region followed his triumphal progress across Europe and Asia, proud of its native son. They were in England and Scotland for two weeks, in Ostend, Brussels, and Waterloo. Then they spent six weeks in Paris, where Honey enjoyed the compliments of noblemen and her elderly bridegroom bought a Panhard-Levasson 24-horsepower motor to take them around. Madame Melba visited the honeymooners. Monte Carlo saw them briefly but the banker did not play at the tables. Pyramiding coal stocks didn't seem like gambling. Coal was something real, a crop that came out of the ground for mills to feed on just as cows eat hay. Postal cards came back from Marseilles to say that they were leaving for Egypt and Bombay. Sanitary conditions weren't very good but Mr. Thompson had thought to have cases of distilled water sent ahead to the various stops on the trip. Uniontown heard and approved. Wasn't it just like J. V. to think of everything like that to look out for his health? The travellers went to Mhow, Chittoor, Ajmer, and up to the Khyber Pass; and Honey was photographed in a rickshaw in Japan where she was buying art objects by the case to send home to Uniontown. It was a good time to get them because Japan was at war and patriotic Japanese families were putting priceless treasures on the market.

Meanwhile, in Uniontown, Congressman Boyle's beautiful estate on the National Pike toward Brownsville was being gotten ready to receive the fabulous Honey. It was the place that Mr. Thompson had wanted to buy for Mary who preferred to live near the bank. The local paper for May 26, 1903, had announced the sale before his marriage to Honey in August. Now while he was abroad the house was being turned inside out to make it a proper show place for his bride and the treasures she was bringing back from abroad.

The Thompsons came back to Uniontown on the 4:19 Pennsylvania train on the afternoon of November 8, 1904, and went to the McClelland House. At 4:45 J. V. was at the polls casting his vote, shaking hands with everybody, and not a bit changed except that Honey had dressed him up. The Uniontown papers faithfully recorded the itinerary of the wedding tour so happily accomplished. The bridal pair had travelled 58,652 miles; 34,750 miles of it over water on 26 different boats. It had taken 125 days to negotiate all those oceans, seas, and rivers. Mr. Thompson hadn't even been seasick, his bride only once. That was when they were on a Russian boat, the *Czar,* on their way from Constantinople to Alexandria. It seems they ran into the Euroclydon, the same wind that tossed the Apostle Paul around so dizzily on his way to Rome, and while they were in its clutches even the ship's doctor was ill. The only three who weren't were the captain, the Russian consul, and J. V.

In December there was a party for two hundred in honor of the bride at the turreted brick house in the grove on West Main Street where Ruth Sheplar, Josiah's sister, lived. The rooms were banked with palms and smilax for the occasion; there were white roses, Easter lilies, and lilies of the valley in the parlor; hyacinths and carnations in the library and a big centerpiece of American Beauties on the dining-room table between candles with red shades. A Pittsburgh caterer served an elaborate collation in red and white, and while the guests ate their ice cream, molded in flower shapes and served in little red cups, and nibbled red and white frosted cakes and candies, an orchestra played softly behind palms on the stair-landing. Honey was magnificently dressed and took pains to be charming. She was going to invite them all to her house as soon as it was ready.

The Oak Hill housewarming had to be delayed to give Honey time to settle her treasures from Europe, Africa, and Asia. Finally invitations went out to 250 guests for a reception from nine to twelve on New Year's Eve. It was Uniontown's first chance to see the wonders of Oak Hill and, even if it did look more like a museum than a house to live in, the effect was impressive. The reception hall was a copy of an English baronial home with a magnificently carved staircase draped with oriental rugs. The fireplace was so tall you could walk inside it, and half a day could be spent admiring the exquisite Japanese trinkets in the cabinets. An ivory screen from Cairo, inlaid with mother-of-pearl and ebony, received special mention in the newspaper account of the wonders at Oak Hill the next morning and would be noted in the news again years later when it went under the auctioneer's hammer. In the Louis XVI room, where an orchestra played, there was a silk rug bought at a staggering figure from the Oriental museum in Cairo. The ladies took off their wraps in the Flemish room with its heavily carved pieces and marvelled at the doors and woodwork inlaid to match the furniture. Everywhere there were flowers sent from New York; orchids in the dining-room, glittering with gold furniture that had cost $17,000 and had come from a Doge's palace in Venice; sweet peas and pink roses in the breakfast room; and bowls of American Beauties against the panelling of the library and in the halls. And Honey's mother had come to Uniontown from New York to stand in the receiving line along with Lida Grimm, the oil heiress from Franklin, Andrew Thompson's fiancee.

In the months that followed Honey was much in the news. She entertained for thirty at the country club in a handsome imported Empire gown of black lace over white lace, embroidered in silver sequins and fastened with a jewelled buckle. A magnificent collar of diamonds and emeralds and a large black picture hat finished the costume. She glittered with diamonds, sitting in a box at the West End Theatre when Robert Mantell and his players came to town. Mr. Thompson equipped a handsome stable for her; then she asked for a private race track to exercise her horses on. She got that, too. It amused her to ride down Main Street in a tally-ho with a trumpeter tooting a horn. Her French chauffeur raced through town scattering traffic. When McAfee and Senator Penrose visited at Oak Hill he drove them the mile and a half from the house to the McClelland Hotel in seventy-five seconds.

She gave a Japanese party with Japanese servants imported for the occasion and kimonos for everybody. When she invited guests to swim in the pool in the glass-roofed conservatory with its palms and flowering vines, she furnished bathing suits and silk stockings. Pittsburgh Sunday papers showed the mistress of Oak Hill on the terrace with her wolfhounds and made much of her dinner for forty at the Sewickley Horse Show. Her retinue included two or three maids, a special hairdresser, a chef, secretary, footman, a head stableman and half a dozen grooms. She wore her most gorgeous furs and diamonds and had an exquisite little Japanese maid with flowers in her hair to trail her everywhere she went, but it was no use. Pittsburgh Society matrons were frosty and she got no prizes for her horses.

Honey found that while she lived in western Pennsylvania she had a better time when she stayed on her own ground. After that she imported her entertainment and her friends. An English company gave *As You Like It* and *A Midsummer Night's Dream* on the lawn at Oak Hill.

When she had done everything she could think of to Oak Hill she amused herself briefly by furnishing Friendship Hill, Albert Gallatin's old place at New Geneva. J. V. had acquired it in a deal but hadn't planned to use it for himself until Honey began fixing it up. She induced Karen

Rahlen, a young Swedish woman in Paris, to close her studio and come to Uniontown to give her music and art lessons, but every time she planned to begin studying she thought of something else that would be more fun. After a while Mlle. Rahlen grew tired of wandering around Oak Hill alone and went back to France.

Nothing could keep Honey in the Coke Region long now that the novelty of showing off was gone. She hated the coal smoke that tarnished her gold furniture and left soot on the window sills no matter how often it was wiped off; and she hated the stodginess of the people who had no more idea of how to play than had her middle-aged husband. When you were young—well, still in the thirties—with a bottomless purse, New York was the place to live, or Palm Beach. Paris was even better. She really got attention there, especially the time when she had paintings of herself used as menu covers in fashionable restaurants. Her only triumph at home was to bring Paderewski to Uniontown. She hired a special locomotive to haul his private car from Pittsburgh, and it was said that she paid him $2500 to come, $500 more than he got for his Pittsburgh concert. People in the Coke Region talked about it for a long time and remembered that Honey was so resplendent for the occasion that you could hardly tell which one to look at.

Mr. Thompson spent most of his time at the bank as before except for a brief sally into politics in the spring of 1906. There had been muttering through the state that Boss Penrose had picked governors too long. Why not let the people choose their own for a change? Penrose, quick to feel the public pulse, promised to keep hands off at the Republican Convention in June. The different sections of the state advanced the claims of their favorite sons for the honor and a lively campaign developed. The Coke Region put forward its great man, J. V. Thompson, and it looked for a while as though his chances were good. A special train carried 740 Thompson supporters to the Convention in Harrisburg on June 6. The banker was already there, but a lieutenant saw to their entertainment on the way down, put a twenty-dollar bill with the compliments of Mr. Thompson in the pot of all the poker games that developed, and paid everybody's fare. Harrisburg was appropriately draped with Thompson banners when they arrived and the delegates descended to what looked like triumphal acclaim. Then the Philadelphia delegates appeared, seven trainloads of them, shouting for Edwin S. Stuart. Penrose had picked his man after all. When the votes were counted, Stuart had 250, Thompson 55. That was the coal baron's only excursion into politics.

By 1909 he was nearly always alone in his million-dollar palace, but he was working as he had never worked before. His secretary remembers that sometimes the press of detail would get on her nerves and she would worry to Mr. Thompson about the matters piling up ahead they hadn't started to work on yet. Then he would say, "Let's do our work just once." And that was the way he did it, grinding steadily ahead, dispatching details as he came to them and not worrying about them afterward. His expense account was terrific. The wedding trip had cost nearly a million; Honey's emeralds and diamonds took another seven figures, and you couldn't spend lumps of coal like dollars. When she came home she brought strangers with her that he didn't like, suave, titled foreign women who made him feel heavy and old, and an endless procession of handsome, idle boys. They might be as harmless as they looked, but they certainly were a nuisance. Sometimes there were parties that lasted four months. He didn't like the roulette wheel spinning in the game room off the library or the routine of wines in the evening. The only way he could get a chance to sit down with the evening paper was to go down to the old Redburn house where he used to live with Mary.

Honey, for her part, was bored to death with the way her husband thought of nothing but work and his blessed bank. What was the good of having $70,000,000 if you sat at your desk all night and never had a good time? The only way she could get his attention was to worry him. One way to do it was to refuse to sign the necessary papers when he was ready to close a coal deal. He'd notice her then because he had to have her signature to make the transfer legal. At first she charged only $15,000 for a signature but once, when there was a lot at stake, the rumor went out that she held him up for $200,000.

The situation had become impossible. Honey was living at the Plaza in New York; her husband was juggling coal property in Fayette County. Finally on the twenty-first of January, 1913, the Pittsburgh papers announced with headlines and photographs the divorce of Uniontown's coal king from Honey Hawes in an edition which never reached Uniontown because the local consignment was bought up and disposed of. The settlement was a million dollars in cash paid to Honey's attorney at the First National Bank Building. The proceedings, it appeared, had been under way since May, 1912, when a subpoena was served on Honey in Connellsville, but the final decree had been delayed until January 20, at Mr. Thompson's request, to allow for some property settlement.

Uniontown saw no more of Honey, who was not to enjoy her million long. The increasing weight, that had begun as nothing more than a threat to her beauty, brought on by too much high living, was becoming dangerously abnormal. The news sifted back to the Coke Region that Honey could no longer trip around on her tiny little feet; she was dying of elephantiasis. When the papers published the news of her death late in the twenties they said that she had come to weigh six hundred pounds. Perhaps it was true. And they maliciously added that an interesting clipping had been found among her effects, snipped from a New York paper for 1898, five years before her marriage to Thompson. It read:

"Ambition to attain everything makes me take these measures. In return for wealth and cultured surroundings I will make a man happy. Identity must be known and honor assured before interview. Object: Matrimony.

"Twenty-One."

With it was wrapped an amorous letter from a hopeful suitor in Jersey City.

The second Mrs. Thompson had bequeathed what she had left of the million, about $700,000, to a home for wayward girls. So the orphanage idea hadn't been a fiction after all. Reading about it, people in the Coke Region who had resented the tooting of her trumpeter as she clattered through town on the tally-ho and the exotic court of outsiders she gathered about her at Oak Hill remembered tardily that after all she had been generous to her less fortunate relatives around the county. She had had a nice way with people. When she used to stand in the receiving line she didn't glance ahead to see who was coming next, and the way she looked at you made you feel as if you were the only person in the room. No matter what you heard about her, when you talked to her you forgot what it was.

CHAPTER VII

THE WRECKERS

IT IS DIFFICULT TODAY TO GET AN UNPREJUDICED IDEA of what Honey was really like behind the flamboyant showing off. People hereabouts believe that it was the million-dollar cash settlement she demanded, coupled with her extravagant living over ten years, that crowded J. V. Thompson into deep water and gave the powerful interests who had jealously watched wealth pile up in the Coke Region the chance they were waiting for. When the storm broke two years later, Thompson's solid equities were enormous, but it was cash he needed.

When the decree was made public there were still two good years to go. The First National had a surplus of $1,650,000, capital of $100,000 and advertised itself proudly as

First in the City
First in the County
First in the State
First in the United States

and it was not an empty boast. It was the financial heart of a tremendously rich industrial district. According to a survey made by the *Pittsburgh Gazette Times,* June 16, 1907, Uniontown alone, with a population of about ten thousand, boasted thirteen millionaires, eleven men and women whose fortunes amounted to from half a million to a million, and eighty persons with assets from $100,000 to $500,000.

There were still about 40,000 acres left in the old Connellsville Coking

Coal Basin and about the same in the Klondike Basin.* And even if production went on according to the present rate, there would be no serious depletion of coking coal for sixty years. After that there was the enormous coal reservoir of Greene and Washington Counties—a natural extension of the Connellsville Field—to draw on. In 1912 the Connellsville fields had produced 48 percent of all the coking coal mined in the United States, a daily production of about 2,000 carloads, even though Pennsylvania had only one-twentieth of the nation's coal deposits.

And the Region could hope to hold its lead because, added to the excellence of its deposits, it had a dollar a ton freight advantage. No wonder the Coke Counties were getting richer and dirtier every year. In the ten years from 1881 to 1890 they had produced 41,200,000 tons. From 1903 to 1913 they had produced more coke than had been mined *in the history of the country.* By July of 1913 they had already turned out a quarter as much as in the whole ten-year period from 1881 to 1890, and 183 plants with 37,744 ovens were making more as fast as they could.

A man could make quick money by going into immediate production after the purchase of a coal tract so that the sale of coal and coke paid the outlay for machinery, cost of development, and taxes. But as the Connellsville field became depleted, its nearness to the Pittsburgh furnaces and its excellent quality would send the price up. The Pennsylvania inspector of mines in 1912 reported that fifty acres of coal land were being exhausted every day. Even though 1913 was a dull year, the rate had jumped to fifty-five acres a day. If a man could afford to wait and pay taxes on his holding until the market rose, he would make a good deal more than if he mined at once. And while he was waiting, money in coal land was safer than in a manufacturing investment where a shut-down meant deterioration of machinery and plant. Coal in the hill was indestructible and the demand was sure to come because when it once entered into industrial use it couldn't be melted up and used over again, like iron. When it was burned it was gone, and more had to come from somewhere for the hungry furnaces.

Mr. Thompson and his associates were holding their properties for the day when steel would really go into action. Anybody could see that a dollar seventy-five and a dollar-eighty were too cheap for coke, but times were slow all over the country. School teachers and storekeepers, farmers and laborers continued to bring their money to Mr. Thompson at the First National to have him invest it in coal land for the coming rise.

An insurance agent remembers that in those days he had hard sledding trying to sell policies. When he approached a man using the security-for-the-

---

* Boileau estimate: *News Standard Supplement,* October 21, 1913, "Coal Land Values of the Connellsville Coking Coal Bed of Southwestern Pennsylvania." John W. Boileau was one of the most able and efficient coal experts of his time.

future angle he would meet with: "I gave my money to J. V. Thompson to invest in coal land for me and it's better than any bank." To the question: "Did you get a note for it?" he'd get the answer, "I don't need one. Jo's got a good memory." It was phenomenal the way J. V. never forgot anything. If he met a boy in the bank with his father when he was twelve years old, he'd call him by name without a minute's hesitation if he didn't see him again until he was twenty-one.

The banker was buying heavily for himself in Greene County, Washington County, and West Virginia. When he made a down payment on a farm to fill out a coal block, often the owner said, "Take the money to invest for me," and J. V. gave him a note for it and then borrowed on the land. It took increasing cash to keep the structure from tipping over, and that meant more and more coal sales had to be made before the time was ripe.

Henry Clay Frick of the United States Steel Corporation made known that he would like to buy some coal property and asked the Uniontown operator to come to see him. According to the report that later went the rounds, when Thompson called at the steel company office he found Thomas Lynch instead of Frick waiting to see him. Frick himself was in the next room. Thompson intimated that he was accustomed to dealing with the principal in a deal of that kind and asked for the steel magnate himself. Lynch, deeply offended, told the chief that Thompson would not deal with him, whereupon Frick invited Thompson into his office. Mr. Lynch, he explained, was in charge of his coal activities, but he would discuss the matter with Mr. Thompson himself at lunch. But they had gotten off on the wrong foot.

Thompson felt that Frick had gotten above himself now that he was a capitalist and lived in George Vanderbilt's house in New York. Even if he did own a lot of railroad shares and steel stock he had come out of the Coke Region just the same as Thompson had and he got his start in coal. Now if he wanted to buy some, let him do his own talking just like anybody else.

Frick's reaction was equally understandable. He was no longer active in the Frick Coke Company but he had a good man to run it, one as eager for profit as he had been back at the turn of the century. Now he was tired of fighting labor and fighting capital. No matter which he was up against, it was tooth and claw. The armed deputies and the trains of strikebreakers pouring into the Coke Region; the homestead strike and the sinking of the *Little Bill* in the fray on the river when they brought in the boatload of Pinkerton's men; the great battle with Carnegie when his fortune was at stake—all this belonged to a long time ago. So much had crowded in between, the sharpness of the remembered scenes dimmed like an old photograph.

Carnegie had maneuvered him out of his coke company and the steel company, too, for a while, but in sixteen months he was back and the merger with United States Steel made him stronger than ever. It had taken a few years to fortify his position and then, with a solid backlog of a hundred thousand shares of preferred steel stock and fifty thousand shares of common, he had branched into railroads. There had been a time when he was the largest individual holder of railway securities in the world. And after he first came to New York he used to collect bank directorates just as now he was collecting Old Masters. He was building a palace to house them at Number One East Seventieth Street. It would be his home, too, during his lifetime, but after that it was going to the city of New York. He was much more interested in the new house at the moment than in coal land back in the Coke Region. He was narrowing down his interests these days but he kept his place on the board of directors of U. S. Steel and of his friend Andrew Mellon's banks, the Union Trust and Mellon National in Pittsburgh. Tom Lynch was doing very well with the Coke Company and, remembering how bitterly he had resented Carnegie's meddling in the old days, he let him have a free hand.

When Frick talked over the coal deal with Thompson at luncheon, Thompson asked $5,500,000 for the property. According to the story, Frick said, "Cut off the $500,000 and it's a deal," and Thompson answered, "$5,500,000 is my price!" They parted without coming to terms. There was a cold streak in J. V. when it came to business and he was a stubborn man.

All over the country money was scarce. Nevertheless, on July 6, 1914, after the enactment of the Regional Bank Law, the First National declared a dividend of 700 percent, otherwise it would have had to take stock in the Reserve Bank to an amount in excess of its capital stock. E. S. Hackney, the cashier, announced in the press:

"This is a condition that obtained in a very few instances, as the proportion of surplus to capital in the First National Bank of Uniontown, Pa., existed only in a few rare cases in the United States."

In spite of the fine record of the First National, word was seeping through financial circles that Uniontown's coal baron had incurred the displeasure of the United States Steel Corporation. Suddenly the New York capitalists became wary of loaning money to him, and Pittsburgh banks that had always been glad to honor his paper were polite but regretful when he asked for loans. After all, if Frick and Lynch didn't like him, they had all the enormous prestige of the Steel Corporation behind them; Thompson had only the independent operators back in the Coke Region. The home folks responded loyally when Thompson asked for help and as the pressure increased they gave again and again, but a series of little set-backs kept turning the tide the wrong way, or maybe it was just the Hard Times all over the country that did it.

There had been talk for some time that Thompson was getting too far from shore. As Frick grew richer he had consolidated his holdings where he could keep an eye on them. Thompson knew he was spread out too far, but Honey's demands culminating in the million-dollar cash settlement necessitated taking long chances in the hope of quick returns. He owed the Union Trust a good deal and the Mellons were not easy people to deal with if one were hard pressed. People had been saying that U. S. Steel, Union Trust Company, and the Pennsylvania Railroad ran the state of Pennsylvania, and sometimes it looked as though they were right.

Thompson, aware of his danger, wanted to retrench but circumstances kept forcing him in deeper. The men at the Coke works were able to work only part time now because the demand was so slack. The lay-offs were staggered so that they came to town on different days, first from one side of the county and then the other. In November and December of 1914 there was a steady drain on the bank's resources. An employee of the First National remembers that in the last sixty days before January 18, 1915, the foreign laborers, mainly from the Frick plants, began drawing out their savings. When questioned as to why they wanted to carry away their balances in cash the answer was, "Super says Big Bank going to fall!"

As the pressure on the bank continued Thompson had to raise more and more money in the limited area where he could get it and pay high rates of interest for it, sometimes as much as 30 percent. The more he paid the more he had to pay, because people naturally reasoned that Thompson must be needing money badly to give so much for it. So increasing numbers of depositors withdrew their funds and Thompson needed still more money to cover; so it went round and round.

One of the depositors remembers: "One day my father told me that I'd better draw my money out of the bank. Mr. Thompson had just been to a friend of his wanting to borrow money and he offered so much interest to get it that the man didn't know whether to let him have it or not. He asked my father what to do and Dad told the man not to loan Thompson the money because he must be getting in a bad way or he wouldn't need to offer so high a rate.

"I didn't like to draw my money out all at once, it seemed so mean, but after that I didn't put any more in the Bank and when I had to pay anything I gave a check for it and tapered my account off little by little."

By January 16 the First National had paid out $600,000. That week end J. V. Thompson, according to an employee who worked with him on the financial statements that had to be prepared, went to Pittsburgh to get a loan to tide the bank over. He had a big deal pending with Frick but he had gotten no money from it yet. If he could get an accommodation loan for the bank emergency, everything would be all right.

"The First National need never have failed," says one of the bank employees, "if people had done as they agreed. We worked on the Honor system in the bank and Mr. Thompson was used to trusting people. At the Mellon Bank they told him to go home and stop worrying; they'd have the money in Uniontown on Monday morning. So he thought everything was all right and came home. Then it didn't come and we had to close. He thought we could open right away, because he'd get the money from Frick but when the bank closed, the deal was off."

The closing of the First National caused surprisingly little commotion at first. The *News Standard* made a modest announcement on January 18:

> "*Hitch Causes First National To Close for a Short Time—Possibility of a Run on Well Known Institution Causes Officials to Take Precautionary Measures.*
>
> " 'BUT BANK IS IN GOOD SHAPE NOW
> " 'CLOSED TEMPORARILY BY THE BOARD OF DIRECTORS—
> J. V. Thompson, Pres.
> " 'WASHINGTON SAYS DEPOSITORS WILL BE PAID 100 CENTS ON THE DOLLAR.'
>
> "The First National Bank of Uniontown failed to open its doors this morning but it is thought they will open this afternoon or in a few days at the latest. At 11:15 Mr. Thompson authorized the posting of the above notice on the bank's doors."

The following announcement appeared in a box on the same page:

> "Washington D. C. January 18.—The Comptroller of the Currency announced the suspension of the First National Bank of Uniontown, Pa. The bank is now in charge of Bank Examiner Sherril Smith who is expected to submit a report of the bank's assets and liabilities shortly. The bank, the comptroller stated, has been in an unsatisfactory condition since March 1912, although much of its indebtedness has been liquidated through the efforts of the Treasury department. It is believed, the statement concludes, that all depositors will be paid eventually 100 cents on the dollar."

So Honey must have known that J. V.'s affairs were becoming precarious when she asked for her million.

To bolster morale, Frank M. Semans, Jr., assistant cashier, announced that the bank owned more a million dollars worth of unencumbered real estate;

bills receivable, notes, etc., aggregated more than $2,000,000. The liabilities to depositors totalled only about $1,300,000. The officers and directors of the bank, the paper stated, stood ready to pledge their own private fortunes as security to the patrons of the bank. Local business men were offering cash, one of them $50,000.

The Poles, Czecks, Russians, Italians, and Bulgarians could not understand what had happened to their money but remained quiet. There was only one arrest, a foreigner, who went around showing a bankbook with a deposit of $350 and could not be made to understand that his money was safe even though the doors of the bank were closed. A burgess at the police station assured him that it was safer than in his pocket. By next week business would be going on the same as usual.

Actually the Golden Days were over.

The closing of the bank was like an acid burn, a surprise at first and an annoyance; then it began to eat in. Simultaneously a lot of people thought they would play safe by applying for judgments where an equity was in danger and there was a rush for the prothonotary's office. That night the clerks worked until two o'clock making up the papers. When they went home they had entered 66 judgments totalling $300,000 against 133 defendants. A fresh batch was waiting for them in the morning.

Something had to be done or the economics of the Coke Region would be in chaos. The day after the crash J. V. Thompson, Judge Van Swearingen, and two of the large unsecured creditors did it. Fuller Hogsett and David L. Durr, whom Thompson owed $90,000 and $400,000, petitioned the court to appoint receivers to protect their debts and keep the secured creditors from wasting the estate in a scramble to collect so there would be nothing left for the unsecured creditors.

The local papers assured the public that the move had been made to conserve Mr. Thompson's property and protect the unsecured creditors. No one need be alarmed. Mr. Thompson had $70,000,000 in assets, mostly coal lands, to pay a total indebtedness of $22,000,000 of which $7,000,000 was unsecured. The principal danger was the depression of coal values if a hit-or-miss flood of executions in creditors' judgments dumped thousands of acres of coal land on the market all at once. And to bolster morale further the paper quoted Mr. Thompson's answer in the application for receivership.

"I aver that if my assets can be conserved and the same prevented from unnecessary sacrifice, that all my creditors, secured and unsecured, can be fully paid within a reasonable time.... I admit that the danger of my estate being thus sacrificed is imminent and very great and hereby consent to the appointment of receivers to take charge of my said assets as prayed in the bill of complaint."

The kernel of the whole receivership ordered by Judge Van Swearingen to hold back the importunate creditors lay in the sixth paragraph. It sounded as dry and legal as the rest of it but it had fangs.

"All creditors of the said defendant ... are hereby enjoined and restrained from bringing and also from further prosecuting suits or actions at law ... against the said defendant; from entering judgments and issuing executions or attachments against the said defendant without leave of the Court first obtained."

Eight other men went into similar receiverships within the next few days, involved through accommodation endorsements for Thompson. Now that the pillars of the Coke Region were tumbling down the situation became increasingly complex. Of the J. V. Thompson notes, some were made by the coal baron himself, some he had endorsed, some he had endorsed with others now in receivership; then there was a complicated series where part of the endorsers were men not in receivership who might be pulled down, too.

The strain became unbearable for one of the coke company superintendents, trustee of the fortune of his grandchildren. Now that their money seemed lost in the general collapse he went looking for Mr. Thompson with a gun. When he didn't find him, the old man came back to the garage behind his pillared mansion and shot himself.

In the spring someone advertised that he was willing to buy Thompson notes at a 20 percent discount. Anxious creditors wondered if an attempt were being made to get control to force the sale of Thompson coal lands. When asked about the advertisement, the man who sponsored it said he had allowed his name to be used but otherwise he knew nothing of who was doing the buying. He would give no further information.

March went by and still the bank didn't open. On April 8, John H. Strawn was appointed permanent receiver and took up the collection of its complicated indebtedness. Mr. Thompson was often in New York trying desperately to sell the choicest of his coal land to the U. S. Steel Corporation and Standard Oil. He asked $40,000,000. They offered $19,000,000. He dropped to $34,000,000 and they went up to $21,000,000. There they deadlocked. Meanwhile taxes and interest were piling up.

On April 13, 1915, some of the small creditors through Attorneys Tuit and Dumbauld openly challenged the receivership which prevented their suing the estate as impairing the obligations of contract and being a suspension of the laws of Pennsylvania. They got nowhere at the moment.

The Thompson estate was losing money fast through its unwieldiness. It was like a mastodon mired in a swamp, sinking under its own weight. When the appraisers filed their report on July 12, it had sunk a few million. According to their figures it was worth only $65,367,758 now but there were still 141,413 acres of coal land. If only the price would go up!

The coal king was optimistic. "Every financial expert, every manufacturer of any size, every banker of experience in the United States, believes the next four to six years will see the best times we have had in this country," he said and shuttled back and forth between New York and the Coke Region trying to make his prediction come true.

The receivership kept hitching along under the hammering of Tuit and Dumbauld. It won a continuance from June 14 to August 14, and then to September 15. Just after the noon hour on September 11, a motion for its discontinuance was brought before the court. For the first time in the history of Fayette County a motion in open court was made, seconded, voted upon and the court decided by counting the vote. Of the twenty-five attorneys, eighteen voted for giving Thompson a six months' continuance of the receivership, two voted against it, and the other five withheld their votes, not having clients involved.

The first crack in Paragraph Six came the middle of the next month with a test case involving a small debt when the Supreme Court directed Judge Van Swearingen to hand down a decision allowing the plaintiff to sue the estate. Further, the Supreme Court ruled that the petition of forty-five members of the Fayette County Bar supporting Judge Van Swearingen's position in withholding the right to sue had no proper place on the record. Outside pressure, hard to combat, was now in a position to threaten the receivership.

The struggle had now taken a definite pattern. If the creditors could be held off until Mr. Thompson could dispose of his property, his debts could be paid and there would be money left over; but it looked to the Coke Region as though the people with money to buy what he had to sell and a use for it, wanted him to fail so they could buy at their own price. Thompson's associates were the solid people of the district, hundreds of small investors, widows, minors, teachers, and small business men. It was the Coke Region fighting to save a value they knew was there that was being artificially depressed by a force they couldn't lay hands on. J. V. Thompson was their general. If he lost, so did they.

The weakening of Paragraph Six was a serious defeat but the local bar association gamely stood in the breach to stop a catch-as-catch-can race to be the first for judgments. They stalled about accepting suits. By the twenty-first there were none yet and they agreed to hold off until the twenty-fifth and later if possible. At the same meeting they named a committee to look out for the creditors and still save Mr. Thompson if it could. The plan, tentatively worked out, would give a permanent creditors' committee, to be appointed later, power to administer the estate and save costly litigation and bankruptcy costs.

That day also the court gave the Bank of Charleroi permission to sell $32,000 worth of securities to satisfy two ten-thousand-dollar notes. Anything left over was to go to the estate. The dissipation of the Thompson collateral had begun.

By November 16 the prothonotary's office was flooded with long rows of blue-covered documents filling the desks. Already there were fourteen hundred suits against Mr. Thompson and his associates, five hundred against Mr. Thompon singly. All of the personal receiverships were affected, so suits against them had the same status. In one day Sheriff Mart Keefer served eleven hundred writs of assumpsit on J. V. Thompson, the greatest number ever served on an individual in the United States to that date.

In addition to the press of legal business and trying to negotiate coal sales, he was constantly harried by small insults. Late in November a Uniontown blacksmith seized his automobile on a writ of attachment for a trifling debt. His mail brought threatening letters warning that his house would be bombed, promise of personal violence. Part of the trouble was due to the misunderstanding of foreign creditors who thought they were depositors at the bank when actually they held private notes from the cashier of the Foreign Exchange division. The First National paid no interest on deposits so when foreign workmen wanted to have their money in the Big Bank and still get interest, the cashier sometimes accepted their money as his own private loan and pinned his note in their bankbooks. It was a perfectly legal transaction, only later they didn't understand that it was not the First National and Mr. Thompson who owed them. The morale of the community was breaking. Overwork and anxiety were to blame for some of it and there were those who, rather than make the necessary adjustments, shut their doors and quietly drank themselves out of their troubles. The coal operator who stood at the storm center only worked harder than ever. Somehow there was a way out of the maze and he was going to find it. People were beginning to urge him to go into bankruptcy but he stoutly refused. He was, however, willing to work with a dependable creditors' committee.

The lawyers on the two subcommittees assigned to the Thompson matter had been giving their time and paying their own expenses travelling back and forth to New York trying to work out a practical plan of refinancing the estate. The result of their work was the formation of the J. V. Thompson Creditors' Association. The attorneys who formed the Association represented $9,000,000 in claims. Now the problem was to persuade the people whose money was at stake to agree to file their claims with a permanent creditors' committee when it was formed. On December seventh the suits went to judgment but the morning paper announced that the local attorneys were in no hurry to press for executions until they knew what the Creditors' Association was going to do. Paragraph Six still held, even though part of it had been overridden and a stiff legal battle might be expected before it was lifted.

Fayette County had a pretty good Christmas after all. The European War was beginning to be felt in steel and that meant coke, so 80 percent of the ovens were in operation and the workmen of the Region had money for turkeys even though Big Business was in a jam.

A flu epidemic was raging so the organizers had trouble finding men to go on the permanent committee, but when the personnel was finally announced, a year and a day after the closing of the First National, a wave of optimism swept the district. It was an imposing list aimed to inspire confidence. The great Samuel Untermeyer of New York, "famous for securing the rights of minority stock-holders and the property interests of the unfortunate, correcting corporate abuses, curbing monopoly exactions and the enactment of remedial legislation," would head the committee and act as its counsel. Now if only the New York capitalists would buy something so that Mr. Untermeyer and the committee would have money to work with.

Even as far away as Fairmont, West Virginia, people felt that Mr. Thompson's cause was theirs. An article in the *Fairmont Times* for January 20, 1916, called attention to the fact that Mr. Thompson was the largest taxpayer in West Virginia and noted approvingly that he was a sober Presbyterian who would do no business on Sunday. He had made thousands of widows, orphans, and landowners prosperous and he had acted as guardian without recompense of sixty-seven different sets of orphan children. "Upwards of three thousand honest, patriotic, peaceful citizens, residing in one of the finest agricultural, industrial and manufacturing communities in the United States are living daily in fear of bankruptcy proceedings and the loss of home and property. They are not asking alms, nor are they at War, but asking to be loaned on unquestionable security money with which to preserve their holdings, protect their homes and support their families."

Meanwhile new trouble had broken out at home. On a Sunday evening a deputy arrived in Uniontown and went to evening service at one of the churches. Later he registered at a hotel. In the morning the visitor dealt out twenty-six subpoenas, summoning all the officers of the First National except J. V. Thompson and J. M. Hustead, most of the employees of the bank, and a dozen prominent Fayette County businessmen to appear before the Pittsburgh Grand Jury the first of February. All books and papers relative to the bank had already been taken either to Washington or to Pittsburgh.

In spite of the judicial inquiry, the hopeful mood engendered by the formation of the brilliant Creditors' Committee prevailed when the witnesses took the train for Pittsburgh. The Creditors' Association had become the not-very-mobile fighting unit of Coke Region strategy, the permanent committee its war council. Business was a lot better. On the first of February the Frick workers got a 10 percent increase in wages; the next day the independents followed suit.

In Pittsburgh the federal inquiry into Mr. Thompson's affairs got under way. The upshot of it was that on February 4 the Grand Jury authorized the indictment of J. V. Thompson on seventeen counts, mostly relative to a matter of public funds loaned by the county treasurer on a personal note to Thompson, and a series of small technicalities. The inquiry came at a bad time for the Creditors' Committee, working hard to build up confidence so that the people would deposit their claims.

The *News Standard* rallied loyally to Mr. Thompson's defense with an editorial aimed to combat the unfavorable accounts in Pittsburgh papers.

"These men do not know what a slave's life Mr. Thompson has led for the last fifteen years to carry a load that was undertaken with a view to preserve the great mineral wealth of this community for the people of this community instead of New York bankers and exploiters. These men do not know that if any of Mr. Thompson's banking operations were questionable, the absence of criminal intent was understood. . . . These men do not know that in borrowing money to carry on his gigantic operations, Mr. Thompson played no favorites, but that in the crash he carried down with him his brother, his sisters, his sons, his nephews and his nieces."

The Creditors' Committee seemed to be getting things in hand in spite of the distractions. On the second of February the final draft of the Depositors' Agreement was ordered to be printed and distributed and the Committee received power of attorney from J. V. Thompson to settle his affairs. The plan was that three banks should receive the claims filed by the creditors; the claimants would receive certificates representing the proportionate value of their claims while the claim itself was held in escrow. The secured creditors would naturally be paid first, then the unsecured. What was left would go to Mr. Thompson. The first unsecured claim was deposited on the fifteenth. By the twenty-eighth they were coming in at the rate of $200,000 a day.

There had been a lively newspaper war on between the Region and the big Pittsburgh dailies ever since the federal indictment of Mr. Thompson, the city papers whooping with delight as each new trap opened for their quarry, the Region papers loyally defending their man, reiterating over and over the things everybody knew if he would only be patient and stop to figure out the situation as it was and not as the Wreckers were determined to make it.

With the excitement caused by the federal investigation temporarily in abeyance, another bomb exploded. On the last day of February, when claims were coming in fast to the Creditors' Committee, Attorneys Tuit and Dumbauld of Uniontown attempted to let loose a flood of executions on the estate by attacking the validity of the famous Paragraph Six. The occasion was the matter of a $4,000 judgment in the settlement of an estate. They demanded an execution immediately, also leave to intervene in the receivership. According to the contention of Tuit, the receivership amounted to a suspension of the legal remedies for the enforcement of the obligations of contract. Also he contended that the court had no power of chancery and should never have issued the receivership order in the first place. It was prejudicial to the rights of creditors, and meanwhile the estate was being dissipated by taxes, sacrifice of collateral, etc.

The opposition was really going into action now. Subpoenas appeared again on the twentieth for Uniontown people connected with the bank and the county treasurer's office. Four days later the Federal Grand Jury sitting at Erie reopened the bank case and returned a new presentment of thirty counts against J. V. Thompson. When Judge Orr received it he threw the courtroom into a furor with the announcement that he was not in sympathy with the action of the district attorney's office in submitting the evidence on which the return was based; he doubted the legality of the presentment, and reserved the right to quash the indictment when presented. The jurors who had been all ready to return the indictment immediately, filed out confused by the hubbub, came back for further instructions at 3:00 P.M. and did not return the indictment until 4:30, a half-hour after the regular closing time. Attorneys McKean and Umbel, acting for Thompson, were able to get the case put over until November because their principal was too busy with the Creditors' Committee to prepare the data for his defense. The nub of the latest charge against Mr. Thompson was the misapplication of the county treasurer's deposit, but that was old stuff by now. The fillip for the press was a hint of embezzlement and abstraction.

The Pittsburgh papers said "I told you so!" but the Region editors stood their ground. According to the *Morning Herald* for March 25:

"What many believe is little short of a conspiracy against J. V. Thompson and this community encountered a distinct and deserved check yesterday in Federal Court when Judge Charles P. Orr denounced pending proceedings and reserved the right to set aside the indictment which was requested by the Grand Jury. What is attempted to be done savors too much of persecution to meet the approval of Judge Orr.

"An indictment was returned in Pittsburgh some time ago covering the extended investigation into local affairs. The same matters are brought up again at Erie without the knowledge or consent of the Court.... It is believed that the Erie action is an attempt to bolster up what is realized as a weak case.... That such persistance is shown strengthens the local suspicion that there is a deep laid plan behind the whole affair. This plan calls for more and more desperate measures as efforts for rehabilitation of the financial affairs of the community ripen successfully from one step to the next. Each time a critical stage in the pending movement is reached, a mine is exploded.

"Some of these nefarious acts have been connected up closely with powerful interests which seek to destroy this community and batten upon its wreckage. It is suspected they all originate in the same cunning brain and find their well-spring in the same cupidity.... Balked of the possibility of wrecking and looting his holdings there seems an effort on foot to pillory and punish Mr. Thompson.

"Nothing has been overlooked in this attempt. Distorted and untruthful news stories have been sent broadcast in an effort to work up sentiment against him. Months have been spent in investigations and probes of every character by officers of the Department of Justice. The net result has been an indictment returned in Pittsburgh which even those who secured it do not believe will stand the acid test of a court trial, and a presentment in Erie denounced from the bench.... In the meantime there is universal inquiry as to the men and motives behind the various moves which have been made."

In April it seemed as though things were looking up. There was a second 10 percent raise in wages. Ninety-five percent of the unsecured claims were in the hands of the Committee; and Receiver Strawn at the First National had $150,000 to distribute as a 10 percent dividend to depositors. On April 12, Martin Drahula, a foreigner, happily drew out $5.50, 10 percent of his balance at the closing. Now with a good-humored crowd lined up at the teller's windows to cash their receipt-slips it looked like old times.

If only the Creditors' Committee could sell something now to pay the taxes that were piling up! Early in May the Thompson attorneys were able to secure an injunction to halt the sale of a block of Greene County land advertised for $200,000 tax arrears. The 1914 returns had not been given them until 1915. Thus, through the delinquency of the assessors, they had not yet had the two-year period allowed by law before the property could be sold. But what about the land to be sold for taxes in Fayette County in June unless money came from somewhere? The seventy-page report of the receivers filed May 19 was reassuring but equities would not satisfy the tax collector. The appraisers valued the entire estate at $65,714,305.99 with an excess over total liabilities of $32,535,443.57. However there was only $605.87 on hand in actual cash, and anxious creditors said that the Thompson indebtedness was growing at the rate of $7,000 a day. Certainly his collateral in the hands of secured creditors was being sacrificed at an alarming rate. On the twenty-second of June, in Mr. Thompson's answer to a West Virginian's suit to collect three notes—two for $3300 and one for $15,000, it came out that the plaintiff, without obtaining permission from the court or notifying

Mr. Thompson, had sold bonds turned over by the banker as collateral and valued at $25,000 for $17.50.*

The test case threatening the receivership held the stage during the early days of July. The great Mr. Untermeyer was coming to Uniontown to take charge of the defense himself and when he had set the receivership firmly on its feet, he would also have paved the way for the coal sales that the Creditors' Committee needed so desperately. The trial was set for the eighteenth. By ten o'clock the larger courtroom was packed, with people standing along the walls. Mr. Untermeyer arrived about eleven only to disappear again for conference. He didn't look very imposing, a nervous squinty little man with a jaundiced complexion. The court announced a recess until 1:45 P.M.

While the visiting lawyers went to the Summit for lunch, the crowd waiting for the show milled about the hot corridors at the courthouse, careful not to go too far from their seats for fear they would lose them. Mr. Thompson arrived, heavy-shouldered and stooped, and took a seat with members of the Creditors' Committee in front of the jury-box close to the press table. Attorneys Tuit and Dumbauld took their places at the plaintiff's council table; Mr. Untermeyer, John M. Freeman of Pittsburgh, and W. J. Sturgis went to the other one. Dignified Judge Van Swearingen, who had issued the receivership, was the presiding judge.

Untermeyer was formally made a member of the Fayette County Bar and the battle began in earnest. Mr. Untermeyer pointed out that the reason that the estate had been taken under the guardianship of the court was to safeguard the interests of thousands of investors, big and little. Over fourteen hundred of the unsecured creditors of this great estate that now hung in the balance had banded themselves together to save the property from useless sacrifice. They represented 98 percent of the unsecured claims against the estate. In all fourteen hundred judgments had been filed, and *only one* had appeared to intervene. It only amounted to $4,000, but the whole fabric the motion would pull down, if granted, was $13,000,000.

"What is the purpose of this intervenor—to bring down the house of safety?" queried Mr. Untermeyer. "Is it possible that some influence we know nothing of, who possibly desires to secure the rich estate at sacrifice prices, is behind the intervenor?"

He talked an hour and twenty-five minutes, his yellow skin turning slowly red as he hammered point after point home. Tuit's reply was brief, and court adjourned at 4:18. A few days later Judge Van Swearingen

---

* The figure is taken from a news item in the Thompson Scrap Book at the Uniontown Library with the date July 22, 1916 written in ink at the top. The bonds consisted of $10,000 worth of Tower Hill Connellsville Coke Co. general mortgage 5½ percent bonds and $30,000 worth of Isabella Connellsville Coke Co. first mortgage 5 percent bonds.

refused the petition and sustained the receivership; Tuit and Dumbauld promptly filed exceptions and later appealed. The receivership was safe for the moment but if its validity were to be always under fire, prospective buyers for the coal lands would keep on waiting to see how things came out before parting with their money and that would defeat the purpose of the receivership. Even though Paragraph Six still held off the executions, supposedly until property sales would have amassed a fund to take care of them, the sales were not being made. Unless money came from somewhere quickly the real estate would go under the sheriff's hammer and the secured creditors would make away with the rest of the collateral.

While the Committee was straining to save the West Virginia properties from tax sales and at the same time get together money to hold off the secured creditors, Judge Knapp of the United States Circuit Court suddenly knocked over the West Virginia end of the receivership. The Committee had just worked up a sale to the Hope Natural Gas Company which would mean some money as soon as the receivership was settled. Now when the verdict came out the wrong way it was anybody's land, depending on who got there first. Friends and relatives of Mr. Thompson dashed down to Monongalia County with claims amounting to $1,500,000 and saved it. And the Committee squeezed out enough money to halt the West Virginia sales by November 30.

The Coke Region had really big news on December third, the birthday of the Creditors' Association. The Frick Company was to have 12,000 acres of the choicest coal lands, the Greene County tract lying along the Monongahela. The price mentioned was between six and seven million dollars, about $550 an acre, but it would take $4,000,000 of it to pay the deferred interest and taxes to the secured creditors. The price was much shaded, considering that it was the cream of the holdings with a coal vein running nine to eleven feet thick, with water transportation down the river. According to the newspapers' information 1,400 of the 12,000 acres bought by Frick belonged to the Fastman tract. The Creditors' Committee had had to option the field at $750 an acre and would have to make up the difference over the actual purchase price from the proceeds of the larger sale, but although it cut down the profit some, they had to do it if they made the sale at all. Frick wanted the coal for the $18,000,000 by-product plant at Clairton which would probably be in operation in a year, using 15,000 tons a day. It was said that by barging the coal down the Monongahela, the Frick Company would save forty cents a ton in freight rates or $6,000 an acre less than their present delivery costs.

"Since the Frick sale practically all of the leading steel and iron concerns in the country have come to Uniontown asking for coal," the Uniontown paper announced hopefully. "Large corporations who need coal and others who are anxious to get into the coal business as a result of some of the amazing profits that have been pocketed during the past six months are optioning large independent fields *in the event that Thompson's coal is unavailable except at the market price."* * Surely the jinx was off now. To add to the general hopefulness there was another wage increase affecting about forty thousand miners, a 30 percent advance over last year.

Nineteen-seventeen started off with industry charging ahead. On January 13 there was an announcement that Bethlehem Steel had optioned 12,000 acres of coal land in Greene County at $600 an acre, the highest price on record for a block of that size. There was talk of a new railroad in Greene County to tap the big coal reservoir. At least engineers were looking the ground over. As it was, the tremendous demand for coke overstrained the common carriers. By the middle of February there was such a tie-up of thousands of loaded cars from Pittsburgh to the seaboard that a suspension of coke and coal freight loomed. The First National announced that it had $135,000 ready to distribute among its depositors. The business of the embezzlement investigation seemed to have flattened out but Mr. Thompson had enough to worry him with the receivership case coming up at the spring term of court in Philadelphia. With a dozen men in unsteady receiverships that would stand or fall with Thompson's, there was a hundred and fifty million dollars' worth of property in doubtful status. If that could be set to working normally, the coal country could take full advantage of the boom.

The Thompson case was causing heads to turn all over the East. It was the largest personal estate over which a court had extended its domination since the establishment of courts in this country and the first time that a court had exercised such broad powers over the property of an individual, although in the case of firms and corporations it was not unusual. The original restrictions had already been modified one by one, until now all that stood between the creditors and the issuance of executions for sheriff's sale was Judge Van Swearingen's Paragraph Six that had so far been indestructible.

In April while the home folks awaited the verdict there was a good deal of speculation about the validity of the Frick sale if the receivership were set aside. It would be too bad for the creditors if they weren't going to get the six million; Frick was all right either way. If the receivership held, he had the finest of the coal lands under contract. If it didn't he would probably get them just the same at a cheaper price.

When the decision was handed down on May 7 it meant the end of the friendly receivership. "The bill filed for the appointment of receivers is dismissed for want of jurisdiction to entertain it and the proceedings thereunder are vacated and set aside." The receivers who had been thus im-

* Author's italics.

properly appointed were directed to file their account immediately and the cost of the appeal was to be borne by the defendants. Another big slice of Mr. Thompson's money. It had been all outgo instead of income since 1915, but when the figures of the final account were released the estate still amounted to $63,166,866.14, with $31,964,457.60 more than the liabilities. All the same there were those who seriously urged bankruptcy at once as the only way to save the property.

Mr. Thompson had another idea. If the proposition he was working on with a western group turned out as he hoped, they would buy the outstanding claims for fifty cents on the dollar, which would mean more all the way around than if every man dived in for himself.

At a meeting of the Fayette County Bar Association on May 9 to decide what to do while waiting the ten days necessary before creditors could officially proceed with executions, the conservative faction pointed out that there was now $13,000,000 in indebtedness against those affected by the abolishment of the receivership and that at sheriff's sale, if the unsecured creditors were to get even one cent on the dollar, the personal property would need to sell for $130,000, whereas it would probably not bring more than $30,000.

Five days after the setting aside of the receivership, in order to be on the safe side—if there were a safe side in the confusion about to be let loose, the Creditors' Committee took actual possession of all the Thompson property—the Highland Building in Pittsburgh, Oak Hill, Friendship Hill and the receivers' offices in the First National. Then they sent a deputation to St. Paul to confer with the James J. Hill interests, reported to be willing to pay $5,000,000 for the unsecured claims.

That May of 1917 coal was selling at five dollars a ton and operators looked for it to be ten by fall. The home papers were wondering why somebody hadn't thought of operating the Thompson coal fields to take advantage of the market. At five dollars a ton, an acre of Pittsburgh vein was worth $60,000 loaded on the cars, and wasn't it queer that thousands of acres of this very coal had been going begging at $300 an acre for the last three years? Right now men were breaking their backs to work three- and five-foot seams while Mr. Thompson's immense holdings, part of them the finest coal property in America, were forced to lie idle. This property was tapped by the Pennsylvania Railroad, the New York Central, and the B & O; and it had miles of frontage on the Monongahela by which coal could be shipped to the Gulf of Mexico and South America. They were willing to pay $20 a ton for it down there. The freight to the Panama Canal was only $3.00 a ton and the coal gotten out ready to ship cost the producer only about a dollar.

"Let's do a little figuring!" urged the *News Standard* on May 12. "J. V. Thompson has 140,000 acres of coal, 140,000 acres of coal will mine 2,240,-

000,000 tons of coal. 2,240,000,000 tons of coal at the prevailing price of $5.00 a ton will bring ELEVEN BILLION TWO HUNDRED MILLION DOLLARS or almost twice as much as the recent seven billion dollar War loan of the United States, the largest single war credit in the history of the world.

"The Pittsburgh Coal Co., the largest coal company in the world, values its unmined coal at FIVE CENTS A TON. At five cents per ton J. V. Thompson's unmined coal, if owned by the Pittsburgh Coal Co. WOULD BE VALUED AT $112,000,000 ON THE BOOKS OF THAT COMPANY!

"The Monongahela River Consolidated Coal and Coke Company values its unmined coal at ten cents per ton. So do practically all the coke producing companies in the Connellsville Region. At ten cents per ton J. V. THOMPSON'S UNMINED COAL WOULD BE WORTH $224,000,000 ON THE BOOKS OF THESE COMPANIES!

"One cent per ton on J. V. Thompson's coal is equal to $22,400,000 or $2,000,000 more than the value of all the plants and equipment of the Pittsburgh Coal Co., a $64,000,000 corporation with a bonded debt of $30,000,000.

"THREE CENTS PER TON ON J. V. THOMPSON'S COAL WOULD DEVELOP THAT COAL, PROVIDE IT WITH PLANTS AND EQUIPMENT SUPERIOR TO THOSE OF THE PITTSBURGH COAL COMPANY, pay every penny of Mr. Thompson's debts and provide the operating company with a working capital of $9,000,000.

"Because Mr. Thompson cannot pay his debts there is grave danger of this immensely valuable coal being sacrificed,—sold perhaps for less than it was bought for from the farmers twenty years ago. Thompson's proposition is too big for the small fellows to handle, and the big fellows are waiting for the crash they think will come.

"Everything considered, Mr. Thompson is THE OWNER OF THE LARGEST AND MOST VALUABLE COAL DEPOSIT IN THE WORLD. It is the pick of what is left of the coking vein deposits of the famous Pittsburgh nine-foot vein. So long as there is danger of this coal being sold under the sheriff's hammer, the interests which need this coal won't buy it and Mr. Thompson hasn't the capital to develop it, notwithstanding the fact that coal was never in greater demand than it is today.

"If sold under the sheriff's hammer, J. V. Thompson's coal won't bring two cents a ton."

The aging coal baron was working unheard-of hours, trying to be everywhere at once. He had caught the trick of dozing in his chair at off minutes without losing the thread of conversation; even when he was talking with people his tired eyes closed but just when he was thought to be asleep they opened, and he went on with the business. Sometimes he nodded a minute in the middle of a column of figures but his pencil point kept the place and in a minute he went on without a fresh start.

There was a widening split in Coke Region loyalty now as outside interests drove the wedge deeper. People were saying that Jo Thompson was so desperate now you couldn't take his advice any more; he'd tell you anything if it would help his own affairs. One of the creditors who had staunchly supported him had a chance to try him one day. She was one of the few who had not registered her claims with the Creditors' Association. Instead she entered her notes for collection in Morgantown and employed a lawyer who she knew had managed West Virginia business for Thompson to handle them. The attorney told her not to sign with the Creditors' Committee or any other group without consulting him, and she hadn't. One day Mr. Thompson asked her how it happened that she was not represented with the other creditors. She told him frankly that she had entered her notes for collection in West Virginia and showed him the lawyer's letter, asking what he would do under the circumstances. He read it carefully, folded it in half and then in quarters while he sat thinking. Then he said slowly, "Well, when I hire a lawyer, I generally try to do what he tells me." He was the same Jo Thompson he had always been.

In June his furniture and personal belongings came near to being sold but the Committee saved them temporarily with the plea that they weren't Mr. Thompson's any more and technically hadn't been for a year.

The Hill deal was much in the papers, bitterly attacked by some of the unsecured creditors. Why, with coal and coke soaring, should they be satisfied with the paltry forty cents on the dollar the Hills were offering? They were western railroad people, so what did they want with Pennsylvania coal? And would somebody make it clear about what was going to happen to the accommodation endorsers if the Hill deal went through? If they were considered creditors and paid 40 percent of their endorsement liability, then they would lose only 60 percent of the value of the notes. If they were not, there was nothing to prevent any interest which took over the notes at whatever discount from collecting a 100 percent from those who only put their names on Mr. Thompson's notes at his request to help him out.

On June 28 Mr. Thompson made a statement concerning the pending negotiations and as usual he took the long view, trying to preserve the interests of the small investors in the coal market.

"The consummation of this sale will mean that the First National Bank will be able to pay every cent of its indebtedness and far more important than this, will mean that coal values in this area will be maintained. Some of my largest unsecured creditors own coal which would be forced to meet a surfeited market were these holdings dumped broadcast, without an attempt to preserve the values now attained. . . .

"Even though forty cents is but the final outcome of the present transaction, the necessity for preserving this mobilized coal reserve intact is far more vital to holders of coal land than the temporary loss they would sustain by reason of the sale of their claims."

The Hills were offering to pay $5,000,000 for the unsecured claims, retire the $840,000 trust fund in full, and take up $2,000,000 worth of collateral held by Pittsburgh banks for a debt of $800,000. They would also redeem the stock in two coal companies. Payment to the unsecured creditors would be made in installments with $500,000 to start with, then nothing more for a year; after that, $500,000 every six months. Friends of the deal urged it as a last chance.

Opposition to the move was what finally split the Coke Region. By the middle of the month it had grown to such proportion that the harassed Committee looked for an injunction to tie up proceedings; still it would take $3,000,000 worth of claims to block it and so far the opposition had only marshalled about $2,000,000. On July 23, Louis Hill, president of the Great Northern Railroad, and his associates came to town to look over the property. When he left it looked as though the sale was assured.

Five days later the Coke Region was stunned by the announcement that a petition involuntary in bankruptcy had been filed against Mr. Thompson in Pittsburgh in the U. S. District Court. Mr. Thompson had at last agreed to the bankruptcy proceedings to halt a huge sale of collateral, $4,000,000 worth of securities, being offered by the Farmers Deposit National Bank and the Union Trust Company to satisfy a million-dollar debt. The bankruptcy action came only three and a half hours before the sale would have taken place.

The Region had gotten used to expecting major shocks just when it seemed that a solution had been found to the Thompson dilemma, but when the expected happened the repercussion was no less keen. If the persistent opposition that struck now here, now there, could keep the hydra-headed Thompson estate in confusion long enough, people would lose confidence that it could ever be rehabilitated. The last step would be to defame the agents working to salvage the local economy. Already a bitter bickering had broken out between the local papers and the creditors were separated into angry factions. Coke had gone as high as $16 that summer. Whose fault was it if not the Committee's, they demanded, that the Thompson lands lay idle?

On September 7 the court formally adjudged J. V. Thompson a bankrupt and referred the case to J. G. Carroll, referee in bankruptcy in Fayette County. When the schedule of Thompson's assets in bankruptcy was published, the liabilities had risen to $39,368,098.11 and the assets had come down to $57,474,593.71. The unsecured claims were now over $19,000,000, just about the same as the secured claims, and taxes had run up to $475,000. The Union Trust Company of Pittsburgh had a claim of $1,500,000; J. R. Nutt of Cleveland about $1,800,000. The shrinking of the assets and mounting of the liabilities was understandable considering there had been enormous expense and little income since January, 1915, constant litigation, receivership expenses, and a steady dispersal of collateral for months, but the papers howled. If there were $19,000,000 in unsecured claims instead of $13,000,000 as everybody supposed, then the Hill money, if they ever actually got it, would mean only nineteen cents on the dollar, not forty. Mr. Thompson must have some more assets that he wasn't telling about or else the Committee had been wasting the property.

When the bankruptcy hearing got under way on November first, Charles Tuit questioned the insolvent coal king exhaustively for a hint of the concealed assets that people were talking about: a $200,000 insurance policy, exorbitant attorney fees, gold-mining stock, a private deposit box full of bonds. When the hearing dragged to an end the prosecution had turned up no hidden assets. The only fact established was that much of Mr. Thompson's collateral had been seized and sold and that due to no fault of its owner, the estate was wasting away.

As the months went by J. G. Carroll proved an able and impartial referee. The case dropped out of the papers but now and then there was a substantial coal sale. The bank paid out just as Mr. Thompson said it would, but as part of the liquidation Receiver Strawn sold the building. After that the Fayette Title and Trust Company moved into the First National's marble quarters. When everything was wound up there was even a premium for the stockholders.

But the last act of the economic drama was not to take place in the Coke Region, and the irony of the thing was that this total war, entered into so gallantly by the butcher, the baker, and the candlestick-maker, should end in defeat that happened so quietly in an artificial twilight that people didn't realize what had happened until a long time afterward.

In 1919, without fanfare, the case was taken from the capable handling of Referee Carroll and put under Pittsburgh jurisdiction. People in the Coke Region never knew much about what happened after that. The unsecured creditors eventually received about twelve cents on the dollar and it appeared that the property had been taken over by three holding companies, the Airshire Corporation, the Gallatin Land Company, and the Piedmont Coal Company. Nobody knew who was operating behind the dummy directors and they still don't. People who had been rich and were now poor wondered how much the bankrupt coal baron had salvaged for himself. Maybe he had come to terms with them in some kind of an undercover deal. The Federal investigation into Mr. Thompson's honesty had come to nothing for want of a case, but maybe he had foxed everybody. There are those who believe that he did. The people who worked intimately with him deny it hotly.

The Coke Region had ended up just where it did with the Whiskey Rebellion back in Washington's time, beaten, divided into distrustful factions and full of confused bitterness against Those on the Outside.

CHAPTER VIII

TWILIGHT AT OAK HILL

AFTER THE BANKRUPTCY AND THE REMOVAL OF THE
Thompson estate from the jurisdiction of the Fayette County Courts,
the ruined coal king lived on at Oak Hill, but the Piedmont Coal Company
owned it now. They had bought all his holdings, real and personal, in 1920,
including the big coal tracts in Greene and Washington Counties and northern West Virginia for $5,500,000 to settle some of his obligations. In the
good years he had had the foresight to get hold of virtually all the land on
which the great Clairton steel and by-product plant was built, but that
went into the pot to satisfy his creditors, too.

Pasquale, the butler, and his wife Angelica, the cook, who had been with
Thompson ever since the days of Honey's regime, kept house for him. He
was always busy with plans for a come back but the coups he planned failed
to work out. When he wasn't covering reams of paper with figures he
worked on a mass of genealogical data that he was compiling for a family
history. His eager mind still drove his body unmercifully even though he
was past seventy. When he went to Gettysburg to search some family
records, at the end of a day with the files he begged the Court House attendants to let him keep on with his work after closing hours. When they
insisted that the building must close at the appointed hour, the old man
countered with: "Is there any rule against locking me in? Then I can go on
with my work and you can let me out in the morning." In the end he had
his way.

There was one more court battle to fight before he could enjoy the peace of old age. Lida, the Princess of Thürn and Taxis in Austria-Hungary, daughter of his sister Lenora Nicolls, wanted an accounting for a trust fund that Thompson had undertaken thirty-six years before. According to the newspapers, Nicholls had wanted to leave half his fortune to his brother-in-law because it was through him that he had made his money. Thompson generously said it should all go to Lenora and Lida. When the estate was settled he undertook the management of the property in trust and more or less looked out for Lida, as well, who had grown into a dashing young lady, beautiful and headstrong with a flair for the sensational.

Her first marriage to Lord Fitzgerald, a handsome Irish officer, ended in divorce, but Lida got the custody of their three sons and a handsome property settlement. Thompson went to England to help her through the proceedings and afterward managed the property that came to her through Fitzgerald to her advantage. One of the Fitzgerald sons, a twin, had been blinded in infancy through the carelessness of a nurse. After the break-up of the Fitzgerald menage, the blind boy spent most of his time at his grandmother's old house in Uniontown. Lida continued to live abroad and presently became the Princess of Thürn and Taxis. Meanwhile, back home, her uncle lost his money and with it the patrimony he had in trust for her. On the face of it it seemed useless to sue the old man now that he had been through bankruptcy, but the story of concealed assets kept going the rounds. The Princess wanted her money.

In 1928 the Orphans Court of Fayette County directed Mr. Thompson to pay the Princess's estate $126,000 principal and $89,000 interest or go to jail. The old man was arrested on the train for New York City, taken off at Altoona and returned to Uniontown. His lawyers begged for him to be allowed to make the New York trip. Maybe he could raise enough to meet the obligation if he could see the men in the money market. He was released.

Later the Princess instituted an embezzlement suit against him in the name of her blind son and the case went to trial. Sixty-two character witnesses appeared for Mr. Thompson—doctors, lawyers, farmers, creditors who had lost money through the collapse but didn't feel that he was to blame for it. The verdict was Not Guilty.

Nothing daunted, the Princess pressed the Contempt suit against Thompson because he had not paid the trust fund according to the court order. About Christmas time in 1930 the old man had to stand up before the judge and admit that he could not pay. Mr. Thompson shook hands with his lawyers and followed the sheriff from the courtroom. When they entered the prison the veteran coal man who had once run the county turned toward the cell block.

"No, Mr. Thompson," said the sheriff, "come this way!" and took him to a pleasant bedroom in his own apartment. The Coke Region likes to make its own interpretation of the Law just as it did back in the eighties. The sentence had not said anything about bars for Mr. Thompson, just that he must go to jail. His lawyers promptly invoked the mercy of the court because Mr. Thompson was going blind and needed to be under a doctor's care. A few days later the financier was released, a free man, and his long siege with the courts was over.

The next day he entered a Pittsburgh hospital to undergo an operation for cataract. Soon after the announcement that the operation was successful, Mr. Thompson made the front page again by confirming the rumor that there was a third Mrs. Thompson; in fact there had been for some fourteen months.

Ever since Honey left, J. V. had spent little time with women although the press helpfully suggested alliances every now and then. About the time of the Princess's suit there were rumors that he had married Rose Stillwagon Maloney, a Pittsburgh woman. At least he had been seen with her in the East End, carrying a market basket. She was a good deal younger than Mr. Thompson, the widow of a Connellsville coal operator who had died leaving her with six children and a little coal land. Then the developments of the Princess's suit became the topic of the day and the press forgot about Mrs. Maloney. Now it came out that they had been quietly married in New Cumberland back in 1929 when J. V. was seventy-five years old.

The public never knew very much about the third wife but the nurse who cared for Mr. Thompson in his last sickness says that she and her children gave the aged coal baron some of the greatest happiness he had ever known. J. V. hadn't cared about money itself, only the game of making it; he had loved power while he had it but it only got him into trouble. The Presbyterian farm boy from Menallen Township had grown old without having leisure to enjoy a home. He was too busy getting a start while Mary was alive. Honey had made Oak Hill into something that was a cross between a museum and a country club; after she went it was only forty-two rooms of echoing loneliness. The Coke Region that Thompson had loved as he had never loved any individual had lost confidence in him. When he sat in his oak-panelled hall in the evenings he could hear the echoes of furious voices shouting for their money in the black days of 1915. He hadn't meant to hurt any of those angry people. The bank had paid out dollar for dollar with interest and $600 a share for the stock when par was only $50, but he could still hear the voices.

Rose Maloney changed all that. She had been in love with J. V. Thompson when she was a little girl. Her father was in the coal business with the wealthy Mariettas but his own capital was small. Once when he was in a pinch he went to Mr. Thompson to ask for a loan and the banker gave it to him without security. After that his word was gospel in the Stillwagon house and when he came to see her father sometimes, Little Rose thought he was the most desirable and elegant gentleman in the world.

When Fate finally brought them together his fortune was gone, his health was shattered, and he was going blind, but she was still in love with him. There was nothing to make news after the fact of their marriage was announced. Sometimes they were at her home in Pittsburgh, sometimes at Oak Hill. The lawns were growing up to weeds and chickens pecked in the geometrical shadows under the skeleton roof of the conservatory but it was home as it had never been. Rose's children adored him.

He never gave up hope that he would retrieve his fortune and then he was going to pay back what he owed and do great things for Rose and the children. He sat in his study with the pictures and statuettes of Napoleon interspersed with photographs of the family, Andrew's girls and Rose's, and planned how to maneuver a change of fortune. About all he had to work with was an interest in the cemetery land on Main Street, but he'd think of something.

One day when he was looking up genealogical data for his family history downtown in the prothonotary's office, he collapsed and was carried to the hospital. Old J. V. was outraged that his body would let him down when he had important work to do. Against the doctor's orders he insisted on going home. He was going to New York next week to work up a big deal and he could get well faster at home with Rose. But he didn't go to New York, and after that there was a succession of nurses.

When Miss Roselle came to care for him in June, 1933, he was delirious. The toes were gone from one foot with diabetes and a great hole had eaten into one arm. He was blind, and, in spite of all the precautions they could take, bed sores had developed. When she came he thought she was Miss Nellie, a nurse his mother had had.

"I can't seem to get used to calling you by your right name," he told her when he was better.

Miss Roselle is a stately gray-haired woman of seventy now and still nursing.

"I'd have nursed Mr. Thompson for nothing just to have known him," she says. "He was two men in one body. I've heard of such things but I never saw it before. Some days he was so gentle and sweet, and then there'd come a day when he felt he had to get to work. Even lying there helpless his will was so strong you felt he could do anything. 'Miss Nellie, can't you get me some medicine that will get me out of here?' he'd say. 'I'll take anything you want me to only I've got to be in New York by the eleventh!' That was his lucky number. The bank building has eleven stories, you know. He was so proud of it, and always remembering how grand it was when it was new. 'My father wanted to build a little one,' he told me, 'but I said "No. When we build we'll build big and the town will grow to it. Everything that goes into it will be the best we can get." We aren't licked yet,' he'd say. 'One of these days we'll get together and they can't stop us. There's a school teacher downtown that's paying interest right now on money she borrowed for me to invest in coal for her. I'm not going to let her lose by it.'

"He didn't seem to bear ill-will against those who had ruined him. I never heard him talk against Frick. He said if Honey had signed the contract on a big sale he had when he needed to put it through, things would have been different. He couldn't sell without her signature but she said her price for it was a million in cash and a divorce. The deal had to hang fire while he raised the money and everything went wrong. The only people he ever seemed to feel vindictive about were the Mellons. Once something was said about a biography of one of the Mellons coming out and he said, 'Have we money enough to get it, Rose? I'd love to have you read it to me, only I expect if it had been me that wrote it, it wouldn't sound just the same.' "

The house was getting out of repair and there wasn't anybody to do things but the Pallinis, Pasquale and Angelica. They didn't wear uniforms any more and they worked like beavers, raising dahlias and chickens to sell to help out. Somehow Angelica found time to fix beautiful trays for Mr. Thompson and if he had been her father she couldn't have loved him more than she did. The water pipes had gotten out of order so Miss Roselle couldn't get hot water for her patient except as she carried it up from the kitchen. She had her meals in the breakfast-room because the regular dining-room with its tarnished gold furniture was closed. On the way downstairs she used to make the rounds of the rich bedrooms of the second floor just to look at the rugs, the marquetry, and the framed needlework that Honey had collected. It was a lonely place now, deadly quiet.

Once when Mr. Thompson was having one of his days of wanting to hurry up to get at his work Miss Roselle said, "There are no Alps to you, are there, Mr. Thompson?"

He thought a minute and then he answered, "Why do you say that, Miss Nellie?"

"Because Napoleon said there were no Alps to him and sometimes you make me think of him."

Nothing she could have said would have pleased him more. In those last days he was so grateful for any chance kind thing. One when he was suffering a lot she said, "Mr. Thompson, you are the most patient man I ever saw!"

A little later he asked, "Miss Nellie, will you open the safe and bring out the book you find on the left-hand shelf?"

It was just where he said and she brought it.

"Now will you please write: 'Some people may have had a brother as good as my brother William Thompson, but no man ever had a better one.' "

He was quiet a minute and then he went on, "And would you mind writing in there what you said just now about me? I'd like to have you."

It pleased Mr. Thompson because Rose's children would always kiss him when they came in the room. Miss Roselle remembers, "Once I said to Mrs. Thompson that they ought not to do it any more when he was so sick. It wasn't safe.

" 'Then it's a risk we'll have to run,' she said. 'I'd never tell them not to.' There was nothing she could think of to make him happy she didn't do."

Andrew came in the summer and said that the creditor who owned Oak Hill had a buyer for the house and wanted possession by October if his father could be moved somewhere else.

"Your father won't be here in October," Miss Roselle told him; and he wasn't.

He died about eleven o'clock in the morning, September 27. Mrs. Thompson had gone to Pittsburgh on business that had to be attended to and there was no one there but the Pallinis and Miss Roselle. She noticed early in the morning that he took a turn for the worse and sent for Mrs. Thompson but, although she came as fast as she could, he was gone when she got there.

Fayette County, smarting under the loss of its wealth, had made the old coal baron its whipping boy. Now that he was dead the *Morning Herald* came out with a generous editorial:

"Thompson was coal and coal was Thompson. No man had his intimate knowledge of coal, particularly of Western Pennsylvania bituminous.... Until 1915 he carried with him to the heights many individuals and a great domain.... A few months before the World War would have created for him a more fabulous empire the whole structure was broken.... Already past 60 years, he set out to rebuild the shattered structure. He battled forces which brought about his apparent destruction; scoffed at failing health, illness and even blindness....

"He knew defeat. He accepted it only to appraise it. He used it as a base upon which to try again."

The family arranged a funeral befitting his former high estate and the embittered Coke Region grudgingly attended. From ten to two o'clock before the service the body lay in state in a plain bronze casket on the rostrum at the First Presbyterian Church that the old man had supported so generously as long as he had anything to give. He had come a long way since he sat in his father's pew there beside Lenora and Will. Mary Anderson had gone a little way with him on that journey and had given him sons.

Honey had given him trouble. Now looking back over the pattern of his life people could see that she had taken more from him than money.

There was an impressive roster of honorary pallbearers marching in solemn procession: James A. Farrel, former chairman of the board of directors of the United States Steel Corporation; Charles M. Schwab, chairman of the Board of Bethlehem Steel; J. H. Hillman of the Hillman Coal and Coke Company; Karl Bickel, president of the United Press Association; Senator James J. Davis; Judge A. H. Sayre of Waynesburg; the four Fayette County judges and the judge emeritus. Dr. Ralph C. Hutchinson, president of Washington and Jefferson College, assisted Dr. William Hindman, the local pastor, with the services. Thompson had served the college forty-four years as a trustee and endowed it with a hundred thousand dollars during his prosperity, the whole amount of the heritage he received from his father.

With the funeral over public interest centered on the will. Now the hidden assets would come out. It was a disappointment to those who had insisted that the old man had quietly laid away for himself funds that should have gone to its creditors. There was nothing of direct monetary value to bequeath. In a long document with a genealogical preamble he gave minute instructions where to find the keys to his desks and portfolios, formally adopted Rose's five minor children with directions that henceforth they should bear his name, and disposed of his keepsakes. Rosemary, his favorite, was to have his genealogical records and some signatures he had collected of signers of the Declaration of Independence, among them two rare ones of Button Gwinnett and Thomas Lynch, now in the care of the secretary of the Pennsylvania Historical Society; the children should share his books, and the insurance would go to his wife.

In chronicling it the newspaper recalled that since 1915 Thompson's shares of First National stock with $100 par value had paid $850 each, but the Piedmont Coal Company owned them along with the house.

Now that J. V. Thompson was dead arrangements were made to dispose of Oak Hill and realize on the value of its furnishings. A gigantic auction was to begin on Thursday, October 26, but during the four days preceding the house would be open so that prospective buyers might inspect its treasures. Over the week end queues formed at the entrance doors and visitors were admitted in batches of from fifty to a hundred so that the art objects might be viewed without crowding. Some sixteen thousand people filed through the rooms in the first days after they were opened to the public. The Coke Region had been racked with a three-cornered labor war since July and most of the big mines were still closed and heavily picketed. The wind-up of the Thompson affairs was a breath of the old times, and Fayette County, tired of industrial bickering, enjoyed it to the full.

A circus tent appeared on the Thompson lawn, wired with a powerful lighting system so that the auctioning might continue until eleven o'clock each night until everything was disposed of. The great sale was to start at eleven o'clock in the morning in deference to Mr. Thompson's fondness for the number. It had been the custom at Oak Hill for the butler to mark the passing of the lucky hour by eleven strokes on an East Indian bronze bell. Even after Mr. Thompson's death he went through the ceremony every day as usual as long as the house was intact.

The last night before the dispersal of the personal possessions there was a thorough rummaging of cupboards for secreted assets. There had been difficulty all week finding the right keys to desks and cases in spite of Mr. Thompson's instructions. There was supposed to be a shawl that had belonged to Dolly Madion in a Louis XVI cabinet that Honey had left behind but it hadn't been opened in twenty-one years because she took the keys with her; and the standing desk where Mr. Thompson used to work to keep from falling asleep was hard to get into. But for all their searching they found nothing but personal possessions characteristic of the owner: an old photograph of Honey wrapped in the Pittsburgh paper that announced the divorce—one of the edition that never got to Uniontown; a book of original entries of the Court of the King of England written in 1688; clippings and memoranda. Joseph H. Bialas, Rose Thompson's attorney, opened a mysterious leather-covered satchel that had belonged to the old man but it contained "nothing of present determinate value," only old letters, worthless stocks, and legal documents. Apparently the one-time millionaire had died possessed of about fifty dollars.

At eleven o'clock the next morning, suave gray-haired C. Lawrence Cook took his place on the auctioneer's stand, backed by a conglomerate display of silver, china, paintings, and oriental rugs. The crowd on hand was gratifying. A thousand collectors had poured into Uniontown for the event and the cars parked on the lawns bore license plates from all the eastern states and as far west as Illinois.

"Ladies and gentlemen!" he said, "You are here today to participate in the final distribution of a collection of riches gathered by one of the most colorful figures of the century. Examine each piece carefully, bid advisedly and don't overlook the fact that nowhere in this country or Europe has a more rare selection of antiques, rugs, furniture and books been assembled in this generation."

The sale was on. The first bid was made on a square lace cover valued at $150. It went for $18. A Chinese urn with silver mountings on bronze that had cost $250 brought $36; a pair of antique lamps appraised at $500 went to a Baltimore collector for $70. A $600 pair of silver candlesticks ran up to $350. The famous furniture from the Louis XVI room was offered individually. Of the Aubusson chairs, worth $1300 apiece, the first sold for $225, the second for $245, and the third for $150. The $15,000 ten-by-twelve rug went at $655. Somebody carried home the great ivory sword for $65 that Thompson bought in India on his wedding trip. Some of the small objects brought fancy prices, however; hand-painted wine goblets sold for $10 and mere saucers for $5.

Lunch was served on the grounds at noon; plain-clothes men mingled with the crowd, and the auctioneer at intervals warned his patrons to watch out for pickpockets; the attendants carried out vases and bric-a-brac to sell to the waiting crowd in the tent while camera flash-lights flared to catch famous dowagers in the act of reaching for their booty.

"I'm not going to tell a story about these furnishings," said the polished impresario in charge of the sale, calmly estimating his audience, "because you know these things, how they got here and their value as well as I do. There is nothing cheap here, ladies and gentlemen, nothing cheap!"

When the confusion was over and the litter cleared away, Oak Hill was dead. The house was there, echoing and drafty, and the trees where Honey's hammocks once swung in the shade, but now it was in the process of changing character to emerge as the Mother House of the gentle black-robed Sisters of St. Basil the Great.

J. V. Thompson lies in an unmarked grave next the stone on which he had carved for Mary:

> "No pearl ever lay
> Under Oman's green waters
> More pure in its shell
> Than thy spirit in thee."

The Coke Region still cannot forgive him for losing his money and theirs that he helped them to make.

CHAPTER IX

THE COSSACKS

AFTER THE LIVELY DISORDERS OF 1894 THERE WAS NO big strike in the Coke Region until 1922, although from 1917 a tide of dissatisfaction was rising. The miners promised not to strike during the war but as prices skyrocketed they asked Fuel Administrator Harry Garfield for a wage adjustment. They didn't get it.

As soon as the Armistice was signed they petitioned President Wilson to help them negotiate a better contract, but he declined to interfere. The operators were saying that the war was not really over until the Peace Treaty was signed, but that might take a long time and, meanwhile, with their wages artificially held down and prices unrestrainedly going up, they were not sharing the good times.

The year 1918 saw the peak of production, 579,000,000 tons. The demand for higher wages grew louder but got no real attention until Setember, 1919, when the United Mine Workers in convention presented demands for a six-hour day and five-day week with an ambitious increase in tonnage and yardage rates. When nothing came of it, John L. Lewis, international president, issued a strike call. The Administration countered with restraining injunctions so drastic that Lewis and the labor leaders called the strike off; but the men went out anyway and tied up 71 percent of the country's coal-producing capacity long enough to secure a 14 percent wage increase while a three-man commission investigated. In the end, although they didn't get the six-hour day, the commission allowed an increase of twenty-four cents a ton for mine-run coal and a dollar extra for day men.

During the war the total of producing mines had swelled to 9,000 with a capacity of a billion tons. That was too much even for war time. With a slackening of the steel market, coal sales would decrease sharply and some of the mines were bound to be crowded out of business. After 1920 the operators began to retrench and showed no disposition to renew the recent wage contract. Instead they proposed wage cuts that precipitated the strike of 1922. John L. Lewis called a strike for April 1 that brought out over 460,000 miners, presently augmented by 158,000 anthracite workers, who had been faced with a 21 percent wage reduction. The Coke Region was not organized, but 100,000 men in the Connellsville-Somerset district came out anyway.

The trouble brewed in the Slovak societies, some of whom, remembering 1894, had written into their by-laws that no member could work when a strike was on or be a strikebreaker. The movement sprang up spontaneously all over the Coke Region. A strike meeting announced for the Slovak Hall in Masontown drew hundreds more than the building could hold and the roads were black in all directions with men coming to sign union cards.

The usual disorders followed. Tipples burned; bombs tore up fanhouses and railroad bridges; there were wholesale evictions; strikers beat non-strikers, shot and were shot by deputies. There was shocking brutality on both sides so that neither group came out of the conflict with any credit. Whatever happens in the Coke Region is apt to come in a particularly violent form. It is a district without a common denominator, made up of racial and industrial factions. There are so many old grudges to settle, so many people in unstable equilibrium—too close to the bottom and too close to the top.

When the strike was in its sixteenth week the country felt the pinch in earnest. Some 618,000 miners were out in the country, which, considering the size of miners' families, meant at least 3,000,000 directly or indirectly in industrial revolt. Harding's efforts to settle the matter did not induce the men back to the pits; neither did the troops sent to central and western, Pennsylvania to guarantee protection. The settlement when it came was, in effect, a postponement. There were to be no wage cuts for the present and the old scale would continue until March 31, 1923.

The coal demand continued poor, necessitating a continuation of the retrenchment policy, and although the existing wage scale hitched along to 1924 and then got a four-year extension by the Jacksonville Agreement, signed by the U.M.W. and operators from Illinois, Indiana, Ohio, and western Pennsylvania, actually it lasted only about a year longer. In August, 1925, operators cut prices and wages to get what little business there was and trouble began in earnest. Before the strike of 1927 was over, a hundred operators and 100,000 Pennsylvania miners were involved with practically every bituminous mine in the state shut down tight, most of them to be reopened on a nonunion basis. Four thousand commercial mines went out of business as production * went down and down and finally hit 308,907,000 tons in 1932, the lowest since 1904. The coal industry was sick and the patches were in a bad way.

The miners lived in closed company-owned towns, just as they had back in the eighties and nineties, ruled by deputies and the recently organized coal police and didn't like them any better than they ever had. The houses were convenient to the job and did not cost much, but when they lived in them it was on sufferance without freedom. A man had to do his work and submit to the discipline or get out. Nobody could enter a company town without a pass, and if the coal policeman was not in a good humor that day, he might not give it. A man wasn't liable to like living in a place where somebody coming to see him might not get in. Some patches were stricter than others but one Fayette County lease on record sounded as though the tenant might entertain no one but the doctor, the undertaker, and the mourners for a funeral. According to its terms the man renting the house "further agrees not to use, allow, suffer, or permit the use of said premises, or the private ways or roads through and over other lands of the lessor used to reach said premises from the public road, for any purpose other than going into said premises from the public road, and out from the same to the said public road, by himself and the members of his family; and, further, to do no act or thing, nor suffer or cause the same to be done, whereby the public or any person or persons whomsoever may be invited or allowed to go or trespass upon said premises, or upon said private ways or roads, or upon other grounds of the lessor, except physicians attending the lessee and his family; teamsters or draymen moving lessee and the family belongings into said premises or away from the same; and undertakers with hearse, carriages and drivers, and friends, in case of death of the lessee or any member of his family." †

The company-patch system was like the script-company-store combination, something that came into being to solve a temporary problem but outlived its usefulness. The private town had come about in a perfectly natural way. When a coal company developed new territory it needed housing for its employees at the mine, but unless the company itself provided it, nobody else would. Even if the miners could afford to build their own houses, which they could not, they would not want to tie themselves down before they

---

* *Pennsylvania Labor and Industry in the Depression*, Dept. of Labor and Industry Special Bulletin No. 39 (Harrisburg, 1934), p. 41.

† J. P. Shalloo, *Private Police*. The American Academy of Political and Social Science (Philadelphia, 1933), pp. 97-98. Also *Report of the U. S. Coal Commission Transmitted Pursuant to the Act Approved September 22, 1922*, Part I, pp. 9-11; 169-170.

knew how the new mine was going to turn out; neither would outside capital risk a housing project in an outlying district for the same reason, knowing that when the coal deposit was exhausted it would have a patch on its hands that would be hard to get rid of. So the companies built their own villages on company property, closed to the public, and ran them their own way.

As the system developed, the miners in the patch houses were much farther from town than the actual miles that separated them. They lived on feudal islands in the county but not of it, for the sole purpose of mining coal. Naturally the county was not disposed to pay for policing the unincorporated patches so the companies that owned them had to do that, too. For a good many years the bituminous operators employed deputies to keep the peace, protect company property, and keep the mines running, strike or no strike, but after 1922 coal and iron police, commissioned by the governor, became increasingly numerous.

The miners called them "The Cossacks" and "Yellow Dogs." Probably no organization of police officers in American industry has ever been so widely denounced and hated. The patch dwellers had no love for any kind of policemen for that matter, whether they were county deputies or state troopers, because when they were called to protect company property they seemed like the company's allies.

Anthracite operators had been using commissioned coal and iron police since the Act of 1866 supplementing the act authorizing railway police made it legal for coal companies to secure state commissions for their own privately paid police officers. Under the Coal and Iron Police Statute the governor had the power to appoint police officers upon petition of the coal company, although he might refuse to do it at his discretion, and he had power to revoke the commissions issued at any time. To begin with, the commissions were issued free of charge but after 1871 they cost one dollar each with no time limit until Governor Pennypacker's administration, 1903-1907, when the duration was limited to three years. There was no investigation of the need of issuing the commissions nor of the character of the men who got them. When the state had its money and the subscription to the Consitutional oath required by law, it forgot about the business. In effect, from 1871-1929, the state farmed out its police power and made no investigation as to how it was used. Until the Pinchot Investigation in the twenties there is no record of a commission being revoked, although plenty might well have been, judging from the way the miners hated the coal police and the generally bad name of the organization. Probably the coal police abuse was no worse than the delegating of police power to deputies (over whom there was even less control) by county sheriffs, some of whom grew rich on commissions and kick-backs. Under the deputy system in 1910 in one coal

HONEYMOON—J. V. and Honey Hawes Thompson in India. J. V. is at Honey's right

J. V. THOMPSON RETURNS TO HIS NEW HOME

HONEY THOMPSON IN A KIMONO SHE BROUGHT FROM THE ORIENT

OAK HILL—This mansion was later to become the Mother House of the Sisters of St. Basil the Great

SWIMMING POOL AND CONSERVATORY—As they appeared in the last days of J. V. Thompson at Oak Hill

FURNITURE AT OAK HILL   ONE OF HONEY'S IMPORTATIONS

WHERE PADEREWSKI PLAYED AT OAK HILL

ROADSIDE PICKETS—There were barricades on the roads and pickets at the plant

PICKETS AT THE PLANT—Every plant was a potential trouble spot twice a day when the shifts changed

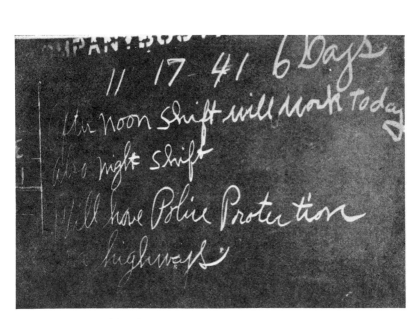

POLICE PROTECTION

PICKETS ON THE HIGHWAY—Complaints from drivers of halted cars poured in to the powerless county officials

COKE-OVEN DWELLERS—During the depression the very poor moved into empty coke ovens

COKE-OVEN HOME INTERIOR

DRESSING ROOM

KITCHEN   AT HOME

MINERS STUDYING THE PENNCRAFT HOUSING PLAN

county the sheriff is reputed to have received $30,000 in a single month as his share of his deputies' salaries.*

At best the company town presented a difficult problem for law enforcement, made up as it was of a number of alien groups who could not understand each other's languages and spoke little English, bound together only by their common occupation and a common grievance when there was a strike. To be a success, a coal policeman would have needed to understand several varieties of Slovak and Italian but not belong to any of the nationalities he supervised. The way it worked out he didn't understand his people nor they him, and too often he put across his ideas by flourishing a gun.

The first sizable coal police organization in the bituminous field, set up in 1926 for the Pittsburgh Coal Company by Captain John G. Searsh, formerly of the railroad police, seems to have functioned without friction as long as it was run by its organizer; but as economic tension heightened in the tumultuous period from 1925 to 1928 coal police were employed in great numbers chosen for size and courage rather than administrative ability. There were no coal police in western Pennsylvania in 1925 but the number had risen to 2,115 by January, 1927, and 3,002 in November of the same year. Their lot was not easy. County officers were apt to consider that coal police were not real police and would give an unfavorable verdict when one of them brought in a prisoner. So another abuse sprang up in the practice of carrying culprits, not to the nearest magistrate but to the one they could do business with, and charging the prisoner mileage for the trip. Sometimes coal police feuding with county officers held offenders in private lockups and turned them loose when they got ready, without benefit of a judge's services; or they refused to allow county officers to serve warrants in their bailiwick.†

In time of strikes the coal policeman was in real and constant danger protecting the mine machinery and buildings and looking out for the "finks" (strikebreakers) who went through the motions of keeping the plants running without producing much coal. Sometimes these were bona fide workmen, former employees willing to work nonunion to feed their families, who would have given good service if they could, but a good many were professional finks who went from strike to strike recruited by agencies specializing in industrial trouble. New York and Chicago were the principal sources of emergency strike labor along with Cleveland, Columbus, and New Castle.‡

Professional finks fell into two classes, the "nobles" or strikeguards and "scabs" who theoretically replaced the absent workmen in the distressed

* J. P. Shalloo, *Private Police*, pp. 89-90.
† *Conditions in the Coal Fields of Pennsylvania, West Virginia and Ohio*, II, p. 3201.
‡ *Report of the La Follette Commission Investigating Civil Liberties*, Report No. 6, p. 65; 92.

industry. The nobles invariably looked down on the scabs but on occasion, each was proficient in "heating up a job," that is, egging on hostilities between labor and management to keep a dispute going so their jobs would last longer.

When picket lines were thinning out, old hands at strikebreaking knew that if a few of them set upon a striker his friends would come running and there would be a free-for-all, so the settlement would be postponed a little longer, and the plant guards would be increased with less individual hazard; or throwing stones through the windows of union headquarters was a good way to assure action if the job seemed about to end. Sometimes finks had to pay back part of their salary to strike lieutenants but too often they made it back by helping themselves to company property. Thus in many cases the strikebreakers imported to end a dispute worked against the company, made the strike last longer, and increased the violence.

The coal demand was slackening steadily. In the general gloom the locals of the United Mine Workers, whose roots had never been more than superficial in the Coke Region, gradually died out, their demise hastened by the unsuccessful strike of 1927.

In February, 1928, of seventy-one mines, employing between 20,000 and 21,000 men, operating nonunion between Connellsville and Brownsville, all but four had previously been union mines.* Spokesmen for the United Mine Workers appearing before the Interstate Commerce Committee in January, 1928, blamed the railroads for bringing pressure on the coal companies to terminate the Jacksonville Agreement. They were out to break the union and they told the coal companies what they would pay for coal, take it or leave it. Operators cut wages to meet the railroad demands and ran the mines with strikebreakers to do it.

After the wage cut of January 10, 1928, the minimum wage paid by Pittsburgh Coal was $3.30 a day for outside labor, $5.05 for inside; but while the Jacksonville Agreement lasted the maximum was $7.50 a day. On the average the men were employed about 160 days per year, which meant a total income of about $1,200 but at least $150 had to come out of that to pay for powder, tools, and supplies, which meant only about $1,050 per man.†

According to the union statement inviting a congressional survey, when the companies cut wages they said that reduced rates for labor would allow them to sell more coal and give steadier employment but, even with the cut, the men were on half time or less. When they refused to work under the new wage scale, 8,000 of them were evicted in the dead of winter and the union had to build barracks to house and feed them. The union was housing 1,896

---

* *Conditions in the Coal Fields of Pennsylvania, West Virginia and Ohio,* I, 35.
† *Ibid.,* p. 8. Statement dated Jan. 17, 1928, signed by George W. Lewis, legislative representative of the U.M.W., in support of Senate Resolution No. 105.

families, in a total of 4,708 rooms, and the rest were scattered in temporary quarters.

"The U.M.W. is the one and only restraining influence in this country that prevents the New York Central and other strikebreaking interests from hammering coal miners' wages down to the poverty and starvation level," urged the union leaders, whose grievance was particularly against operators mining for the free market.

The Senate Investigating Committee that presently appeared in the western Pennsylvania coal country upon the union's invitation found the company towns in a dismal condition. The visiting senators interviewed miners, union leaders, coal police, county officers, reporters, operators, superintendents, and bosses—everybody who had anything to do with the industry—and piled up a stack of contradictory statements and affidavits hard to reconcile. The fact of the matter is that in large measure both sides were telling the truth from where they sat. In a district with so many mines operating under different companies a wide range of conditions prevailed, particularly in housing, just as they do today. A report on Pittsburgh, specializing on statements from the Strip, would not be representative of the city, however true the individual pronouncements. Neither would a survey centering particularly on Schenley Heights. The truth would lie somewhere in between.

The findings of the Investigating Committee fill two fat volumes, *Conditions in the Coal Fields of Pennsylvania, West Virginia and Ohio,* which make much more interesting reading than their sober covers would lead one to suspect.

The report of investigation from which the following quotation was made was signed by the late Senator R. Gooding of Idaho, who was chairman of the Senate Investigating Committee, and by Senators W. B. Pine, Jesse H. Metcalf, Burton K. Wheeler, and Robert R. Wagner: *

"... The Committee then visited the home of Clarissa Englert at the union barracks nearing Horning No. 4 mine. Mrs. Englert told the story of the iron and coal police shooting into a group of school children in which two of her children were coming home from school. The brutality of the coal and iron police shocked every member of the committee. ...

"Your committee left Pricedale fully impressed with the fact that the morals there were in a very demoralized condition—that the men and women were running wild and that no effort was being made by the authorities to curb these immoral conditions. In fact, the committee found generally that no effort was made to invoke law and order or to maintain police protection except through the iron and coal police and they were found to be the outstanding ones who showed little regard for law and order or for the improvement of morals. The committee found generally

* *Ibid.,* I, 345-364.

that the operators themselves paid little if any attention to the morals of the community and made no effort to improve them....

"Everywhere your committee made an investigation in the Pittsburgh district we found coal and iron police and deputy sheriffs visible in great numbers. In the Pittsburgh district your committee understands there are employed at the present time between 500 and 600 coal and iron police and deputy sheriffs. They are all very large men; most of them weighing from 200 to 250 pounds. They all are heavily armed and carry clubs, usually designated as a 'blackjack.'

"Everywhere your Committee visited they found victims of the coal and iron police who had been beaten up and were still carrying scars on their faces and heads from the rough treatment they had received. Your committee found more or less evidence of bootlegging in the places it visited; and in one community especially it seemed as if the morals of that community had been broken down entirely."

The following is from the statement of J. D. A. Morrow, president of the Pittsburgh Coal Company, refuting union charges about patch conditions.

"Senator Gooding is quoted in the newspapers of Feb. 27 as saying: 'Conditions which exist in the strike-torn region of the Pittsburgh district are a blotch upon American civilization. It is inconceivable that such squalor, suffering, misery, and distress should be tolerated in the heart of one of the richest industrial centers in the world....'

"In this language the Senator did not particularize. He did not tell the reader that the committee visited but a few of the hundreds of towns in western Pennsylvania where mines are operating steadily. He made no mention of these mining communities where men, women, and children are living under excellent conditions. He gave the uninformed reader the impression that all mining towns in western Pennsylvania are pigpens. He made no distinction between the clean, electric-lighted, well kept villages of the Pittsburgh Coal Company with their paved streets, their filtered tested water, their synthetic garbage disposal, their approved sanitation, and the shacks of temporary strike colonies located elsewhere. We feel that a grave injustice has been done this company in this respect. We resent and deny the implication that our non-union employees live like hogs, and our employees resent the reflection on their personal habits and manner of living....

"We believe that liquor has been introduced into our town, in spite of our efforts to keep it out, by persons who desire to handicap the production of coal in our mines, increase accidents there, cause turmoil and disorder in our towns and generally demoralize the community as a part of their illegal attacks upon this company....

"During the period of open-shop mine operations by the Pittsburgh Coal

Co., there have been 159 arrests made from liquor-law violations in our mining villages. Of this total, 107 were employees of the Pittsburgh Coal Co., 5 were proprietors of boarding houses on the property, and 47 were bootleggers and nonemployees....

"All the $800,000 expense for police and deputies to which the company has been put since it started its mines open-shop has been made necessary by the presence and activities of pickets, organizers and representatives of the United Mine Workers of America in and around our properties...."

In answer to questions by Senator Couzens, Mr. Morrow testified in regard to the coal and iron police employed by his company: *

"...It was a measure of necessity on our part. Continual picketing of our properties, constant threats directed at our employees, almost daily instances of brutal assaults of our workmen, the burning down of our houses, the dynamiting of residences of our people at night, and a long unending succession of conscienceless depredations upon our open-shop workmen, who are exercising the right to choose their own place and condition of work; who are exercising the liberty guaranteed them under the Constitution of the United States finally compelled us to take measures to protect ourselves and our men.... This company has faithfully endeavored to employ capable, trustworthy, dependable men. We may not have succeeded in all instances ... but today we have a body of men trained and experienced in work of this kind, of whom we are justly proud. Of the 104 commissioned coal and iron police in our employ at present, 66 have had military service; 19 have had service in the State police of Pennsylvania; 6 in the Pennsylvania highway patrol; 7 have served as municipal policemen in various cities; 4 have had experience as railroad policemen; 9 are former deputy sheriffs; 5 have been special police officers for corporations serving in capacities other than coal and iron police; one man has had service under the United States Department of Justice; one under the United States Immigration Service and one in the United States border control....

"In spite of complaints against the coal and iron police registered with this committee, we know that the men of our force have exercised great restraint and patience in the face of insult, provocation, and even assault by union sympathizers."

Horace F. Baker, president of the Pittsburgh Terminal Coal Company, testified before the Committee as follows: †

"The bitterest complaint of the union has been that coal companies employ coal and iron policemen about their properties. On the other hand, it may be said that the greatest single item of expense which this coal company has had to bear to protect itself against members of the United Mine

---

* *Ibid.*, II, 2643-2645.
† *Ibid.*, II, p. 2775-2800, for statement with Exhibit and Affidavits, etc.

Workers of America is the expense of maintaining these police. Such police in the employ of this company have cost it $200,000 in round figures since April 1st, 1927.... This company, I can assure you, would be only too happy to discontinue at once all such police, if the union would cease war against the company or the Government provide protection....

"Since April 1927, our operations have been one continuous story of abuse, violence, sabotage, and disorder of every kind inflicted upon the company and its employees.... An examination of the motors and mining machinery of this company made immediately after March 31, 1927, and before any new employees were taken into the mines, disclosed that great numbers of the mining machines had been injured and haulage motors put out of commission by acts of sabotage. This must necessarily have been the work of the union since no other persons had operated the machines or up to that time had been in the mines....

"Attempts have been made to destroy the mines and machinery of the company by the use of dynamite and by so tampering with the electrical equipment as to make it self-destructive.

"This company soon after April 1, 1927 began to recruit a force of police for the protection of its employees and its property....

"In recruiting its police we desire to state that this company has exercised the greatest care. The history, characters, and general reputations of all applicants have been investigated before such applicants were received. It is not humanly possible to recruit a large force of men in a short time without finding an occasional one who will not act under all conditions in the manner expected of an ideal police officer. A few incidents have occurred involving police officers of this company which have shown certain of such officers to be unworthy of the trust reposed in them. In every case the offending officer has been summarily discharged and his commission caused to be revoked. It is submitted that such occurrences have been remarkably few when the trying conditions under which the police of this company worked at all times is fully understood...."

"April 12, 1927: On this date the first families of new employees moved into No. 8 mine with the result that a riot was narrowly averted and serious trouble was prevented only by excellent handling of the mob by coal and iron police, who held their tempers under very trying circumstances. The truck bringing in the first furniture was stoned, the people were assaulted, and all the windows of the houses in which these families moved were broken by rocks thrown by former employees who occupied nearby houses owned by the coal company....

"Jan. 28, 1928: C. E. Young was employed as coal loader at No. 4 mine and lives at Bruceton. He arrived at Bruceton on the Baltimore and Ohio train at 9:30 P.M., carrying groceries in each hand. As he moved away from the train six men approached him and one of them hit him on the forehead, then another man hit him. He dropped his packages and started to run. Then he was hit from behind and knocked into a deep pool of water, which was covered with ice. They threw rocks at him and pushed him with poles trying to push him under the ice, all the while calling him names. He called for help and part of the men ran away toward the union barracks, and the rest down the railroad. After they left, he crawled up on to the Pittsburgh and West Virginia Railroad tracks, becoming unconscious and was found by a coal and iron policeman who had heard him yell for help. He was then taken to St. Joseph's Hospital, where he was confined for four weeks having sustained a fractured skull."

In evaluating the following excerpt from a statement from Washington County, it is well to remember that in the twenties bootlegging was by no means confined to the coal country and in this instance many of the people in question were European, accustomed to drinking wine at any kind of social gathering as well as with their meals; also that in a mining community a single man is apt to employ a cook and live with her if he likes her, not because he means to affront the institution of marriage but because the arrangement is a convenience understood by both. The same sort of thing was prevalent among the boaters on the Erie Canal. The patches being so largely Catholic, Roman or Eastern, a marriage is supposed to be for keeps and is sealed by the blessing of the church.

"COMMONWEALTH OF PENNSYLVANIA
COUNTY OF WASHINGTON, ss.

"Before me the subscriber, one of the justices of the peace in and for said county, personally came——————,* who, being duly sworn according to law, deposes and says: that he is 28 years of age, and now resides at——————, Washington County, Pa. That about Dec. 15, 1926 he went to work at——————Mine No. 1 of the——————, said mine being operated on a non-union basis. That he left his employment at said mine on or about Jan. 13, 1927. That he returned to work at said mine on or about April, 1927, and again ceased his employment Dec. 10, 1927. That during the period he was employed at said Mine No. 1 he was domiciled with his common-law wife at house No. 345, the patch being commonly known to those living thereat as——————.

"That the conditions obtaining at said mine showed that the people employed there were given to all manner of vices, selling and dispensing of liquor, with the knowledge and consent of the authorities of said mine,

* *Ibid.*, II, 3160-61. Names have been deleted as unimportant to the point.

gambling being practiced at a large number of houses, prostitution generally prevailed among the Negro miners and the presence of venereal and kindred diseases making it bad for the health of the community.

"That at the following houses miners lived with women not their wives: House 355 occupied by———————and his woman; house 322 by ———————and a woman; house 349 by———————and a woman. Others living with women not their wives were———————,———————,———————and one nicknamed———————in house No. 50. That the men living in houses Nos. 74, 63, and 64, at said mines were living immoral lives with women of shady character. In house No. 320 at said mine was a notorious place of prostitution and bootlegging, and was operated by one———————. That house No. 336, a place of low character was operated as a dance hall by one———————. That one———————operated a house of ill fame and dispensed of bootleg liquor in his house at———————. That the following houses were places where liquor was sold and dispensed of freely: houses Nos. 82, 315, 322, 324, 328, 332, 349, 354, and 358. That absolutely no effort was ever made by the mine officials and coal and iron police stationed at said mine to restrain or prosecute the very common violations of law. That in one instance where a non-union miner had gone over to join the union, he was prosecuted for violating the liquor laws but the contraband liquor was disposed of in some manner by the coal and iron police and never offered in evidence.

"That while he, deponent, was at said———————mine No. 1 approximately 120 non-union miners stopped work and affiliated themselves with the United Mine Workers of America. Twenty-six of these men were arrested, charged with no other offense than that of having joined the union. That of the 26 men arrested 4 were charged with carrying concealed deadly weapons and were held to answer before the court of Washington County, Pa. The other 22 were kept confined in jail for about 24 hours and then discharged.

"That at the hearing accorded the 26 men it was openly testified by the coal and iron police that the men were being arrested for joining the union.

"That as long as Negro miners worked at said mine under the open-shop conditions they were permitted to carry concealed weapons upon their persons, in and about their homes, revolvers, handy-billys, and blackjacks, and other offensive weapons. The coal and iron police permitted all this (and) made no effort to restrain the men.

"———————

"Sworn to and subscribed before me, this 26th day of Jan. 1928.

"———————Justice of the Peace.

"My commission expires first Monday in January 1934."

The senatorial committee talked with evicted miners being cared for in union barracks and found that they were also being offered food by a group who called themselves the Pennsylvania and Ohio Relief Committee whom the union leaders distrusted because the men who brought the provisions tried to stir the strikers to mass picketing. Some of the miners refused the groceries offered by the strangers because they didn't like their talk. "We want to obey the law," Smiley Chaltak, local representative of the U.M.W. told the investigators, "but that is what those fellows wanted to do, mass picketing, and you know what that would likely bring about."

Further inquiry into the affiliations of the Pennsylvania-Ohio Relief Committee showed that they were allied with the International Labor Defense Association, distributed *The Daily Worker* at their meetings, and had been connected with the Colorado Miners Strike guided by the I.W.W.'s, with which the United Mine Workers had had nothing to do. In their speeches their recurrent theme was "The Government is against us," and besides mass picketing they advocated the violation of injunctions, nationalization of the mines, a five-day week and six-hour day, the formation of a labor party, and organization so that strikes might become national affairs, no longer confined to small districts.

The private police system began attracting so much unfavorable publicity to Pennsylvania, particularly after the congressional inquiry that Harrisburg became uneasy. The widely publicized case of a miner named John Barkoski, of Tyre, Pennsylvania, beaten by three coal police so severely that he died, made definite action inevitable. Finally in April, 1929, after considerable backing and filling, the legislature passed the Mansfield Bill to replace the old coal and iron police statute.

Subsequent events have shown that the attempt to better conditions in the closed mining villages by minor changes in the coal police organization was like trying to cure an ulcerated tooth with pain pills instead of extracting it. Later when the patches were free to the public like other villages, subject to county instead of private officers, the conditions in great measure righted themselves.

The Mansfield Bill recreated the coal police system all over again but changed the name to Industrial Police and made the requirements stiffer for applicants for commissions. It also required the posting of a $2,000 bond with the government for the faithful performance of duty, but allowed the corporation hiring the candidate to pay it, and endowed the privately paid industrial police officers with the same power as those of a city of the first class, meaning Philadelphia. Keepers of jails must receive prisoners arrested by the industrial police but the new law failed to say anything about taking a prisoner to the nearest one. Governor Fisher appended twelve further regulations, among them a ruling that industrial police should not use undue violence in making arrests, nor should they unnecessarily display or use weapons or profanity. Their uniforms were to consist of suits of forest green with dull bronze buttons and military caps. They might also wear puttees if they cared to. In summer it was permissible to leave off the uniform coat and wear a green outing shirt with black buttons and a black bow tie. And whether the officer wore suit, coat or summer shirt, whenever he was on duty he must display prominently upon the left breast a badge at least two and one-half inches high in the shape of a shield bearing, besides the inscription "Industrial Police," the name of the company employing him and his own serial number. The regulations for industrial police uniforms were designed to differentiate them clearly from state troopers and stop once for all the passing of responsibility back and forth between the two organizations, each one blaming the other when something went wrong.*

As far as the coal towns were concerned, an industrial policeman was only a Cossack in a smart uniform. Pennsylvania's ulcerated tooth was as painful as ever. When Governor Pinchot returned to office in 1931 he promised to get rid of the private police. In his earlier term the fee for issuing commissions went up from one dollar to five dollars and on his orders there was a thorough investigation of the system, but although one coal company's private police lost their commissions as unfit persons, the great mass of evidence collected was never made public. Now in 1931 he had a bill submitted whereby the industrial police would become the Pennsylvania Protective Service auxiliary to the state police and available to unions as well as to corporations. It was a well-intentioned, poorly worked out bill, promptly defeated. Thereupon Governor Pinchot used the powers he already had to abolish all outstanding commissions and refused to issue any new ones. Thus in effect the industrial police system stopped functioning on June 30, 1931.

Uncommissioned deputies, responsible to nobody but those who paid them, took their places but by that time the Coke Region was thinking more about the hard times than about coal town government.

As might be expected the depression came sooner and lasted longer in the Region than in other parts of the country. The beehive coke business, marginal at best, is used to recurring lean seasons and the miners serving it manage to live through them somehow, but this time the pinch went on interminably and it didn't help to know that the rest of the coal fields were suffering too.

It wasn't just the little fellows who were taking a beating. The corporations were going down as well in a welter of depreciated coal paper. Big banks swallowed little banks and were swallowed by bigger ones in a frantic exchange of securities to stave off collapse, until, of the forty operating in

---

* See J. P. Shalloo, *Private Police*. Also Bill No. 979, File of the Senate (Pennsylvania) Session of 1929, approved as No. 243 Laws Of Pennsylvania, 1929, pp. 546-49.

1929, only ten were still going in January of 1933. At the other end of the scale the very poor moved into empty coke ovens and joined hunger marches on Uniontown. The relief rolls were enormous and local committees solicited coats and shoes for children who could not otherwise go to school. Sometimes the state and federal aid ran as high as $100,000 a month for Fayette County with a population of less than 200,000; the Red Cross and the Quakers helped out, but things grew no better. Some of the big operators were carrying their people at the company stores and in the patch houses but the burden of debt piling up that must be paid sometime was impressive. The Frick Coke Company alone had extended $840,000 in store credits to its employees for whom there was no work.

For the moment there was uneasy peace in the Coke Region because vitality was at its lowest.

CHAPTER X

A HOUSE DIVIDED *

MAY, 1933. HITLER WAS DEMANDING EQUALITY OF ARMS in the Reich; Gold Star mothers from twenty-five states made a sad pilgrimage to France as guests of the United States Government; and England worried because thirty-nine-year-old Edward Windsor, Prince of Wales, was still unmarried. He seemed to prefer American dancing partners, and the press hinted that an American might yet be his consort.

In the United States banks failed, bread lines formed, and kidnappers snatched victims where it was profitable. Franklin D. Roosevelt, the new President, was juggling the nation's economics with a program which, besides stabilizing finance, proposed to initiate a new set-up between capital and labor and bring about National Recovery with leisure and money for everybody.

Now, in the spring of 1933, it looked as if at last industry, prodded by the new Administration and the press, was picking up. The Pittsburgh Coal Company's production increased from 22,000 tons a day in March and April to 30,000 tons in late May. The H. C. Frick Coke Company's active plants worked three or four days a week. River and rail shipments jumped 316,640 tons over the April tonnage but coke continued slow, waiting for steel to

---

* In this chapter dealing with the Coke Region's last stand to remain aloof from the national organized labor movement I have relied in large measure for the narrative of what actually happened and how the people who live here felt about it on the local press because in this district where partisan feeling runs high, the home newspapers make every effort to be as accurate as possible.

pick up. Finally Frick ordered 150 ovens in blast at Continental No. 1 on June 20 and began cleaning up Leith and Crossland. By late June, ten of the twelve open hearths at Monessen were being fired and the captive mines owned by the steel companies, whose output went to the parent plant, looked toward a busy season. There were not enough boats to move the coal; in twenty-four hours sixty-eight steel barges that had been chartered down the river for eighteen months passed through Pittsburgh after being called home.

The independent coke producers still hung back, waiting to see whether the demand were real or only to refurbish depleted stocks.

"It is conceded that there are twice as many mines in the country as are necessary to supply normal peace-time demand for coal," worried *The Morning Herald* of Uniontown. "It is obvious that there are substantially twice as many miners. We do not see how the Recovery Act can sufficiently provide staggering or spread of employment to absorb all of this surplus and yet provide all workers and their families with sufficient income to maintain American living-wage standards."

One thing was sure: the relief rolls were decreasing. In three weeks two thousand families were withdrawn as the men found work, and many came of their own accord to ask to be taken off the list. And most startling news of all: On June 5 the Frick Company, who had always declined to deal with employee committees, voluntarily inaugurated a workers' representation plan anticipating the collective bargaining provisions of the National Recovery Act.

Under the new plan, similar to one already in use by the Bethlehem Steel Company, a workmen's committee made up of not more than ten nor less than five would participate in consideration of mine problems affecting themselves: continuity of employment, wages and piecework rates, hours of employment and working conditions, health and sanitation, safety and prevention of accidents, economy and waste prevention, athletics and recreation. The rate of representation was one workman on the committee for each three hundred in large plants, one for each one hundred in small ones. They would work in conjunction with a committee of management which might equal but not exceed the workmen's committee, and jointly they would consider appeals and arbitrate complaints.

There was to be a 10 percent increase in the wage scale too, effective July 1, based on payment by weight instead of by wagon as soon as scales could be installed. The pay increase would affect 6,000 men for the present but if all the plants were in normal operation, as they soon might be, it would mean between 15,000 and 20,000 persons affected. From now on fire bosses would receive $5.50 a day, track-layers and assistant timbermen, $3.70, mine laborers, $3.55; drivers, rope riders, cagers, hoisters, and timbermen, $4.25 for eight hours; pick-coal miners who furnished their own explosives and drilled the holes would get 48.4 cents per ton.*

The new wages would buy a lot of groceries at prevailing prices. At the Frick Company store Calli hams were 9¢ a pound, prime steel chuck roast 10¢, boned and rolled veal roast 17¢, tenderloin steak 25¢ a pound, two- to six-pound hens 22¢ a pound, and a two-pound roll of butter was 57¢.

Changes were happening fast all over the Region. Pittsburgh Coal inaugurated a similar company union, and Republic Steel and Buckeye Coal Company, a subsidiary of the Youngstown Sheet and Tube Company, announced 10 percent increases for their mines before the month was out.

The burst of good feeling was not destined to last long, however. A four-day strike at Rainey's Clyde mines called 1,300 men out on June 20. The same day the men at Republic threw down their tools, and they were followed by those at the Oliver mine of the Pleasant Valley Coal Company.

After the walk-out John L. Lewis of the U.M.W. announced that the Union was now ready to deal with the operators under the collective bargaining provisions of N.R.A. but that they had made no move to get in touch with him. If they did not do so at once, General Johnson was going to take action against them. The Pittsburgh Coal Company had already been informed by Washington, said Lewis, that their recently organized company union would not be recognized.

Simultaneously local labor leaders warned that the recent walk-out showed what was going to happen if the U.M.W. were not allowed to represent the workers. Patrick Thomas Fagan, president of District No. 5 of the U.M.W., promised that they would try a peaceful solution first, but if that didn't work they would strike. The company unions of Frick and Pittsburgh Coal Company were "out and out attempts to evade the law" and would not be tolerated.

Union spokesmen had been raising the cry that Pittsburgh Coal Company was discharging and evicting miners for union activities. President Morrow flatly denied it. An employee of his company was free to join any union he chose; he was also free not to join any union if he did not want to. Men who lived in company houses must not be objectionable residents and if it was necessary for the company to evict a tenant they did so at their own expense to a house outside the mining village. There were no evictions in the wintertime.

* Coke Scale New Wage July 1, 1933

levelling per oven,	machine		$0.1850
watering "	"	"	$0.0982
cleaning "	"	"	$0.1059
bricking "	"	"	$0.06
drawing coke per oven	"		$0.1345

There was a good deal of confusion as to what the collective bargaining clauses of the National Recovery Act meant. The questions at issue were: who was to act as agent for the miners in the formation of labor contracts, and what would be the standing of minority groups of nonunion men. If the U.M.W. succeeded in forcing a closed shop on the operators, independent miners would have no standing at all. There were three types of mines involved: the steel-captive, the utilities-captive, and the commercial mines whose output was sold in the open market.

General Johnson's explanation did not help much. "It is the duty of this Administration," said the Industrial Administrator, "to see that all labor, organized and unorganized, gets a square deal. ... It is not the duty of the Administration to act as an agent to unionize labor in any industry ... and it will not so act. ... Labor ... has the right to organize and bargain collectively; the law also recognizes the right of individual workers to bargain for their own conditions of employment."

Thomas Moses, president of Frick Coke Company, and J. D. A. Morrow of Pittsburgh Coal Company maintained that their company unions constituted collective bargaining. They were willing to deal with a minority group, if a properly accredited one wishing to be represented by the U.M.W. developed, but they did not propose to run a closed shop.

The U.M.W. organizers had been conducting a whirlwind campaign in the Coke Region, and now, armed with sheaves of new membership cards, they maintained that they alone should represent the miners. The newly formed company unions stood in the way and must be destroyed.

Thus far the Frick employees had been cool to the advances of organizers. They couldn't see why they ought to pay tribute to a lot of slick talkers from outside just to be able to say they belonged to a national union when they were already the best paid miners in the state, with as steady work as any in the Region; and when there was no work to give them, the company took care of its own relief. If a man got hurt the company wasn't tight about doctors and compensation either. Then, too, he had a chance to better himself if he stuck with them because they passed out the good jobs by promotion and after twenty-five years he got a pension. The patch houses were drafty but they only cost from six to ten dollars a month and if a man wanted to buy a place of his own he could borrow money from the company cheaper than the bank would lend it to him. And every year he got a chance to buy United States Steel Stock, with a bonus in addition to the regular dividends for the first five years, as part of a Profit Sharing Plan. It looked to him as if the outsiders hanging around the edges wanted to muscle in on what he had.

A four-county labor meeting scheduled for the Reagan-Lynch field in Uniontown on Saturday, June 25, was the U.M.W.'s first show of strength.

Deputations began pouring into town by 10:30 in the morning. The crowd of ten thousand milling on the flat in the June heat included men from the Scott's Run district in West Virginia, two hundred women and children from the Oliver plants, and a delegation who had walked all the way from the river district at Belle Vernon. The issue at stake was not wages this time but a fight for complete unionization and the closed shop.

"When you leave here today," William Feeney of Charleroi, provisional president of the newly formed District No. 4 of the United Mine Workers, composed of Fayette and Greene Counties, told the miners, "Go back and center your battle on every mine in Fayette County, particularly the Frick mines, and organize them 100 percent!"

And underlying all the speeches was the assurance that the Washington Administration was behind full organization of the coal fields.

Meanwhile the northern and southern operators were trying to work out a master code that would satisfy capital, labor, and General Johnson. The northern operators, representing western Pennsylvania, northern West Virginia, and eastern Ohio wanted the southern companies in Kentucky, Tennessee, Virginia, and southern West Virginia to raise their rates and give uniformity to the business but the Southerners were making a code of their own. So was the group led by John L. Lewis.

The U.M.W. proposed a $5.00-a-day basic wage scale for miners; $4.00 for outside labor and a five-hour day and six-day week. Thus far the operators who had been induced to subscribe to the union code represented only 25 percent to 28 percent of the nation's tonnage. The Northern Coal Control Association, headed by Morrow of the Pittsburgh Coal Company, claimed to represent operators who produced 150,000,000 of the 206,000,000 tons of coal mined in 1929, the remainder being accounted for by captive mines whose output went to the steel and utility companies. The majority of the operators wanted a code providing five eight-hour days and a good many of them did not want to deal with John L. Lewis in any case, so the code-writing got nowhere while General Johnson, distracted with trying simultaneously to regulate the automobile industry, steel and garment workers, and all the rest of the businesses big enough to be complicated, threatened to call the operators into Washington and impose a code if they didn't hurry up and settle their differences. Meanwhile industrial Pennsylvania seethed with strikes, an increase of 400 percent for the second three-month period of 1933 over the first three.

In the middle of July the situation was further complicated by the resignation of Dr. A. M. Northrup, secretary of labor at Harrisburg, who charged Deputy-Secretary Charlotte E. Carr with fomenting strikes.

"After careful study," announced Dr. Northrup, "I do not believe this is the time to foment strikes when the working man is desperately in need of employment and the employers so seriously handicapped by industrial conditions." He considered it his right to be able to administer his department in an impartial manner. "Not being permitted to conduct my office according to this standard I respectfully submit my resignation."

Governor Pinchot pooh-poohed the idea that it was Miss Carr's activities that had disrupted the Secretary of Labor's office but the press in reporting it recalled that it was Governor Pinchot who had imported Miss Carr from New York and turned her loose on the department. For that matter, Mrs. Pinchot herself was encouraging strikers in the East.

Late in July, Fayette County began to engage the attention of outside organizers, slipping under cover through the ranks of workmen like quicksilver. Strangers in the district, they complicated their trails by working on the opposite side of the Region from their boardinghouses.

One day a woman representing the Pennsylvania Security League appeared at Star Junction distributing a controversial leaflet called *Black News*. A little later she encountered a Frick policeman on company property and, upon being told that she could not proceed without a pass, she said that she intended to go from house to house in the mine village, pass or no pass.

The local paper reported the incident briefly, adding that the lady received the freedom of the patch with permission to visit the company's model town of Grindstone as well, and then forgot about her for more interesting subjects. Two hundred men at Gray's Landing had gone out on strike, tying up seventy-five ovens, in spite of a 15 percent pay raise July 1 with more promised for August 1 and no rent to pay on the company houses for the current month. Now they were parading two or three times a day, demanding recognition of the U.M.W.

There were minor disorders over the week end of the twenty-third following a clash between miners and deputies at Maxwell, but the violence that ushered in the strike proper on Tuesday came as a surprise. About 2:30 in the morning a crowd of a hundred pickets and their families at Colonial No. 3 manhandled two deputies. Soon after five o'clock there were barricades on the roads and picketing at the three Colonials; the deputies used tear gas; the strikers threw sticks and stones and overturned automobiles of workers. Some of the men had already gone into the mine and knew nothing of the disorder up above but they found out when the shift changed and a fusilade of rocks met them at the pit mouth. Two brothers, who had gone into the mine expecting no trouble, got back to Hopwood with their car riddled with bullets. Another miner, knocked unconscious by a rock as he drove away, lost control of his car and crashed into the ditch from which he was carted off to the hospital.

By night there were five more casualties to keep him company; the Frick belt system connecting the Colonials and Maxwell mine was tied up and there were serious inroads in the southern system made up of the mines at Buffington, Filbert, Footedale, and Gates. Leckrone and Edenborn were still all right, but along the river Jones and Laughlin's Vesta plants Nos. 5 and 6 (as well as the Emerald and Edwards mines) were out.

So far the picketing had mostly been done by workers from neighboring mines, some of them as far distant as Washington County, but the seeds of discord had been sown. To help them grow, in some instances men wearing masks and armed with clubs went through the company towns hammering on doors and offering the householders a choice of signing a union card or taking a beating. With only six state police detailed to the sector, the matter was impossible to deal with.

Governor Pinchot ordered Troop A of the Pennsylvania state police to Brownsville. They arrived the next day and began to disarm pickets blocking the roads, thus collecting an assortment of clubs, sticks, rubber hose weighted with iron, and some 1,200 pick handles. It was a rainy day but the strikers stuck to their posts in their wet shirts. Only a few of the leaders, dashing from point to point shouting orders through megaphones, had raincoats. Some of the parties stopping cars stretched American flags across the road, other carried huge posters of President Roosevelt.

Sheriff Hackney of Fayette County appointed one hundred new deputies; and the H. C. Frick Coke Company, with eight mines crippled, opened eight new ones, some of them long idle, and threw 2,000 new men into the breach to close the gap of lost production.

The pronouncements from Washington were conciliatory. Donald Richberg, chief counsel for the National Recovery Program, who had represented organized labor for years, urged that "both employers and workers stop efforts at rapid organization of either open or closed shop unions in order to gain a temporary advantage." It was not the time for provocative discord when the utmost cooperation was necessary. In the opinion of Industrial Czar Johnson, both sides were to blame. Companies who had not hitherto consulted their employees formed company-dominated unions with unseemly haste, but, on the other hand, union organizers were trying to force men into their ranks by telling them that they could not get the benefits of the National Recovery Program otherwise.

"There is no doubt," he admitted, "that a small amount of real racketeering is going on, efforts to incite the workers from a basis of outright Bolshevism."

Meanwhile on the battleground the rival factions made conflicting claims for strength. The labor leaders said that they had 95 percent of the Frick employees signed up; 99 percent of Jones and Laughlin's men and 96 percent of those at Pittsburgh Coal Company's mines. The strikers believed that their actions were in accord with the N.R.A. and that union organization was more or less demanded. The U.M.W. union was thus the appointed collective bargaining agent and if it were not recognized not a mine would be in operation next week.

On Thursday there was less violence. The troopers were keeping the roads open and there were no cars molested except one in the Colonial district, which, with Maxwell and Filbert mines, was the worst trouble spot. Filbert was running but badly crippled; the windows were shot out of the tipple at Grindstone (Colonial No. 4) by gunfire from the hillside; and the company moved the livestock from Colonial No. 1, preparing to close it down tight.

In the afternoon Superintendent William Merwin of Colonial No. 3 was surrounded by a crowd of about forty pickets as he attempted to drive his car from the company road into a red-dog * highway to reach a distant part of the plant. He allegedly fired several shots into the ground and the crowd fell back. That would have been an end to the matter but for the fact that Elizabeth Wight, the *Black News* distributor, was on the picket line. She raced into town to wire Governor Pinchot that she had been fired on by the Frick Company's superintendent at Grindstone.

Pinchot had been trying since Tuesday to induce Sheriff Hackney of Fayette County to sign a waiver of a type known as the Lansdale Plan † whereby Hackney would withdraw the county law enforcement officers and turn over the management of the strike to him. Hackney replied that he was willing to cooperate but he could not abdicate the authority because, even with state troopers in charge, legally the county was responsible. Instead he issued a blanket proclamation which seemed about to make it possible for the men who wanted to work to do so. Officers were to disperse and prevent the loitering or gathering of three or more persons at a time on highways, public property, and vacant lots.

While the proclamation was being tacked up around the county, tension visibly relaxed. The strikers planned to comply with the order but to keep on picketing by placing their men five feet apart but it looked like the end of the road barricades. The operators rejoiced because there were plenty of men eager to work if they could get to the pits, and orders were piling up.

The day had been fairly orderly except for a brawl at Buffington which was chiefly the result of the presence of women on the picket line in spite of the state troopers' orders. When the men who wanted to work tried to go through the ranks of the strikers, the women seized the men's dinner pails

* Red-dog is a mixture of partly burned coal, slate and ashes from a dump that has been on fire.

† The Lansdale Plan, used in a hosiery strike at Lansdale, Montgomery County, Pa., "established a precedent under which State Police could take complete charge of a strike area without being brought under local influences which sometimes made themselves felt upon the sheriff and municipal officers in a strike district." See Carr, *Labor and Industry in the Depression,* Special Bulletin No. 39, p. 46.

and threw them against telephone poles. A nonunion man's wife saw her husband being chased by a woman picket and flew into her, whereupon there was a general free-for-all with stones and tear-gas bombs flying.

The use of gas in economic warfare is a widely accepted if unpleasant practice whenever tension erupts in riot, judging from the range of industries purchasing it. The compounds most commonly used either singly or in combination are CN and DM, milder forms of gases used in World War I.*

CN, tear gas, is a white or gray crystalline solid with an odor like locust blossoms which, if breathed in sufficient quantity, so inflames the eyes that one cannot open them for several minutes. A strong concentration may cause unconsciousness, make lips crack and bleed, irritate the throat, and initiate digestive disturbance that may last as much as three days.†

DM, sickening gas, is just what it sounds like judging from a sales circular of the Lake Erie Chemical Company which sells it under the trade name KO.‡

"What does KO gas do to the victim:
(Note—The effect of the gas varies considerably with different individuals and of course with the amount inhaled.)
1. Violent nausea and vomiting.
2. Sense of suffocation as if several men were sitting on chest.
3. Intense pain in chest and head.
4. Above effects last, if subjected to a good dose for several hours to a whole day, but without producing permanent injury...."

The compounds encountered in the open air are apt to be more infuriating than dangerous, like wounding a bull still at large.

That night Pinchot, armed with the Wight telegram, took things into his own hands. If Hackney would not voluntarily waive his authority and withdraw the county enforcement officers, he would take charge anyway. From now on the state police, who had been an effective quieting agent, were forbidden to cooperate with the sheriff. A sharp exchange of telegrams ensued in which the governor charged that Hackney was to blame for the disorder in Fayette County and that he had conspired with the H. C. Frick Coke Company to import gunmen from New York. The sheriff's order against assembly would deprive the miners of their lawful right to peaceful picketing and would plunge the county in disorder. Only Hackney stood in the way of his being able to take over the situation. The sheriff hotly denied working in conjunction with the Frick Company and President Moses substantiated it, but before morning Pinchot had ordered 325 National

* For list of purchasers see *The La Follette Commission Investigating Civil Liberties,* Report No. 6, Appendix A, p. 209.
† See Edward B. Vedder, The Medical Aspects of Chemical Warfare (Baltimore, 1925), p. 170.
‡ *La Follette Commission Report No. 6,* Part 3, p. 23.

Guardsmen of the 112th Infantry, conveniently on hand in summer training camp at Mount Gretna, to entrain at once for Brownsville. Ranking National Guardsmen from the district were not allowed to command. Instead the expedition would proceed under the orders of Major Kenneth Momeyer of Erie.

Governor Pinchot's parting instructions to Major Momeyer directed that the troops "protect all citizens in their constitutional rights, enforce the laws of this Commonwealth, and suppress all violence in Fayette County. . . .

"Under your orders, the National Guard must assure their rights to the miners, the mine operators and the citizens generally. The miners have the right to organize and to picket peacefully; and to free speech and assembly. . . . The mine operators are entitled to have their property protected from damage. . . . Above all, the National Guard in all its dealings with the people of Fayette County must be fair and impartial. . . .

"You have been sent to Fayette County to keep the peace, without fear or favor. The National Guard of Pennsylvania will do its duty with malice towards none and with charity for all." *

By 7:30 A.M. the first hundred men were under way in fourteen automobiles led by two highway patrolmen. Two hundred and twenty-five more left by train at 9:30, rode interestedly through the hot-bed of trouble at Smock, Rowe's Run, and Grindstone (the Colonials), where the strikers cheered them, and arrived in Brownsville at 4:30 P.M. There were 2,500 people at the depot to see them detrain in the Monongahela freight yards, eight coachloads with three baggage cars of equipment. The troops went immediately into formation with fixed bayonets while two machine guns were wheeled into position and a line of guardsmen was thrown around the forming companies. Then they tramped off to set up housekeeping in a field outside of Brownsville while Sheriff Hackney and Commandant Momeyer met and agreed that the county was now in a state of partial martial law.

Assuming that violence had been stopped, Pinchot invited President Moses and representatives of the Frick Company to meet leaders of the U.M.W. in Harrisburg to adjust the misunderstanding.

"We have no misunderstanding with our employes at our mines in Fayette County," replied Moses. "They wish to work but outsiders through violence and intimidation are preventing them from doing so. If the peace officers of Fayette County and the State of Pennsylvania would protect them in their lawful rights against molestation they would be at work.

"I will be very pleased to discuss the situation with you personally and would go to Harrisburg for the purpose of doing so but it must be obvious that I cannot meet Mr. Lewis for the purpose of discussing with him the

---

* Carr, *Labor and Industry in the Depression,* Special Bulletin No. 39, p. 47.

question whether the lawful right of our employes to be free from molestation should be secured."

Philip Murray, international vice-president of the U.M.W., William Feeney, president of District No. 4 (Fayette and Greene Counties) and Patrick Fagan, president of District No. 5 (Allegheny and Washington Counties) accepted the governor's invitation.

Following a lull with oratory over Sunday, violence flared in earnest. After all there were only 325 militiamen, not enough to police the mines on the outskirts of Brownsville. The strike had spread to Greene County and there were now between 15,000 and 16,000 idle with every plant in the district a potential trouble spot twice a day when the shift changed. The men from Buckeye Coal Company's Nemacolin Mine with its model housing had joined the strikers along with those of the Crucible Mine of Crucible Steel and Republic Iron and Steel's Searight and Republic Mines and the Crescent Mine of Pittsburgh Steel. Jamison of the South Union Coal Company and the most recently opened of the Frick plants still ran, but Colonial No. 1, Filbert, and Maxwell were down tight with production greatly curtailed in the Gates-Footedale section.

To start the week two hundred men and women pickets attacked the morning shift at Edenborn when they tried to cross the public road, and in the ten-minute battle that ensued, fought with clubs and dinner buckets, three were seriously hurt. A picket from Allison, who found himself in a strange group of Filbert and Buffington strikers, took a severe beating by mistake, and only the timely arrival of troops prevented a riot at Footedale where four hundred pickets had gathered. Barricades appeared again in the public highways.

Major General Edward Shannon, head of the National Guard, flew to the Coke Region and reportedly told Governor Pinchot that he needed at least two thousand men if he were to keep order; the best the present force could do was to answer riot calls. Pinchot announced that he would send no more troops for the present and so the matter rested. The refusal to send reinforcements meant that with authority withdrawn from county peace officers and the force put in control too small to function, the operators had only their deputies for protection.

Meanwhile the highway system was in a worse snarl than ever. The stopping of cars in the public road in itself was nothing to excite the Coke Region. The coal police had been doing it for years with less excuse; but piling rails and crossties across the roads and hurling bricks into windshields and headlights was something else. Pickets stopped automobiles indiscriminately whether they had local or out-of-state licenses while complaints poured into the powerless county officials. A man on his way to the hospital had been delayed an hour; women in a car from a neighboring state complained that they were halted by Negro pickets and their machine stoned as they fled; a state and county officer's automobile had been held up four times. When the strikers overhauled a miner's car, they really got tough; somebody broke his right headlight, another took care of the left, while others dragged the occupants to the road to the tune of shattering glass in the windshield. And the outside picketeers changed from day to day so beaten workmen could not recognize them and file complaints.

Rioting was general all over the county, aggravated by the strikers' belief that Pinchot was on their side and would do nothing to stop it. When a lieutenant ordered a picket line to disperse at Colonial No. 4 after a striker had thrown a brick, the man warned the officer that he was going to protest to the governor immediately. At Star Junction six pickets were shot and many strikers and miners hurt when a hundred pickets tried to prevent twenty-five workmen, escorted by a dozen deputies, from going into the mine. After the confusion was over none of the injured were able to tell whether they had been shot by pickets, miners, or deputies.

Over at Colonial No. 3 a picket named Louis Padorsky was killed by gunfire from a car and, although a call went out for the militia as soon as the shooting occurred, there was a lapse of three hours and fifteen minutes before a soldier was on the scene. At Footedale twelve soldiers tried to handle five hundred pickets, and all that troublesome Tuesday there was not a militiaman in the Filbert area.

That night for the first time Major Momeyer called on the machinegunners to send them to Palmer where trouble was expected but none occurred, which may have been cause and effect. In the middle of the week Major Momeyer announced that his men now had ammunition but on Monday and Tuesday "all guardsmen were on duty with guns and bayonets but no bullets." Also he now had trucks sufficient to move 140 men with machine guns whereas formerly he had only enough for 60.

But with or without equipment the major was in an anomalous position, ordered to supervise militia in a county whose highest peace officer had not asked for it, backed only by the governor's mandate without a formal declaration of martial law, and with his authority further nullified by express instructions that he was individually liable for any injury to property resulting from the acts of any of those in his command. He was supposed to protect peaceful picketing but the only kind he encountered was not peaceful and unless he had different orders he would have to continue to protect, in effect, the lawless element and thus be a party to keeping citizens from exercising their constitutional right to travel the roads unmolested.

The miners who wanted to work, but were not being allowed to, felt that they were getting scant attention from either the government or the press. After it seemed certain that they could expect no help from the militia, a deputation of three from a Frick Company patch appeared at the *Morning Herald* office in Uniontown to recite their grievances. They were neighbors and heads of families, one with six children, one with seven, and one with nine, all of them with at least twenty years' service for the Frick Company, steady workers exasperated at being kept from earning money they needed.

"Why don't you say that 80 percent to 85 percent of the men want to work but they are afraid?" asked the spokesman. Out of their company town of 450 all but three were in favor of staying on the job, but organizers were going from house to house of miners who worked, threatening to burn their homes and punish their families. Many signed pledge cards under threats. "We have had scarcely any work for a long time," said the men. "Now we were told that the mine would be shut down tomorrow because there could be no protection for the men.... Let Governor Pinchot put on pit clothes and come out here and see for himself. Let him try to run the gauntlet and he will find out what conditions are!"

With the Lansdale Plan working so poorly in Fayette County, the sheriffs of Allegheny, Greene, Westmoreland, and Washington Counties got together and unanimously agreed that they wanted none of it. Pinchot's aide, Stephen Raushenbush, and a representative sent by Secretary of Labor Perkins were in the district investigating, and while they were deciding what to do the Frick Company issued a blanket order closing all its mines for an indefinite period "to prevent more serious disorder to the men willing to work."

Meanwhile in Harrisburg the governor met with the U.M.W. leaders. Lewis did not attend but kept in touch with the conference by telephone. The meeting lasted four hours and out of it came Pinchot's jubilant announcement that he now had the solution to the Coke Region trouble.

"No such step as this has ever been taken before.... It assures a new kind of cooperation to establish peace and good order."

Philip Murray and the presidents of the western Pennsylvania locals had promised that from now on their men would give advance notice of where they planned to picket, parade, march, or hold meetings so the National Guard and state police could "place officers with them to protect the rights of all citizens." There were to be no more parades or marches between 8:00 P.M. and 4:00 A.M.; the miners would not go on private property where the owners objected, and when they did hold demonstrations they would be peaceful. And to dispel any doubt as to what peaceful meant, they declared that "Any act that may reasonably be expected to result in bodily harm or destruction is not peaceful." About 2,000 "union guides," men of good standing in their locals, were to be elected to enforce the Pact and would be distinguished by white arm bands marked U.M.W.

Following the Harrisburg meeting, Pinchot flew to Washington to attend a four-way conference with Lewis, Moses, and Johnson. While the leaders conferred, two Frick deputies went to jail for the shooting of Louis Padorsky. They claimed that they had fired in self-defense when about two hundred pickets closed in on them, blocking the road with an unfurled American flag. The strikers said that there had been no violence but that two volleys barked from the car as it sped through them.

The citizens were worrying about the swelling relief rolls. Just when they were getting less it looked as if twelve thousand miners' families would be added, meaning an increase of at least 50,000 men, women, and children— more than there had ever been in the history of the county. Harrisburg had decreed that local relief officers were not to inquire why a family was in need; the fact that need existed was to be sufficient reason for authorization of relief. The labor forces were concerned with how to get the miners on relief whose credit had not been stopped at the company stores. The Frick Company had made no move to discontinue the credit of idle employees but if they got supplies there, they would have to pay for them sometime, whereas if they were on the relief rolls they would not. A United Mine Workers' meeting in Uniontown advanced the novel suggestion that the Frick Coke Company turn over to the Fayette County Emergency Relief Board money equivalent to the amount of relief it was providing through the extension of credit in the company stores, and the matter continued unsettled.

After the Governor's Pact, groups of pickets announced when and where they were going to mass and march, but the general situation remained unchanged; there was no protection for workers and industry was at a standstill. The emergence of an active Klan organization with blasts of dynamite and flaming crosses gave an added fillip to the muddle, while the rumors of undercover Communist organization grew.

There was big news on Saturday. President Roosevelt had himself made an agreement with the operators and on his order the country's 70,000 striking miners were to go back to work under existing wage agreements without prejudice or discrimination, leaving the controversial points to be solved at the Coal Code Meeting early in August. Weighmen chosen by the miners and paid by them would check tonnage at the mines,* and any disputes that could not wait for the Code could be turned over to a special board of three arbiters made up of Gerard Swope, president of General Electric; Louis

---

* Actually in the matter of the checkweighmen, before the strike was declared the Frick Company, Buckeye Coal Company, and other western Pennsylvania captive operators had agreed with their employees that any of the men who wished to do so might hire their own checkweighmen. Thus in the main the President's Truce was for western Pennsylvania a restatement of a point already agreed upon between officials and men.

Kirstein, a Boston manufacturer representing N.R.A.; and George Berry, president of the Pressmen's Union.

The agreement with President Roosevelt had been signed in two sections, with Pittsburgh Coal, W. J. Rainey, Inc., Rochester Coal and Coke, and John L. Lewis in one; H. C. Frick Coke Company and the National Mining Company in the other, which meant that the principals were now severally in agreement with the National Recovery Administration but not with each other. In effect the Mellon and Morgan interests had parted company on the issue of collective bargaining. The Mellon-controlled Pittsburgh Coal Company and some of the other big commercial companies had signed a truce with John L. Lewis. The Frick Company, a subsidiary of U. S. Steel in the Morgan orbit, in dealing directly with the Administration, preserved intact its refusal to deal directly with organized labor and could be counted on to stage a fight to preserve its company unions. Later news from Washington announced that President Roosevelt proposed to maintain industrial peace in the country at large by a blanket moratorium on strikes until the industrial program got under way, when a tribunal under the leadership of Senator Robert F. Wagner would solve everybody's differences.

The coal settlement looked to the press like a partial victory for the miners. General Johnson was jubilant. According to his estimate 200,000 workers could have been affected by the strike and imperiled the President's recovery program if it had not been settled. Scant storage of coal at factories had threatened the revival of manufacturing on which so much depended, but now the coal would start flowing out of the Region again.

Back in Fayette County people were not so sure. The strikers had closed up everything in the Region but the Olivers, and, financed by relief rations, they could stay out indefinitely. President Lewis's order to the U.M.W. to return to work was not being well received. That night in a meeting of all the union locals of District No. 4 held in the council rooms at the Uniontown City Hall the vote was 123 to 4 against returning to work for the present.

"We have not decided about our strike as yet," they wired President Roosevelt. "Our men will look the situation over and give you a definite decision by Friday of next week."

The day of the Roosevelt Pact a crowd of 10,000 assembled for the funeral of Louis Padorsky, the thirty-eight-year-old war veteran of the Marne, Château-Thierry, and the Argonne killed at Colonial No. 3 on Tuesday night. There were a thousand union miners in the procession, along with a bugle-and-drum corps and color guards, that accompanied the flag-draped bronze coffin from Allison Company town down roads patrolled by militiamen to St. Mary's Slovak Catholic Church in Brownsville.

Inside the crowded building Major Momeyer sat near the widow and three children of the man so suddenly snatched from obscurity to martyrdom, while outside twenty soldiers in steel helmets with riot sticks tramped up and down. Father Yesko's sermon, first in Slovak, then in English, pled eloquently for forbearance and understanding. Referring to the fact that a large percentage of miners are of foreign extraction he said:

"They are not only good workers but they are law-abiding American citizens. They want justice, nothing else. We have Communists, it is true. One out of a thousand. But we must not condemn the others....

"Let there be no more violence.... Use your heads, not your hearts or your emotions.... A corporation is composed of men who have souls and hearts the same as yours, and if properly approached they will grant justice ... and there will be peace and no hunger."

Following the Requiem High Mass, a monster motorcade escorted the body to Connellsville where it lay in state at the American Legion Home until the final services conducted by the Connellsville Post.

The Frick Company had expected to open its mines on the Monday following the President's Pact but at the request of General Johnson and Pinchot they remained closed awaiting the outcome of the miners' meeting that had been set ahead from Friday to Tuesday. Thus far the President's settlement had only succeeded in dividing the union forces. At a labor meeting near Grindstone on Sunday, Martin Ryan, a forty-four-year-old Irish immigrant, emerged as the leader of the opposition to the Lewis faction while state and federal agents tried to heal the schism.

"For this moment let controversy cease!" begged Lewis. "Return to your normal occupations. Give time for the application of reason and logic to your own problems and the problems of the coal industry and extend your cooperation to your government, to your President and to your union."

The Ryan faction proposed to realize their demands first.

Meanwhile picketing went on as usual, augmented by four thousand recruits from Washington County, while the newspapers asked how to reconcile the fact that Fayette County miners, while striking for recognition of the United Mine Workers of America, refused to be guided by the leadership of their national officers.

Feeling had been tamed down a bit by Tuesday and the miners finally agreed to go back to work under the President's Truce. After it was over Edward F. McGrady, an N.R.A. assistant administrator and personal representative of the President, speaking from the courthouse steps told an overflow crowd: "The President guarantees that there will be an end to company unions—that the Coal Code will bar them."

So the men went back to work and the troops looked forward to leaving at an early date. The usual time for their summer encampment had expired and there had been a good deal of conjecture whether they would be released and others sent if the disorders continued. For the time being they were busy patrolling the roads of entry from other counties to keep outside pickets from upsetting District No. 4 now that it was disposed to settle down. The miners were in a good humor. At Filbert they went to the pit behind a band with the women and children marching too.

The question of who was to represent the miners for collective bargaining was still unsettled, but the militia went home and the coal diggers returned to work while they waited for Washington to make out a code that would embody all they asked.

But what was of more lasting importance than the questions under discussion was that men new in the United States, who learned American ways by seeing how they worked out, had come to believe that in their new home it often paid not to cooperate with bosses, whether they represented capital or labor, and that a good deal of violence would be overlooked if they were on the strong side.

II

The peace was short lived.

In August the Coal Code makers reached a stalemate after protracted haggling, while the impatience of the coal diggers mounted. They couldn't see why the business needed to drag on so long. All the talk in the newspapers about the conferences over different rail rates for North and South and the competition of oil, gas, and electric power was just something to stall with while they figured out how to cheat the miners out of the things the President had promised them. They weren't worrying about wages. What they wanted to know was whether the operators were going to recognize John L. Lewis and his union.

"You men have the right to strike if you want to," Governor Pinchot told the miners in his Labor Day speech in Uniontown.* "You have the right to organize into whatever unions you want to; and the United Mine Workers is best, first, last, and all the time. . . . The fight which you and I must fight together is against the grasping money lords, like those who sat down around a conference table in New York in 1901 and ordained that United States Steel should be nonunion; your fight is with the Mellons, the Morgans, the Hoovers, the Reeds and the rest of the money barons who have been running these United States until 1932. . . . So long as I have anything to say about it, the Federal relief funds in my charge will be distributed on the basis of human need and nothing else. . . . Your cause is right. Do not defile it with violence. The man in your own ranks who attempts to provoke you to violence is your enemy just as much as the deputy

* For full text of this speech see "Money Barons Lashed by Pinchot," Uniontown *Morning Herald*, Sept. 5, 1933, page 5.

sheriff who teases you into violence that he may get a chance to fire upon you. ... If you resort to violence then I am against you. ... Don't put me in a place where I must fight against the men I want to help. ...

"I think President Roosevelt and his advisers realize that without prosperity in the coal regions there can be no security anywhere. ... I have told them again and again that here in the soft coal fields is the key to the whole national situation. And I was right.

"Food, water and wood alone rank with coal among the necessities of life. Without coal the whole country would soon be closed down, idle and hungry as well.

"Better times are coming and more of you are going to get work. ... Without your steadiness and self restraint these things could not have been brought about. ...

"I thank you. I congratulate you, and I wish you all good luck—and a dry coat."

On the thirteenth of September the men began laying down their picks. The next day a riot at Gates ushered in a new era of uproar. The plant and company patch lie in a picturesque bend of the Monongahela, reached only by one narrow, unpaved road. The houses occupy a bald bluff with the mine entrance below in a narrow valley on the far side of the railroad. An ugly situation developed in the bottleneck when fifteen men started across the railroad to the lamp house and 150 pickets charged them. The deputies used tear-gas bombs and in the melee sixteen men were wounded, among them a young deputy who had his right arm shot off, allegedly with a dumdum bullet.

That same day miners from Allegheny, Westmoreland, Greene, Washington, and Fayette Counties met at Pricedale and voted to stop work until the Code was signed. The new cessation of labor was not to be considered a strike but a holiday and there would be no picketing. The next day picketing began again in spite of the resolution; requests for protection for non-union miners began pouring into Sheriff Hackney's office and the familiar routine of strikers marching from plant to plant was on. The local police didn't know what they would be allowed to do.

Hackney announced on the front page of the *Morning Herald*:

"Until further notice, by reason of emergency conditions in the county, no further permits will be issued by this office to carry guns."

He had three hundred applications for jobs as deputies on his desk but until the attorney general defined his authority he did not know what action he might take. Governor Pinchot's speech, which had in one breath counseled strike and the next denounced it, made it clear that he assumed responsibility for the situation in the county if there were a recurrence of trouble.

The repercussions of the Fayette County storm had reached Washington and brought an order from President Roosevelt that the Code-makers must finish up their work without further dallying. At last, on September 16, the Master Code was ready. It established a basic wage in the Pittsburgh district of $4.60 with differentials for southern sections and, in a carefully worded clause that had cost weeks of haggling, provided that employees might choose anyone they desired to represent them or they might represent themselves. They had the right to check the weight of the coal they turned out and they need not live in company houses any more or deal in company stores unless they wanted to. Commercial operators might combine to fix prices but the rates they fixed would be subject to the approval of the regional administrative body. Labor disputes must be referred to whatever mediation machinery operators and miners set up.*

J. D. A. Morrow of the Pittsburgh Coal Company, president of the Northern Coal Control Association, who had been the leader of the fight that broke the union in western Pennsylvania six years before, was the first to sign the agreement that in effect unionized all the commercial mines.

The captive mine operators who had taken no part in the code negotiations did not sign the agreement but its provisions were extended to include them anyway. The public waited with interest to see how they would take it.

"We are not going to disobey the law," said the Frick president when he heard that the Master Code was on its way to the President. "We will have to mark time until we can determine just how we are affected and how we can cooperate. There has never been any dispute as to wages.... We had not taken any part in the negotiations over the Coal Code or on wage contracts. We have not said we would or would not sign the Code.... We merely want to know what we are signing." As to the matter of the Frick mines standing idle in Fayette County he announced, "Certainly our mines will not operate until we can work in harmony with our employees and with the communities where our mines are located."

President Roosevelt signed the Code the first of the week following but when he did so, of his own authority, he struck out the "labor interpretation clause" which stated that employees might choose anyone they wanted to represent them.† So the company union question was not settled after all. It looked as though all the long wrangle and final agreement were for nothing.

Back in the Coke Region Attorney Anthony Cavalcante, regional contact man for Governor Pinchot, sent an invitation to Lewis through his principal to come to Uniontown to explain the Code to the miners. They were not

---

* But if a dispute affected more than one region or the general public, the decision would be referred to the National Bituminous Labor Board.

† The President made a further change to permit the appointment by himself of three additional members of the bituminous coal board or to substitute them for government members of the divisional code authorities.

going to work until they knew more about it, especially why the captive mine operators' signatures were not on it.

Meanwhile the coal and coke business was tied up tight with heavy picketing and alarms coming it from all sides. There were sixty troopers in the county with supplies for a long stay but when the superintendent at Jamison mine of the South Union Coal Company, which had never employed deputies or had trouble with their men, asked for protection after finding dynamite in the tipple, the state police chief said he could not send any men unless trouble had actually occurred. So it was going to be the same story all over again—protection of picketing but not of nonunion men or company property.

The paralysis of the Coke Region meant good business at the West Virginia mines and the state authorities down there were keeping armed guards at the border as a precaution against an invasion of Pennsylvania strikers to work up a sympathy walkout.

Meanwhile the long suffering populace of Fayette County was getting anxious to have the matter settled any way at all if only the mines would open. The suspension was costing $75,000 a day in pay-roll; the relief rolls were too big to think about and while the neighboring mines over the hill in West Virginia's Monongalia County prospered, the beleaguered Fayette Coal companies, who bore from 60 to 70 percent of the tax burdens, were losing contract business that would affect the coming months.

Following President Roosevelt's signing of the Code the commercial companies entered into a wage pact with the United Mine Workers, whereupon the labor leaders told the miners to go back to work. Their answer was to vote against returning to the pits until the U.M.W. received full recognition "by leading coal producers in Pennsylvania," meaning the captive operators. So the lull continued while the press watched to see how much authority the union would be able to exert over its new members.

The Frick Company had thus far made no move to resume operations but rumors flew about the Region that new faces had been seen, presaging a surprise opening, perhaps with Negroes from Alabama. In Washington the executives were still trying to adjust code details.

There was no quarrel about wages, hours or conditions of employment because many of the captives already paid generally higher wages than required under the Code but when the coal from captive mines went to their parent companies, they did not think the Master Code price-fixing and sales-agency regulations, with all the extra cost assessments to set them up and maintain them, ought to apply to them.

Finally, the last of September, the Administration tardily announced that the coal companies whose coal did not go on the market would not be included in the marketing provisions of the Code. The next day the captive companies,* who had been waiting for this simple statement, signed the agreement and sent it to the President, although the company union question was still far from settled now that the labor interpretation clause no longer had a place in the Code.

The way was now open for both captive and commercial mines to begin producing coal the first of the week, but on the day when the President signed the Code representatives from U.M.W. Districts Nos. 3, 4, and 5 voted to extend the holiday indefinitely. That afternoon about five thousand miners from Greene, Fayette and Washington Counties, as well as three hundred representatives of West Virginia locals, met near the West Virginia border while the neighboring authorities watched nervously to see that there was no invasion of the district.

"We aren't going to work even if the Code is signed," announced a picket leader from Footedale. "We are not going to return until President Roosevelt gives orders to Governor Pinchot and Governor Pinchot tells John L. Lewis and John L. Lewis tells us. That means we are not going back to work until the H. C. Frick Coke Company recognizes the union."

That last week in September while the Coke Region waited for the outcome of the Washington conferences there was a definite speeding up of dynamitings, brawls, beatings, K.K.K. warnings, and private reprisals. On Thursday there was trouble at Grindstone when families of union and nonunion men met at the company store for relief and each tried to keep the other from getting it. The tide of violence swelled to a climax on Friday when the Coke Region miners undertook to close U. S. Steel's great Clairton by-product plant on the outskirts of Pittsburgh.

As recorded in the *Morning Herald* for September 30:

"In a motley parade of trucks and cars with their insurgent leader, Martin F. Ryan, in the vanguard, the unwelcome army began rolling into Clairton at dawn, swarming about entrances to the steel mill which already was closed, itself a United States Steel subsidiary.

"The husky coal diggers, some helmeted, many in shirt sleeves, stormed the gates of the by-product mill from 6:00 A.M. until 10:00, tearing clothes from some office workers, grabbing dinner-pails from others and all but upsetting an automobile of workers.

"They turned back some workers but officials claim more than 90 percent of the 1800 got to their jobs.

"The plant is across a small stream on company property isolated so that it cannot be approached except by a small bridge. A squad of grim company deputies armed with riot guns stood guard here.

---

* The H. C. Frick Coke Company, Youngstown Sheet and Tube Company, Tennessee Coal and Iron, Wierton Coal Company, Gulf States Steel Company, Wheeling Steel, Republic Steel, Jones and Laughlin Steel Companies, etc.

"Obeying orders of a large force of deputy sheriffs under command of Sheriff Frank I. Gollmar, county detectives and city police, they kept the pickets moving. Some carried American flags, others mouth-organs, banjos and guitars. Labor leader, Steve Patroney, President of the Footedale Local, U.M.W. had an old phonograph horn through which he shouted orders."

That night some 1,800 steel workers slept in the plant on improvised beds while twice their number of belligerent coal miners jeered and shouted outside for them to join them. Labor leaders were confident that by the week end there would be 10,000 on the picket line and when they had closed Clairton they would undertake the mills at Homestead, Duquesne, and Monessen.

In Harrisburg Governor Pinchot began to worry for fear the affair might get out of hand and begged the miners to do their picketing in their own bailiwicks. Unexpectedly the strikers abandoned the steel company campaign but they continued to roam the Coke Region.

Monday, October 2, was the day on which the new wage scale with all the attendant concessions secured under the Code would go into effect. The Frick Company, having signed the agreement with President Roosevelt, posted notices at its plants on Saturday over the signatures of President Moses to the effect that:

"The H. C. Frick Coke Co. will continue its long established policy of paying as high wages and maintaining as favorable working hours of labor and working conditions as prevail in the districts where its respective operations are conducted and will observe all of the provisions of the National Recovery Act applicable to them.... Operations of mines will be resumed as soon as conditions permit."

But the Coke Region miners were not ready to go to work whatever their leaders said. There was too much bitterness for firebrands to work on.

"The agreement with the Captive mine owners is just as firm and binding as the contracts with other operators," urged William Feeney, president of District No. 4.

"It's all over," the A.F. of L. representative assigned to the bituminous mines told them. "Any further strike is without sanction."

"Today you are fighting Coal companies but tomorrow if you remain on strike you will be fighting the Government of the United States," warned Philip Murray. "Today you are conducting a strike; tomorrow you would be conducting a rebellion."

A few miners went back to their jobs, but two days after they were supposed to return to work only two-thirds of the nation's striking coal diggers had complied with the order. Instead, ignoring the U.M.W. leaders, three hundred delegates of the insurrectionary faction met in a small building near Pricedale and drafted a resolution to stay on strike until the district was completely organized. Only one man voted against it. At the end of the caucus the delegates announced the decision to a crowd of three thousand miners assembled on a near-by picnic ground who received it with cheers.

It is easy for outside forces to stir up trouble in the Coke Region but once started they have generally found themselves powerless to control it. The union leaders now had the bear by the tail. If they hung on, the doings of the rebellious locals would probably alienate public opinion; if they let go they would lose all they had fought for. Washington was worried as it became increasingly obvious that the chaos in the Coke Region was not a simple struggle between capital and labor but a free-for-all between laboring men divided between themselves for and against the union with a further schism in the union itself.

Meanwhile Pittsburgh, with coal all around it, found itself in the midst of a cold snap with supply stocks exhausted while householders clamored to fill their empty bins. The miners from the commercial operations would have liked to go back to work now that they had won their demands and the operators were eager to take advantage of the market but roving bands of pickets made it impossible for any kind of coal mine to operate until the employees at the captive mines settled their differences. As yet there were no signs of break in the deadlock.

At Colonial No. 3, Rowe's Run, there was a gun battle when pickets besieged a row of company houses in which deputies were lodged with non-union men. A group of strikers were playing cards under a street light when somebody shot out the bulb. The strikers said the firing came from one of the company houses and the fray was on.

"After the first shots I looked out and saw the flashes of at least 60 shots from the picket lines," said a deputy sergeant. "The first salvo seemed to have been fired in the air. Twenty minutes later the shooting started again. There were more than 150 shots coming from both sides. It was in this exchange that my deputies were hit. It sounded like the Western Front. The next concerted attack occurred 25 minutes later and lasted more than five minutes. At least 300 shots were fired this time."

It was not a pretty story when you realize that women and children were living in the houses under fire.

Near Isabella there was an attempt to wreck a coal train from West Virginia; fire destroyed the main tipple of the Miller Coal and Coke Company; picketing extended to a school attended by children of nonunion miners. An appeal to Pinchot brought the reply: "Unless picketing at school ... produces actual disorder which sheriff or township peace officers cannot handle, state police can take no action. Suggest you notify sheriff so that he may take steps necessary to preserve order."

As a result there was disorder, nonunion men were arrested but state police, acting under orders, refused to assist a constable to serve warrants on union men.

At last District No. 5's eleven thousand men voted to return to work, but they were apprehensive of an invasion from the Coke Region. So far union leaders were having no success getting the Fayette and Greene County miners under control. When the president of District No. 4 tried to talk to them at a meeting at Searight's, the Ryan insurgents shouted him down. On October 15, as a strategic move to prevent further trouble, Philip Murray announced a new provisional president, William Hynes, a former international organizer.

It was clearly time for the disrupted Coke Region to be put back together again. To October the strike had cost miners and operators some $7,845,-000; considering the business gone to other sections, it soared to at least $20,000,000. Had there been no strike the four counties would have produced approximately 5,600,000 tons of coal more than was actually mined. Inasmuch as wages paid to labor constitute about 65 percent of the cost of coal, the men would have received approximately $5,460,000.

Pinchot took a hand in the situation with a message:

"TO THE MEMBERS OF THE UNITED MINE WORKERS OF WESTERN PENNSYLVANIA WHO HAVE NOT RETURNED TO WORK

"You have forced the steel trust to do what it has never done before: give you your own checkweighmen and agree to recognize your mine committees. And now in a letter to the President published in this morning's paper, the captive mines agree to the check-off of union dues. Without the fight you made they would never have done that but there are many miners who want to work in mines which have signed the Code and have signed the agreement with the United Mine Workers of America. These men who want to work must be protected in their right to work.

"I have upheld in every way open to me the rights of the working people of Pennsylvania. I sent the National Guard into Fayette County to preserve the peace of the Commonwealth and prevent acts of violence by deputy sheriffs in the pay of the steel trust. I have defended the rights of miners to free speech, free assemblage and peaceful picketing as guaranteed by law.

"But roving picketing by thousands of persons to prevent union miners who want to work from going to work under the N.R.A. and under union agreements has ceased to be peaceful picketing.

"These roving pickets by intimidation and violence are raising public opinion against the cause of the miners. They are preventing the production of coal which is absolutely necessary if President Roosevelt's Recovery Program is to succeed. They are shifting the soft coal business to other states to the permanent loss of Pennsylvania miners and Pennsylvania industry.

"Therefore I appeal to you who are leaders of idle miners to give up voluntarily this roving picketing. I ask you miners who have been marching from one mine to another and from one county to another to stop. I believe you will do as I ask."

But although Pinchot asked the men to go back to their jobs he refused to allow the names of strikers to be taken from the relief rolls and as long as the state provided their support, the strikers could go on indefinitely. From Washington however there were rumblings that if the men did not start producing coal, federal relief for Pennsylvania would be stopped.

At last the nonunion miners became articulate with an organization of their own called the Miners Independent Brotherhood. Early in October Sheriff Hackney received three petitions from the Colonials which read:

"The following members of the Miners Independent Brotherhood want to work and will work immediately with ample protection afforded. These men do not want to be affiliated with the United Mine Workers of America in any way. These names are not for publication in any newspaper but anyone in authority may see the authentic signatures of these members as signed by them on cards."

There were 716 signers. By the eleventh of the month the organization, armed with a roster of 1,597 members, requested the Frick superintendents to deal with them as a collective bargaining agent. Then they laid their case before General Johnson and President Roosevelt in a letter which charged the U.M.W. of intimidation and Governor Pinchot of playing politics at the miners' expense.

"We don't want relief squandered by the Chief Executive of our state simply to satisfy his selfish political ambition to be our next U. S. senator," they said.

"Men have been clubbed, stoned, and coerced into signing certain union cards. Many men signed to keep from taking a beating; some signed to save their home and property; others signed through plain stark fear of what they pictured in their own minds as to what would happen if they didn't sign."

With the advent of a new union in the field both factions scrambled to gain the blessing of authority in Washington. President Hynes charged that the new organization was company dominated, held on company property, with company superintendents to address the meetings, and said he had laid the matter before the proper authorities. Martin Ryan went to Washington and announced as he was leaving the White House after a conference with General Johnson: "The General is 100 percent with us." Whereupon representatives of the Brotherhood departed to tell the General their side of the story. They went on five dollars given them for gasoline "by a donor not connected with the Frick Company" with fifty cents apiece for spending money, but when they reached Johnson's office a lieutenant told them he was out of the city. A second clerk said he was in and would see them shortly, but, after a little delay, regretted that he would not be able to receive them after all because he had gone out to lunch. They might, however, leave their petition.

The labor leaders had heralded the signing of the Revised Coal Code by the captive operators as a virtual acceptance of the U.M.W. including the check-off of union dues, and announced it to the miners as a fact. Now it developed that Moses and the heads of the steel companies did not consider that their agreement with the President entailed the checkoff at all; so affairs in Washington were still in a snarl.

Apparently both Johnson and Roosevelt assumed that the steel companies had in effect bowed to the union demands but the N.R.A. legal counsel, Donald Richberg, unexpectedly interpreted the Pact according to the understanding of the captive operators.

"The steel men are perfectly correct," he said, "in saying that I told them the check-off was not involved."

In the resulting flurry the labor officials urged Johnson to simplify the whole thing by making the captive operators sign out-and-out union contracts whether they wanted to or not, but observers close to the Administration thought the President would hesitate to go that far. The feeling was growing that the N.R.A. was already a little over the line constitutionally and the Administration would hesitate to throw the steel-owned mines into the courts.

Johnson was eager to be off on a western trip but he hesitated to leave with the coal industry still in an uproar.

"I regard the situation as highly dangerous...," he worried. "I do not want 40,000 to 50,000 men milling around like this."

Finally upon Roosevelt's suggestion, Thomas Moses and Philip Murray met and discussed the deadlock but when it appeared that nothing less than unionization would satisfy the U.M.W. the conference broke down.

In the end President Roosevelt settled the matter with another compromise on October 28. The miners were positively to go back to work and when the National Labor Board felt that peace had been sufficiently restored to permit an impartial election, the men might vote on whom they wanted to represent them. Until then the operators would institute a modified checkoff, take back everyone who was working when the unpleasantness began, and meet with their employees under the representative plan until the election decided who should represent them.

The union miners liked the idea of voting but not of waiting until the N.L.B. judged the district was orderly, thus giving the rapidly growing brotherhoods a chance to add more members. A group of them were in Washington even now laying their case before the President along with a copy of Pinchot's letter refusing their petition for a charter.

The Frick Company had carried out all the requests of the President but production remained paralyzed because the sentiment of the miners was uncertain and the union leaders feared more violence if they tried to open the mines until the situation was clarified. Pinchot had said nothing yet about protection for workers willing to return.

Finally, Roosevelt gave in another point and ruled that the elections might be held as soon as the National Labor Board representatives could set up the machinery. Governor Pinchot could no longer withold protection now that the President was satisfied that the corporations had fulfilled their part of the Pact.

Work began without friction and the state troopers, who had been in the Region since the middle of September, left on the afternoon of November sixth, after a last survey of the plants showed that everything was peaceable. At Grindstone the women paraded to the shaft with their husbands, carrying their dinner pails. The men greeted passing cars and waved farewell at the top with joyful whoops.

The election by which 15,000 workers in twenty-eight mines decided who should represent them took place by mines, the week of November 19. The U.M.W. choice printed on the ticket consisted of the three ranking national officers, John L. Lewis, Philip Murray and Thomas Kennedy; and the three ranking district officers. Nonunion miners might write in the names of their six candidates in spaces provided.

Except for nine Frick plants who endorsed the independent union the United Mine Workers' ticket swept the field. Their victory was complete a few years later when the brotherhoods voluntarily disbanded to relieve the complexity of the situation.

Since then the U.M.W. union has controlled the Coke Region, as much as any outside agency can control it, with the shadow of John L. Lewis growing always a little taller.

He had not cut a very big figure in the district before 1933. Born in Lucas, Iowa, in 1880, the son of a Welsh miner, he fought his way to the front rank in organized labor and emerged on the national scene in 1919 when he took over the leadership of the 600,000 United Mine Workers. Shortly afterward he ran head on into an injunction that set him back for a while. With the Strike of 1922 he had better luck but in the middle twenties, although he was able to wangle the Jacksonville Agreement from the operators, with the depression creeping on he could not hold them to it. When

Roosevelt came in, his union had shrunk to less than 150,000 members. N.R.A. gave him his chance and, with the union firmly on its feet after the strike of 1933, he was in a position to secure major concessions in wage and living conditions for its members.

Without pressure from Harrisburg and Washington he could not have won his battle to unionize the captive mines up the Monongahela and the miners knew it. So, while they gave Lewis credit for being a smart leader, "the best union trader in the country," it was Franklin D. Roosevelt, the personification of the New Deal, who was the hero of the hour. Gifford Pinchot enjoyed a brief personal popularity but he was too much overshadowed for it to help him politically. As long as Roosevelt lived, Coke Region miners would vote for the party that shone with his reflected glory. When Lewis broke with the President in the election of 1940, they loyally supported Roosevelt in spite of Lewis's thundering.

The reaction of the miners to directives from outside continues puzzling. They won't let anybody tell them how to vote, but in union matters they obey Lewis, often with bitter complaint and misgiving but *they do it*. Much as they liked President Roosevelt they would not do as he asked, even in a national emergency, in matters of union policy.

Under the Lewis leadership Coke Region wages have gone up so that a machine operator makes $71.40 for a five-day week, $90.83 for a week of six shifts, and other mine workers in proportion, but *eight times in five years* he has called the men out on strike, so, deducting work suspensions, the yearly take is considerably cut down.

In 1933 there is no doubt but that the miners needed union protection and such organization was taking shape when the U.M.W. began its membership drive; but the independent unions might not have been strong enough to bring about the much needed changes in company-town administration and open the villages to the public. At least the changes would have been slower in coming. For the country at large it has been a calamity that centralization of union organization went quite so far and that the captive mines, whose metallurgical coal is the key to steel production on which so many industries depend, should not have been differentiated from the mines whose coal flows into the open national market from districts with widely different living and operating conditions.

After 1933 the stage was set for the stalled steel production, the idle automobile plants, the power famine and brown-outs that we were treated to twice in 1946.

CHAPTER XI

THE FACE OF DANGER

A SHINY BLACK SEDAN WITH AN OHIO LICENSE IS TRAV-
elling slowly up the Ten Mile Creek Road past the Clyde Mines No.
2 and No. 3. The man and woman in the front seat look interestedly out of
the windows at the smoke-blackened houses, crowded close to the highway,
where men in undershirts sit talking on narrow stoops in the pinkish evening
light. A little way beyond, the valley narrows abruptly where a creek winds
under a wooded cliff across from a group of mine buildings with a sign on
the bank in front announcing THE EMERALD MINE OF THE HILLMAN COAL
AND COKE COMPANY. A steel cable stretched between posts bars the way
to the plant yard.

The man parks the car in front of the barrier and mops his face with a
clean handkerchief, looking disgustedly at the black grime that comes off
with the perspiration. "This is the place all right," he says and gets out.

"There's no smoke," the woman demurs as she follows him around the
end of the cable.

They cross the plant yard doubtfully. To the right lies a small grassy plot
with geraniums and foliage plants fronting a white wooden panel holding
the roster of Emerald employees in Service. Ahead there is a layout of one-
story wood and brick buildings, a headframe, piles of mine posts, black
cinder banks levelled off for dumping cars, and the rails of a tramway
running up a short slope to a wooden building that looks like an old-fashioned covered bridge. The first-aid house by the office is orderly and deserted beyond the screen door.

A pebble rattles dryly down the cliff; a bird rustles getting settled for the night, and the creek scolds over the stones. In one of the buildings a telephone screams into the quiet: One-two-three! One-two-three! No one comes to answer it, but a yellowish spitz appears from behind a low brick shed marked DANGER and begins to bark. Then a door opens and a middle-aged man in overalls comes out.

"Hello!" says the man from the sedan, taking off his glasses to wipe them. "We're staying in Uniontown a few days and we drove over to have a look at this sealed mine we've been reading about. I guess you had a pretty bad fire."

"Yes," answers the watchman. "The worst in years." His voice is grave and low pitched as though he were meeting callers in the hall of a house where someone lay dead. The dog picks up a stick, shakes it, and drops it on the ground in front of the workman. He picks it up, tosses it toward the dump, and she retrieves it smartly.

"Well, could we see it?" pursues the visitor. "I mean the place where it is sealed."

The watchman takes them to a square slab of concrete under the head-frame.

"That's all there is to see," he says; "they take samples of air through that pipe," pointing to a stout casing closed by a valve attached to a wheel. There are five openings to the mine, he goes on to tell them, one of them several miles away, all of them sealed the same as this so no tiny crack of air can feed the flames inside. The workings of the Clyde mines run close to the Emerald underground so they've all been shut down since the fire. For a few days there were some 1,900 men idle in the valley, 640 from the Emerald-Chartiers and the rest from the Clydes Nos. 1 and 3 and the Emerald-Clyde No. 2. The men wouldn't go into the pits for fear the fire, fed by gases, would sweep across into their headings. It took twelve hours to seal the slopes and headings of the Emerald. They put in concrete blocks, covered them with a brattice, and then they plastered over the top. There's no knowing when the pit will operate again, not till the mine inspectors say the air samples are all right. It takes a long time to choke off a mine fire, and then there will be a lot of cleaning up to do.

The man and woman stand staring at the smooth slab that fills the opening where the shaft has been. There is no trace of smoke to hint of the blazing corridors under their feet where men and horses are— Just a piece of stone floor, but to the people interested in the miners down below it meant a finality so complete that there was no hope at all. This is what the sealing of a mine means.

"The papers said there are six men and thirty-two horses still down there," says the woman.

"That's right." The watchman takes the stick the dog brought him and tosses it again.

"As long as there was a way open," muses the woman, "the miners' wives would keep hoping—thinking about men who came out alive in other disasters after everybody thought they must be dead, but when they seal the mine it's taking away their last chance. I know they only do it as a last resort but it seems so terrible to wall men in—"

"They don't care," the watchman says quietly, turning away. "They're all dead."

It was a spark from a grounded trolley wire that started the Emerald Mine fire soon after seven o'clock on the evening of June 7, 1944. It fell into a load of hay intended for the horses that pulled the pit wagons, a speck of light no bigger than the tip of a cigarette, then a pot of fire, and suddenly a whole carload of flame. The men tried to push the car into a worked-out section but the fire got out of hand and consumed the haulageway.

Above ground the volunteer fire departments of East Bethlehem and Jefferson came in answer to the call for help as men swarmed toward the shaft from every direction. Women and children were running down the hill from Chartiers Village, the new Emerald Mine patch, to see what had happened to husbands and fathers. At the four-hundred-foot shaft Fire Chief Albie Tinelli of East Bethlehem sent down four volunteers in the cage with masks on to man three thousand feet of hose, but they had to pull it up again. The bottom was a raging inferno.

Of the 157 men on the night shift in the mine when the fire started, all but six came out within a few hours, most of them by way of the Lippencott air shaft three miles away. Rescue crews from Tower Hill and the Clyde Mines went repeatedly into the pit after the others but the flames drove them back. At the main shaft the women of Chartiers had organized a canteen in the supply shed and were passing out coffee and sandwiches to the men as they came to the surface, smoke-blackened and half suffocated. State troopers held back the crowd of the curious.

All the mine officials were there: Thomas Lamb, superintendent of the Chartiers pit of the Emerald Mine; William G. Stevenson, general manager of Hillman Coke Company; T. P. Latta, superintendent of Crucible Steel's Monongahela River Mine; George O'Brien, superintendent of the mines at Allison and Tower Hill; Richard Maize, state secretary of mines; the district mine inspectors from Waynesburg, Uniontown, and Monongahela City; the Federal Inspector; United States Bureau of Mines engineers; William Hynes, president of District No. 4 of the United Mine Workers; and a party of union officials.

Emerald is a gassy mine and as the flames spread the rescue work became increasingly dangerous. Finally after eighteen hours of fighting a losing battle, the state mine inspectors ordered the sealing of the mine to avoid further loss of life. There was no longer any hope of getting out the men and if the fire were allowed to go unchecked it would consume not only the Chartiers pit but the neighboring mines as well. In the old days, when the Pike Run Mine fire got out of control it burned for ten years; and the old Coal Hill Mine on the south side of the Monongahela River near Pittsburgh that caught fire in 1765, before they made a practice of sealing underground fires, was still burning in 1820 when the *Pittsburgh Gazette* reported that it looked like a volcano. Something like that might happen here unless there was quick drastic action.

Of the missing miners, three were unmarried; one was the father of five children; another, Steve Barnish, a fifty-five-year-old machine operator, left nine children. Calamity struck at the Barnish family and the Hillman Coke Company again before the month was over. Barnish had put his savings into a home in Chartiers Village, the Emerald Mine's new model housing development on the hill above the plant where he had worked for twenty-six years. Sixteen days after the fire a freak tornado whirled down on the white Colonial cottages and neat yards of the patch, and when it had passed all there was left was a fringe of houses on the far end of a rounded knoll strewn with shredded boards, soaked bedding, overturned automobiles, and the graves of houses. Among the dead were Steve Barnish's widow, Mary, and one of the daughters.

The Emerald Mine remained sealed all summer and fall. Meanwhile the Bureau of Mines safety engineers drilled fifteen holes to sample the gases, and by late December it seemed safe to open the shafts preparatory to putting the mine in operation. Under the best conditions it is a risky business to open a sealed mine because even if the fire is extinguished, the heat will have cooked a high concentration of firedamp out of the strata and nearly all the oxygen will have been burned up. Of four explosions in Pennsylvania caused by mine fires, costing twenty-seven lives, three were from sealed fires opened too soon. Sometimes it is impossible to seal a mine so as to cut off the oxygen completely and stop a fire that has been well established, but at Emerald the work had been well done. Six mine inspectors directed the exploration, working in shifts of two, beginning Christmas Eve when the neighboring mines would be idle over the holiday.

The air in the mine showed a concentration of about 40 percent methane (firedamp) with low oxygen, approximately 5 percent. They started the fan slowly because although methane so highly concentrated would not explode, the fresh air coming in would dilute it down to its danger zone of 5 to 15 percent, at the same time raising the oxygen. If a spark flared up when the gases were in the right mixture they would blow the top off the hill.

The bodies when they found them were bundles of clothes and bones, identifiable only by metal check and lamp numbers, two in a puddle of water, the rest under slate falls. They were only about two thousand feet from the shaft, close to a three-way intersection, four men from the maintenance crew, a machine operator, and his helper who had finished work and gotten that far on their way out of the mine. There must have been a time when they could have gotten around the flame by the side routes and so reached the shaft, but when the fire reached the intersection they were cut off. The safest thing would have been to retreat back into the mine and come out the Lippencott air shaft as the other men did. Apparently they waited too long deciding what to do and the fire hemmed them in.

Five or six months after the cleaning-up began, almost a year after the disaster, the Emerald-Chartiers pit was in operation again.

Contrary to public belief the high death rate among miners is due, not to spectacular gas explosions with mass deaths but to the steady, unheralded, picking-off of workers in slate falls. The Coke Region is used to sudden death and the smothering of a miner under a pile of slate and coal will rate two or three inches on an inside page of the newspaper.

"On .... a slate fall cost the life of ...., an employee at the ....'s .... mine. There will be a High Requiem Mass at St. ....'s Church on the morning of .... The deceased leaves a wife and .... children, etc."

In the thirty-three years ending January 1, 1939, 27,064 men died from slate falls, only 8,045 from explosions—77 percent as opposed to 23 percent. Modern mining has gone a long way in the prevention of explosions by enforcing safety regulations removing the causes of hazards, but there is not much a miner can do about slate falls except timber as close to the face as possible, keep the loose slate scaled down, listen for warning cracks, and try to get out from under if a "squeeze" comes. The fire boss tests the roof in every working section before the men go in by tapping it with an iron bar. The miner will check on it from time to time with a pick or hammer, any tool he has handy, but all he has to go by is his judgment.

When the outside air is warmer than the inside air, the ceiling sweats. After a while some of the pendant drops are absorbed and the roof begins to swell and break up. If the tapping brings out a muffled sound, short and stuffy, the roof has taken up water and will bear watching. A drumlike sound means an air cavity, "a fault" up above liable to cleave apart. Solid slate gives back a clack well sustained as the blow travels upward, but the reverberation of the pick may make the roof sound solid when it is not.

Before a fall there are often warning cracks and growls like thunder a long way off and the miner counts on these to tell him when to run; but if the warning comes when he is momentarily somewhere else, he might come back just in time to be caught. Sometimes the roof falls with no warning.

As fast as the "face" is shot down timbermen go to work to prop up the unsupported roof. In the spring of 1945, six of them were working back at the rib line where a crew was finishing up a section in a Coke Region operation. The men had already made a cut into a coal block, worked it out and let it fall, worked out the next sector and let that go down. Then they took one cut out of the third block toward where it was caved from the solid, sheared and shot it. When the machine had loaded out the first cut the timbermen went to put in capped timbers and posts so the track could be laid.

Suddenly there was a rain of loose slate and coal that buried five men. The sixth was just going out to get something he needed to work with so he was already in motion when the fall came and was able to leap clear. The fall had covered the timbermen but did not kill them outright, at least not all of them, because the men who rushed to their rescue were able to talk with one who said he was not hurt but was having trouble breathing. Then the second fall came about five minutes after the first, almost smashing the rescuers, a huge block of black slate, fifteen feet wide and about four feet thick.

The roof had been tapped just before the accident and had sounded solid but the fault was so high, as shown by the thickness of the piece that came down, that the sound failed to indicate the danger. There was no hope of getting the men out after that. It was out of the question to blast, so the only way to recover the bodies was to tunnel underneath and wedge back the slate at the end of the big stone.

As is the custom when there has been a fatality, the mine shut down and only the rescue crew remained in the area. It was dangerous work for them as well as for the engineers who had to map the fall later for report to the Bureau of Mines because the "top was talking" constantly (ceiling shifting around), with big pieces of slate coming down at intervals, some as big as a refrigerator. In the end the survey party had to map the fall twice because it was so difficult to get the measurements, running underneath with a tape measure in intervals when the roof was quiet. The body of the man who had talked to the rescue party was found wrapped around a pit post without a bone broken; he had died of suffocation.

1906-1907-1908 were bad years for explosions both in Europe and America. Those were the days when people thought coal dust had to be mixed with air containing firedamp to explode; so mines rated as nongassy considered that the precautions taken in gassy mines need not apply to them. When unaccountable explosions happened with shocking frequency they talked about the law of averages and "the luck of the mine."

In 1906 the terrible Courrieres disaster in France wiped out 1,100 miners. The next year a series of great mine blasts in England and the United States focussed attention on the need of a serious study of mine hazards. When the Monongah Mine blew up in West Virginia killing 358, the worst American explosion to date, Congress appropriated money for fuel investigations to be conducted under the technologic branch of the U. S. Geologic Survey, the funds to be made available July 1, 1908.

The French and British had already established testing galleries to try to find out what was wrong with their mining practice, and as a preliminary to setting up testing equipment, United States mining engineers went abroad to study their methods. When they came back, they built in Pittsburgh a gallery one hundred feet long by six feet four inches in diameter, principally intended to try out safer explosives. They also conducted chemical investigations of different coals and mine gases in a laboratory on the old arsenal grounds.

As the data on the propagation of explosions increased, the government engineers became convinced that coal dust could and often did explode from a source of ignition without the help of firedamp. If they could prove by actual demonstration that coal dust was of itself explosive and discover the conditions favorable to generating the phenomena, they would have solved the riddle of why nongassy mines blew up.

Tests conducted in the hundred-foot gallery under controlled conditions confirmed the hypothesis, but when commercial operators came to see the demonstration they were unconvinced. Coal dust might explode without firedamp in a fancy testing tunnel with everything figured out ahead of time, but it wouldn't in an ordinary mine. It looked as if the only way to make the scientific findings of the government useful to the industry was to demonstrate under actual mining conditions. Naturally no company would care to hazard an experimental mine explosion, so if the U. S. Engineers wanted convincing experiments they would need a mine of their own.

On July 1, 1910, Congress officially established the Bureau of Mines to take over the fuel-testing under the direction of Dr. Joseph A. Holmes. He began looking for a suitable experimental mine and after investigating a number of abandoned operations, none of which were satisfactory, he finally leased seventy-seven acres of land containing some thirty-eight acres of five-foot coal thirteen miles from Pittsburgh. That summer Bureau engineers began driving entries preparatory to opening a new mine. The coal land lies in the spur of a hill with outcrops around it, adjacent to an abandoned mine separated by a barrier pillar. By 1924 the importance of the mine had warranted such extensive plant and laboratory investments that the U. S. Government bought the property.*

* For map and description of the Experimental Mine see the Appendix B, page 262.

When the Experimental Mine was located in the Pittsburgh district at the northeastern edge of the gas-coal territory that stretches through the Connellsville Coking-Coal Basin into West Virginia, the site was chosen partly because the Pittsburgh bed is one of the largest continuous coal beds in America, of a uniform character and thickness, running from five feet in the north to between seven and nine feet in the south. A second factor influencing the choice was the frequency with which disaster had been visiting the Pittsburgh district.

Ever since the Bureau of Mines inaugurated modern methods of life-saving in mine accidents under the first director, Joseph A. Holmes, it has made First Aid and Safety Instruction an important branch of its educational service. In addition to serving as a laboratory it has become a training ground for mining inspectors and candidates for foremen's certificates. It is so constructed that faults liable to be found in commercial mines can be created temporarily to give classes in mine safety experience in detecting them.

When mining men attend meetings and safety societies in Pittsburgh, often there are demonstrations of the explosiveness of coal dust and the ways to prevent it, with usually an impressive explosion test so violent as to burst out of both mine entrances, hurling cars and splintered timber to the other side of the valley. On occasion Experimental Mine-induced explosions have broken windows several miles away.

The contribution of the U. S. Bureau of Mines testing station to the published body of scientific coal studies includes among other things reports on coal dust and air combinations; permissible explosives; roof movements; ventilation and mine gases; the speed of fire and what the gases are made of travelling ahead of, inside and behind it. And always in demonstration and publication it hammers at the defeatist philosophy that has such a hold on the coal miner, "If my number is up, I'll get it anyway."

Today, after thirty-five years of Bureau of Mines investigations into the nature and prevention of mine accidents, the Pennsylvania bituminous field has an unusually good safety record compared with other parts of the country. The Bureau has no police power in any state and its activities are confined to investigations and recommendations to improve safety practices; but in Pennsylvania there is close cooperation with the State Department of Mines which does have police power and can shut down a mine in a hurry any time until safety regulations are complied with. If a preventable accident happens, the state mine inspector for that district cannot take refuge in the excuse that he warned the management of the hazard but they disregarded it. The authority lay with him to have compelled the removal of the dangerous condition. If a mine has to be sealed it is the state mine inspectors who decide and give the order.

Nobody questions any more the fact that coal dust will explode of itself without the help of firedamp. When mining engineers talk about coal dust they mean material that will pass through a 20-mesh * screen. (If as high as 85 percent of a sample will go through 200-mesh, it is called pulverized dust.) The more volatile it is, the more liable it is to blow up—that is, the kind of coal that starts burning easily in a furnace and is apt to puff back in one's face if he throws a shovel full of slack on the blaze will readily burst into flame in a mine if mixed with air in the right proportion. The fineness of the coal dust makes a difference, and so does the composition of the atmosphere.

Normal dry air contains 20.93 percent of oxygen, 0.03 percent carbon dioxide, 79.04 percent nitrogen, and usually some water vapor and dust. In a mine the balance of oxygen promptly becomes upset and can only be maintained by artificial means. Even if there has been no fire or explosion, the breathing of men and mules takes up oxygen; so do open lights, if there are any. The decay of mine timbers and absorption into the coal and rock strata deplete it still further, and what is left is apt to be diluted with methane, nitrogen, and carbon dioxide from the strata. Even a nongassy mine may become gassy under certain conditions, so precautions must be taken anyway.

When organic matter decays to form coal, it releases a gas that lingers in the pores and fissures until freed by breaking into or dislodging the rock. Sometimes a miner's pick releases a "feeder" that blows out into the room. Unless the miner hears it he would not know it was there because there is no color, taste, or smell to it. His name for it is "firedamp" but the active agent in it is methane, marsh-gas, a light carbureted hydrogen that rises to hover along the roof. While it is not poisonous to breathe, it is capable of blowing mine, men, mules, and machines to bits if anything happens to set it off when it is in the danger range of 5 to 15 percent.

"Blackdamp," carbon dioxide, also comes from the rocks and increases the upset balance of the atmosphere as oxygen is displaced by breathing, combustion and decomposition but is nonexplosive and heavy, lying close to the floor. There is no odor to it but it gives some warning in dimming lights and creating discomfort in breathing with headache and nausea.

"White damp," carbon monoxide, is likely to appear after an explosion when there has not been enough oxygen to burn up the methane-coal dust combination. Like the other two it is odorless, tasteless, and colorless but it is particularly deadly in that it lulls the victim to sleep without his realizing what is happening to him. If a concentration of from 0.12 to 0.16 percent is

---

* For the measurement of particle sizes smaller than ¼ inch it is not practical to measure each particle so a series of sieves of standard opening has been adopted. In this series a 20-mesh sieve has square openings .0331 inches and 200 mesh has openings of .0029 inches.

TESTING FOR GAS—Gas mask crew testing for carbon monoxide with a canary bird in Experimental Coal Mine. Note Hoolamite detector held by man in the foreground

EXPLOSION TEST AT THE EXPERIMENTAL COAL MINE—Flame and smoke are issuing from the main entry pit mouth. Flame generated by an explosion may start at one hundred feet a second but may run up to three thousand feet in a second or two more if conditions are favorable

RESCUE TEAM—Rescue crew entering a mine equipped with approved self-contained oxygen breathing apparatus, electric cap lamps, self-rescuers and flashlights, and wearing protective caps and shoes

RESCUE CREW RETURNING—The crew emerges from the smoke-filled entrance of the Experimental Mine

OXYGEN BREATHING APPARATUS—Gas mask crew is erecting a canvas stopping at the Experimental Mine. Brattice-cloth and brattice-boards are as much a part of mine equipment as picks and shovels

FRESH AIR BASE—Apparatus crew returning to the fresh air base during mine rescue maneuvers at the Bureau of Mines Experimental Coal Mine, Bruceton, Pennsylvania

MEMBERS OF MINE RESCUE TEAM CONSTRUCTING PERMANENT
CONCRETE BLOCK AND MORTAR FIRE SEAL

VISITORS WITNESSING DEMONSTRATION AT EXPERIMENTAL COAL
MINE, BRUCETON, PENNSYLVANIA

breathed for one hour it may produce collapse; 0.5 percent will cause unconsciousness in a few minutes. Carbon monoxide has a great attraction for the hemaglobin in the blood and, given the opportunity, will unite with it more freely than oxygen. But when the hemaglobin is carrying carbon monoxide, the body tissues fail to receive the oxygen they require to keep functioning, so the victim dies unless he is rushed to the outside air. If the poisoning is far advanced before the condition is discovered, rescuers will try to revive him with a respirator using pure oxygen mixed with carbon dioxide.

The term "afterdamp" is the blanket name for the baleful gas combinations apt to occur after an explosion, usually meaning that there is white damp present in dangerous quantities, probably with an accompanying lack of oxygen.

Coke Region mines are not much troubled with "stinkdamp," hydrogen sulphide, although it sometimes occurs in abandoned parts of the workings. It smells like rotten eggs, burns the eyeballs and throat, causes dizziness, and may kill if the concentration rises to a tenth of one percent.

The problem that faces a coal operator is how to prevent coal dust, air, and a source of ignition from getting together in such a manner as to explode. Thus he is in the position of a cat watching for a mouse to come out of three holes at once. He must keep coal dust from rising in a cloud in so far as possible, and when it does fly it must be so diluted with nonexplosive material that it will not burn. He must regulate the air supply to sweep the gases out to prevent explosions and bring oxygen in to keep his men alive, and that poses problems in forcing air underground artificially. Then there is the necessity of blasting coal, running machines, and lighting the mine without supplying an igniting spark.

The answer to the control of coal dust seems to be water and rock-dusting, a method first suggested by government engineers in 1908. It became an official Bureau of Mines recommendation in 1923, after which it began to be taken up by commercial operators. The process is based on a practical formula with a sliding scale according to the volatility of the coal, which gives the percentages of nonburnable material that must be mixed with the coal dust to make it safe. The readier the coal dust is to burn, the more rock dust it will take to keep it from burning; and for every one-tenth of a percent of methane in the air, the percentage of rock dust in the formula rises one percent.

In modern practice in Coke Region mines which produce high volatile coal, the dust must have 65 percent rock dust with it to keep it from exploding, more if there is methane in the air. However if as much as 5 percent of methane is present nobody should be in the mine anyway.

The best rock dusts are pure limestone or pure dolomite, but any noninflammable dust will do, provided that it is ground finely enough to mix easily with the coal dust and that it is low in silica which is dangerous to the health of the men. Tiny particles of silica absorbed into the lungs may cause silicosis, "miners' asthma," which kills quite as well as an explosion, although it takes longer.

If rock dust is to be efficient it needs to be blown all over the underground workings unless they are sealed off or properly fortified by rock dust barriers, and that means rooms, entries, cross-cuts, break-throughs, rock tunnels, slopes, haulageways, everything up to within eighty feet of the face, and that must be kept wet so that no more dust than necessary will fly with cutting and shooting. As soon as a sample of the dust shows that the incombustible material has dropped below the necessary percentage, the dusting has to be done again. In addition the coal pile must be kept wet during loading, the cutterbar has to be sprayed, the tops of loaded cars sprinkled, and the car bodies kept dust tight and loaded solidly enough so they will not dribble coal on the track-bed.

In the old days mine ventilation was allowed to take care of itself. The difference in temperature of outside and inside air was generally enough to keep a draft drawing through the most open parts of the mine. Sometimes, however, there came humid days in summer when the mine air and outside atmosphere were so equally balanced that the natural circulation stopped. Then an artificial draft of sorts was set up by lighting a stove in the bottom of a shaft so the heated column of air would rise, setting the air in the galleries behind it in motion. There was also a good chance that it might set the mine afire.

Later when steam-driven fans were introduced they were used only part-time and then thriftily turned off, allowing firedamp to collect in the interval. Today Coke Region mines are continuously ventilated by electrically driven fans, quickly reversible at will, that force the air into the mine or pull it out as occasion demands.

A current of air left to itself will follow the route of least resistance, blowing freely down haulageways, by-passing the devious network of entries where men are working, unless artificially rerouted by break-throughs in the pillars, and by doors and stoppings. But even then the air in the entries may contain some firedamp. To cut down on the hazard of sparks from making and breaking connections in the trolley cable, the "gathering motor" that collects the loaded coal cars from the entries to make up the loaded "trip" (the train of cars that returns to the entrance) drags an electric cable after itself to supply the power, just as a vacuum cleaner runs by a long cord plugged into the wall in a house outlet. The haulages are so well ventilated that it is safe to allow the motor that pulls the "trip" back to the dump to run on an overhead connection.

Air is unfit for a man to breathe when the oxygen drops below 19 percent, dangerous if it is below 16 percent. Miners used to gauge the oxygen by their lamps burning low but while oil and candles go out unless they have about 17 percent oxygen, a miner's carbide lamp would burn until there was less than 13 percent oxygen, so it was quite possible that he would be dead before the lamp warned him. Today with open lights ruled out of mines, the worker depends on the fan to pump in fresh air with sufficient oxygen so he need not worry about it. He looks to the fire boss with his magnetically sealed safety lamp to assure him that the methane is below the danger point. Either canaries or a Hoolamite * detector will be used if necessary to test for the deadly white damp. A canary can live on less oxygen than a man but it reacts to white damp quicker. If there is 0.25 percent present in the air, the bird will show distress in two or three minutes where it might take ten minutes for a man to react. Men entering a mine to clean up after a fire or explosion will need an all-service gas mask to protect from carbon monoxide but it is useless in low oxygen atmosphere which calls for self-contained breathing apparatus (which gets in a man's way if he tries to do any work). Either device works only about two hours.

On December 19, 1908, somebody went into a fenced-off gassy room with an open light in a Westmoreland County mine and the explosion that followed killed 239 men. In those days men wore carbide lamps, smoked when they felt like it, blasted with black powder and long-flame dynamite and set it off with lighted squibs. Out of eighty-five explosions from 1878 to 1932, forty were from open lights and sixteen from blasting devices. Many open lights were still being used in 1933 in spite of the known hazards but by that time the increased use of electrical machines was the most important factor in causing explosions. In the four years ending in 1931 about 46 percent of the fatalities were a result of electric arcs and the deaths of these men would have been unnecessary if the electrical equipment had been of the proper type, used according to safety rules. Mechanized mines produce more coal in a shorter time but the death rate has climbed with the production. Of the six major disasters in 1940, four of them originated in electric installations. A visitor in a mine usually wonders why so much of it is dark and spooky when there is plenty of electricity available to light it thoroughly, not realizing that every unnecessary connection increases the hazard.

A Washington County miner, working in a poorly ventilated room heavy with methane in November of that unlucky year, 1908, put a charge of long-flame dynamite in a hole and took a chance on "stemming it" (packing it down) with coal dust instead of noninflammable clay. The shot "blew

---

* The Hoolamite detector will indicate the presence of carbon monoxide quicker and register for lower quantities than a canary but there is a good chance that one may not use it until he has breathed a good deal of carbon monoxide. If a canary tips over it will be noticed at once.

out" instead of directing its force into the solid, ignited the gas accumulation, and of the 155 men working only one came out alive, and he was injured. In that period about half the mining accidents could trace the source of ignition to the use of black powder. More recently the death rate from that source has only been about 20 percent of what it used to be, following a long campaign for the use of permissible explosives. In the best modern practice, a professional shot-firer sets off approved short-flame dynamite with an electric detonator but even that has to be handled carefully.

.If there is an explosion, exactly what happens? Supposing a blown-out shot raises a cloud of coal dust not sufficiently diluted and just then a spark crackles from a bad connection on the coal-cutter. The explosion that is born of this unhappy combination produces a shock-wave that travels off through the air with the speed of sound, 1,100 feet a second, stirring up more coal dust clouds as it goes; there is also a "bodily forward movement of the air travelling as a column." The flame generated by the explosion starts out more slowly, maybe only one hundred feet a second, but if the conditions are favorable it may run up to three thousand feet in a second or two more. If the explosion was weak the shape of the flame rushing down a corridor has a sharp point perhaps a hundred feet long trailing fire some three hundred feet behind it, like a long bright sword darting through the middle of the area, possibly not touching the walls at all. As it gathers speed the point becomes blunter and the flame licks out along the sides. If it were going only twelve hundred feet a second, it would still overtake the shock-wave travelling at a steady eleven hundred feet, whirling up dust ahead of itself. So there is another explosion and if there is nothing to stop it, another and another, getting bigger and better all the time.

It is not easy to determine where and why an explosion started from the evidence in a mine afterward. The shock-wave may pick up mine cars weighing several hundred pounds and carry them away from the explosion, but when the flame catches up with the air column, it may reverse the direction of the flying object, sending it back the other way again. In addition, the vacuum created as the gases cool tosses light objects around, confusing the trail.

And what about the potentialities of an explosion in terms of people? The story of Mather is a case in point.

Four o'clock, Saturday afternoon, May 19, 1928. The day shift was finishing up and the night shift going in at Mather Mine, swinging under the new green of the trees in front of the company bungalows, the water in their round buckets sloshing. Men liked to work at Mather. It was a comparatively new mine, only about ten years old, with new machinery, well run, with a capacity of 4,000 tons a day shipped by rail to the parent company in Cleveland. The patch was a model village with a public square, community center, and separate houses in generous yards with flowers and shade trees. There was nothing to rival it in the Coke Region except Nemacolin.

The air was damp with the good smell of spring overlaying the smoke that had hung low through the rainy days just past. Men in pit clothes came out of the lamp house, went to the shaft and belled the cage up. When it came they rang three times for a man-trip, waited until the engineer answered with one bell, climbed aboard, rang for lowering and dropped from sight. More men gathered at the pit mouth and the bell rang again.

Suddenly at seven minutes after four a long roar shook the underground galleries and clouds of suffocating black smoke rolled along the main haulageway of the bottom. The solid rock of the roof fell in strips like plaster. Nick Sharko of the night shift had taken only a few steps from the cage and was hailing a crowd of men on their way out when the blast of air knocked him down. Then hot dense smoke blotted everything out and in the pandemonium he got up and ran the wrong way, looking for the air shaft.

He had floundered nearly a quarter of a mile through the debris before he realized that the sound of voices came from behind him. Fighting for breath, he turned back toward the shaft and collapsed close to the outlet. A group of miners standing by the manshaft above in the yard when the rush of air shot from the pit mouth dashed down the stairs 350 feet to the main entry. The bottom steps were blown away but they slid down the water pipes, picked up Sharko, and stumbled over a man pinned under a slate fall. He was already dead so they left him and carried out Sharko.

William Eaden, assistant foreman, who had been standing by the other shaft a quarter of a mile away, made a quick trip down in the cage, rounded up sixty-two miners from that section, among them his two sons, and got them safely to the top.

When the earth convulsion told of the blast the women and children of Mather came running to the shaft head and there they stayed all night, unsheltered in the rain. The explosion tore the door off the fan house and reversed the fan, but after turning backwards a few times it stopped and righted itself. With the fan system still working and the shaft undamaged the work of rescue began at once, but there were pitifully few to come out after the first few minutes.

After midnight Sunday morning Mike Stefanik and his buddy * stumbled out of the blackness of the bottom and came upon a squad working from the main entry. They tried to hail the rescue party to let them know that they were coming but after more than eight hours in the fumes they could not

---

* In mining parlance a man who works in the same room or entry with another man is his buddy.

speak. When they were borne to the surface the crowd of women at the shaft surged forward, screaming, "Who is it?"

Whiskey brought Mike's voice back. Then he told them in broken English that there was another man of their party alive back there where they had come from. He wouldn't make the dash for the shaft with them, thinking it safer to stay where he was getting some air so they left him sitting on a rail with a lamp in each hand. He could be gotten if somebody went for him quickly. When they had been able to get out without gas masks, surely a rescue party could reach him! The man left behind was his brother-in-law. Wouldn't somebody go while there was still time?

It was hell down there. Fire running in sheets, fire all over, smoke everywhere. It was like a coke oven, but he and his buddies didn't run into the fire, they went away from it.

Mike Stefanik, Frank Krupick—his brother-in-law, and two other men were loading coal in No. 26 butt off the No. 2 main when they heard an explosion close by. It sounded as if it might be in the next heading. One of them went to the main haulage to see what the trouble was, smelled smoke, and shut the door in a hurry to give the warning to the others in No. 26 butt. They waited there a while but the air began getting bad so they decided to try to walk out. They got as far as 21 butt when the smoke and fire drove them back to No. 28 where they lay down on the ground to breathe.

One of the men couldn't see the idea of lying on the wet bottom and probably smothering anyway, so he went out into the "main" where the fumes killed him. After a while Mike and one of the other men thought it was safe to start for the "bottom" again but Frank Krupick got hold of a couple of lamps and stayed behind. This time Mike and his buddy Jack got as far as No. 19 butt, but there it looked as if they could neither go backwards nor forwards. A wrecked trip lay there with dead men all around, their booted feet sticking up every way.

"Look like I can't do nothing," said Mike. "Try to pray. Can't do that neither so I think, 'This is all. I'm finished!' and I lie down on the ground."

But when Mike lay down he smelled good air coming from somewhere so he and Jack tried to go a little farther. When they could go ahead a bit, they did; when they came to a bad spot, they retreated and waited until it cleared a little. Mike didn't know how much time they spent feeling their way along the "main." It was just walk a little and lie down for air until they lost track of the hours. Finally he sat down on a dead mule thinking he'd be lying there too when they found him. Then they saw the lights of the rescue party.

By Sunday, with two hundred miners still unaccounted for, help was pouring into Mather from all over the Coke Region and as far south as Fairmont, West Virginia. Mt. Pleasant, Crucible, Vestaburg, Chartiers,

Orient, Buffington, and Nemacolin sent crews who went into the pit after survivors, headed by experts from the U. S. Bureau of Mines.

There was surprisingly little hysteria among the women. Most of them stayed quietly at the pit mouth watching to see what the cage would bring up but a few went back to their porches to rest in the sunshine that had followed the rainy night.

A few minutes after the explosion C. M. Lingle, general manager of Buckeye Coal Company, heard the news over the telephone and hurried from Pittsburgh to Mather to direct the work until the Pickands-Mather officials could get there from Cleveland. State police were deflecting traffic within a two-mile radius. It was comparatively easy to isolate the area because Mather sits on a hill that is practically an island site bounded by Ten Mile Creek. Food was running low in the local stores but the Red Cross came with supplies and the Pennsylvania Railroad sent in a dining car to feed rescue workers and visiting officials. The town was full of them: D. D. Dodge, general superintendent of W. J. Rainey, Inc.; W. C. Hood, assistant general superintendent of H. C. Frick Coke Company; M. D. Cooper of Hillman Coal Company; James J. Geary of Monessen Coal and Coke; and National and State Bureau of Mines experts. Boy Scout patrols ran errands, carried messages and rations.

One eleven-year-old Scout was so faithful, day and night finding jobs for himself and never seeming to stop to eat or sleep, that finally one of the men, noticing tears on his face, thought he was breaking down and tried to make him go home. But the boy would not leave. Then they learned that his father was one of the two hundred still unaccounted for. Each time a body came up the shaft, he lifted the cloth for a quick glance. Then he went on with his work again. On Wednesday, the fifth day, he uncovered the face of his father, James Dillow of High House.

By 2:00 A.M. Monday the tally showed that of the 273 men in the mine at the time of the explosion 62 escaped immediately afterward from the southwest shaft, which was less affected; 13 were rescued alive from the fatal north side; 38 bodies had been recovered, of which seven were not yet identified, with 90 more still in the mine, found within a radius of a hundred feet. The fate of 70 men still hung in the balance.

The point at which the explosion had been fiercest was about two and a half miles distant from the shaft between No. 15 butt and No. 24 butt where it had tossed fifty-pound rocks around, crushed miners against sidewalls like paper, and turned loaded mine cars into kindling wood. There was not enough left of a string of thirty wagons to start a fire.

The rescue crews had hope of finding some of the men supposed to be near No. 31 butt. If they had bratticed themselves in they were probably alive because the fan had continued working. Brattice-cloth and brattice-board are as much a part of mine equipment as picks and shovels. In ordinary mining procedure they act as curtains to deflect air forced in by the fans to the parts of the mine that might become dead air pockets. In time of danger miners know how to build air locks with them and pen themselves up until help comes if it doesn't wait too long.

Hope faded a little when they came on the bodies of Tom Callagan, the assistant mine boss, and the fifteen men who were with him. He had been working near an airshaft when the explosion occurred. Shortly afterward, he telephoned that his party had made their way to an offset where they were building a brattice to keep out the gases; they were getting some good air and could hold out if help came soon. Apparently the gases had begun to seep into their retreat and they made a run for the shaft as a last resort. They were found 3,000 feet back in the main entry.

Thus far there had been surprisingly little fire as a result of the rock-dusting the mine had received only a week before, but as Monday wore away eleven small blazes had to be put out. Then a stubborn fire in No. 19 butt that had been smoldering under the wrecked trip threatened a whole section, and the rescue crews had to be recalled while firemen fought it with chemicals, mine hose, garden hose, anything they could get to carry water. A fire that gets the upper hand in a bituminous pit calls for strenuous measures, sometimes the dreaded sealing of the mine. The Coal Hill Mine near Pittsburgh burned off and on for sixty-seven years.

By midnight the fire in No. 19 butt was out and the work of looking for survivors went on, although the delay destroyed the likelihood of finding any. The workers advanced cautiously, building air locks, carrying canaries in cages to test the air. Nearly a hundred birds had died already but there was a fresh supply at the surface.

Then at 2:30 Tuesday morning, Bruce Beal of Masontown, working on the Buffington Rescue team, came on Frank Krupick sitting on a rail with his two lamps.

"You no come pretty soon, Bruce, somebody choke me!" he said as they laid him on a stretcher. The air in the room where they found him was tainted with blackdamp but it had not accumulated in sufficient quantity to kill him yet. He was in surprisingly good condition after nearly sixty hours in a living tomb, able to walk from the stretcher to a cot at the shaft head.

"What do I get for my sixty-hour shift?" he asked jocularly as they gave him a cup of coffee. But although he was rational when rescued, soon after he was not. Questioning threw him into delirium and his story had to be pieced out of fragments.

He had wandered through the underground passages in various directions until he came to butt No. 14 where he found good air between two trap doors in an air shaft and sat down to rest. When he tried to rise, he found that he could not. Every time his knees gave way so he thought that was as good a place as any to wait for what was coming to him. He had two long sleeps that he knew of, perhaps more, and each time he waked up he thought he was in the next world. Luckily he had plenty of water. It was dirty but he drank it anyway and kept a wet handkerchief to his nose.

Krupick's body gained strength quickly in the days that followed, but not his mind. On Wednesday he walked to the shaft and went down in the cage unnoticed to look for a coat and set of false teeth he had lost. Finally somebody recognized him and sent him back to the surface to be put under the doctor's care. After that he spent three months in the hospital, came out and tried to work, but he was queer and unstable. He died within a year.

By Tuesday the bodies were being taken out in a steady stream. Undertakers from the surrounding towns prepared them for identification in a temporary embalming room set up in the blacksmith shop. From there they were taken to the Amusement Hall to be placed in coffins and finally to the schoolhouse where relatives claimed them. That day there were group funerals in the village square, solemn High Mass with four priests officiating in the morning, Protestant services in the afternoon.

Relief work in the stricken village was now thoroughly organized. The neighborhood women had set up a cafeteria in the Christian Church for all comers; two sleeping cars, sent in by the Monongahela Railroad took care of the doctors, nurses, and undertakers, while students from Waynesburg College helped with the embalming and drove ambulances.

There was now no hope at all for the unaccounted-for miners. By Wednesday practically the entire workings had been explored and 167 bodies had been recovered. In some cases help had come only a little too late. A group of fourteen miners in the next butt to the one where Bruce Beal found Krupick, had apparently heard the voices of the rescue party and torn down their brattice too soon. They were found dead but still warm, with handkerchiefs over their mouths.

The disaster that had made headlines since Saturday gave first place to the story of the search for Nobile, lost in the Arctic with the *Italia*. Dance marathons made the front page again. Then another survivor came out of Mather, a Negro, John Wade, thirty-eight years old, rescued after 146 hours. He had apparently been wandering dazed through the corridors and thus missed the rescuers. On Thursday, workers searching through slate falls in butt No. 24 came upon what they took to be a corpse in a sitting position. But when they lifted it, it tried to talk. Wade's wife was waiting by the shaft head with a Negro preacher when he came up in the cage. Seeing her husband alive after the long vigil, she screamed with joy and threw her arms around the minister.

"I'm all right now," mumbled the rescued man as nurses laid him on a cot.

His condition was good when he came out of the pit, considering the long ordeal, but he succumbed to pneumonia four days later.

The mine was being cleaned up, making ready for the inspection of the Bureau of Mines engineers who hoped to determine the cause of the blast. Miners from other districts were coming to Mather to apply for the jobs left vacant by the dead. The official check-up showed 195 casualties, 94 newly made widows, and 498 orphaned children.

It was not easy to determine the cause of the disaster. Mather had the reputation of being one of the best-run mines in the state with one of the best engineers in charge. It had modern equipment used in accordance with strict safety rules that went farther than the law required. When the explosion occurred all track roadways had been recently rock-dusted; the others protected by rock-dust barriers. Machine operators used water on the cutter-bars, and only the cable-type permissible mining machines, animals, and approved locomotives did the gathering. The mine was worked on a single panel with full retreat, but in spite of all these precautions 195 men went to their death in it.

Apparently the direct cause of the explosion was the ignition of a heavy accumulation of firedamp that went undetected until too late. The presence of the gas in an explosive quantity might have been due to a failure in the ventilating system or possibly the rainy weather of the past few days kept fumes within the mine that would otherwise have escaped through natural outlets. Mather was known to be a gassy mine but for that very reason extra precautions had been taken. It was an iron-clad rule that all lids of storage-battery motors must be locked on before entering the mine and the key left at the shaft, but after the blast the cover of such a motor, taken in by a haulage crew, lay beside its machine. If it had blown off instead of being taken off, it would probably have gone out into the entry. Either the key had been left in by mistake or it had passed the inspection unlocked. If that was the case, whoever lifted the lid paid with his life and those of 194 others who worked with him.

Some classes of mine accidents are apparently beyond human power to prevent, but tracing back to the final cause of an explosion, the result is invariably the same: The accident happened "because somebody went into a pocket of dead air with an open light," "because somebody left a door open in a stopping so the air by-passed a section," "because somebody took a chance on a shot with nonpermissible explosive," "because somebody failed to check on an electrical connection." *Because somebody—*

The fault may have been in the management or it may have come back to one of the men who was in a hurry or was feeling reckless because he had fallen out with his wife or had lost his girl friend, or perhaps he was one who habitually took chances, trusting to the luck of the mine.

Either way the first cause was the human factor which is elusive to deal with. Some people are temperamentally ill adjusted to work underground at any time but it is hard to tell which ones are just by looking at them. An education program helps; so does the strict enforcement of safety rules, and being certain that a miner can read signs and warnings before he is allowed in a mine.

The fatality rate is far below what it used to be in the disastrous first decade of the century but explosions still occur.* After a big holocaust the accident rate drops for a while because everybody is being careful. Then somebody grows careless and another mine blows up. Am I my brother's keeper? In the coal mines, perhaps more than in any other industry, the answer must be YES!

* During the war stress just past, the year 1943 set an all-time record of only 175 fatalities from all causes in mining 138,200,000 tons of bituminous coal, the best production per fatality ratio in Pennsylvania's bituminous coal history. The first nine months of 1944 were still better with a ratio of one fatality for each 871,000 tons of coal as opposed to the 1943 figure of one death for each 735,000.

CHAPTER XII

POTPOURRI

T IS A QUARTER OF FIVE ON AN AUTUMN AFTERNOON IN
one of the river patches. The day shift has come home and washed up;
supper is over. On the front steps of the yellow brick township school nine
middle-aged women and four men stand waiting in the sunshine, each
carrying a tablet and pencil. The building sits on the edge of a bare knoll
that falls away steeply at the back, where a network of pebbly paths
descends to the manway of No. 3 mine down by the road in the valley. On
the tilted plane of schoolyard in front of the building some of the seventh-
grade boys are playing mushball. To the right, near where the road loops
up from the Hollow, fourteen identical two-family houses the color of gun-
metal lean against a cloud of smoke.

From below comes the sound of a motor climbing the grade. One of the
women goes to the corner of the building and looks down the hill.

"It's them!" she calls.

A man tries the door to see if the janitor has finished sweeping after the
day session of children so the adult class can come in. Inside there are foot-
steps and the click of the lock being released. The door swings open just
as a Plymouth sedan with two men in the front seat and two women in the
back rounds the corner and pauses while the women get out. Then it purrs
off across the flat table-top of the knoll and disappears down the bluff above
the Monongahela where similar classes are waiting in mine villages for the
men teachers.

There is a stir of appraisal as the women cross the sandy yard coming toward the group by the steps. Miss Lessinger,* the teacher, has brought a visitor, a tall thin woman in a gray tailored suit and flat-heeled shoes, an American with graying curled hair trimmed short at the neck and eyeglasses on a chain. Miss Lessinger is more to their liking, full-blooded with flashing black eyes, a big girl ready to laugh and quick to pick up Slovak and Italian words that come in handy to make English more understandable. The Slovak and Italian, Polish and Bulgarian women from the company towns like to go to her school because she makes them feel as if the teaching worked two ways. If she says something in their language and gets it wrong, they tell her and next time she says it right; and when they get their English wrong she straightens it out just as they did for her.

They follow her now down the cool central hall of the building to a classroom at the far end, the women in clean, starched cotton prints, their hair sandy or gray or black, brushed severely back to round coiled buns bristling with hair-pins, all but one with a heavy honey-colored braid around her head and a back-parting. That is Olga Fedovna who recently passed her citizenship examination for second papers. She has been affecting an American hair-do ever since, and the rest of the women don't know whether they like the idea or not. The men following in a knot by themselves have dressed up to the extent of putting on wool trousers and white shirts but they have left coats and ties at home.

When the students have taken their seats, the women in front with the men behind them, and the guest is settled in a desk at the rear, Miss Lessinger begins to hear reading class. The selection deals with a trip to the grocery store where Mrs. Jones buys a long list of familiar staples after inquiring the price of each. She concludes the transaction by offering a five-dollar bill in payment and receiving the correct change in half-dollars, nickels, and pennies. Then she pauses to chat lengthily with her neighbor, Mrs. Brown, further increasing her vocabulary. The words are simple only if one knows them, and some of the mothers and grandmothers frowning over the unaccustomed phrases are learning to read for the first time in any language.

Mrs. Povick, the eldest of the group, a spare old woman with muscles gone loose, her weathered brown skin furrowed with wrinkles like a map in high relief, finishes her stint of reading in a loud, precise voice that aims to reproduce Miss Lessinger's pronunciation.

" 'Good-bye, Mrs. Brown. I hope you will come to see me soon,' " she concludes in triumph and looks over her shoulder to see whether the visitor has noticed how well she reads. The stranger nods and smiles.

Thereupon Mrs. Basik, Mrs. Povick's next-door neighbor, a straight-backed,

* All names used in this chapter are fictitious and are not intended to designate any specific individuals.

freckled blonde woman in her fifties who always smells of *polinki,* rises and begins to drift back toward the visitor.

"Sit down, Marfa!" says Miss Lessinger. "We're going to have writing class now."

But Marfa is trying out her English on the newcomer.

"Would you like to see my marriage license?" she inquires.

The class has turned around with one accord.

"You may show it to the lady after school," says Miss Lessinger, rising. "We have our work to do now. Come back to your place."

But Marfa is almost to the hall door.

"Be back, sure. Go just a minute," she says and slips out with a smile in the direction of the visitor intended to invoke her presence as the excuse for the irregularity.

While one of the women collects the readers, Miss Lessinger joins her friend at the back of the room.

"Marfa always figures some way to get home," she tells her in a low voice. "She wants some *polinki* and as soon as she has it she'll come back."

The class opens its writing tablets and begins to copy over and over the sentences Miss Lessinger has written on the blackboard in handsome copy-book script:

"Washington is the capital of the United States."

"Philadelphia is the largest city in Pennsylvania."

A small dark woman in the front seat by the window yawns loudly and taps the desk with her pencil staring out of the window. She is a Croatian lately come in the class who speaks no English at all. The unintelligible words on the board make her so discouraged that she won't try to copy them. Miss Lessinger goes to the woman, writes her name at the head of the page, makes her understand what it is, and gets her to trace it. Then she starts copying it.

Civics class follows and because this is a special occasion with a visitor they will make a game of it. Two of the men act as captains and choose sides, the opposing teams facing each other spelling-bee style across the room. Marfa returns carrying a folded paper and is chosen before she has a chance to sit down. The other captain gets the visitor to balance her. Then the questions begin, passed from one team to another if a contestant gives a wrong answer.

"What is the highest executive office in Fayette County?"

"How many judges are there in this district?"

The American caller fails in her first chance at the question "Who is the attorney general of Pennsylvania?" and sits down amid friendly laughter. Olga Fedovna, who is almost a citizen now that she is ready for final papers, knows the answer and gives it proudly.

So few miss questions that there is not time to let the game go on until one side outdoes the other. Outside the shadows are growing long and bedtime comes early in a patch. Most of the women have been up since half-past four to get their men off for the early shift. At seven-thirty class is dismissed and Mrs. Basik can at last show the marriage license from her home village in Lithuania, a typed form on a thin quarter-sheet of paper with spidery handwriting in brown ink filling in the spaces. She translates, running her finger along the lines.

"Can read English, too," she finishes. "Read my language; read English. Two kinds."

"You may be very proud of it," says the visitor and Marfa goes away satisfied.

"These people seem to be mostly different kinds of Slovaks," observes the woman in the suit when the last student has filed out. "Are the other patches about the same?"

"It is natural that the Slovaks, Czechs, Poles and Hungarians should predominate," says Miss Lessinger, gathering up her papers, "because the Slavic peoples are the biggest group around here, but in some company towns there may be a concentration of Italians. They are the second largest foreign minority and they like to get together where they can. All the patches are mixed, though."

"How about Americanization?" pursues the observer. "I suppose some villages are further advanced than others?"

Miss Lessinger sits down on a desk top, books held loosely on her hip.

"Yes, some of them are pretty much Americansky, but it isn't always the best things about us that they copy. I can show you what I mean when I tell you about Thanksgiving in two patches I go to. It is a new holiday for them and I thought we ought to feature it a little in class because it is especially American. So I told them how we came to have Thanksgiving and then left it up to them if they wanted to do anything to celebrate.

"When I told the class you saw today about it they said they wanted to have a Thanksgiving party but they didn't make any definite plans about it right then and the next week I heard no more about it. There is another patch where I teach that is what you would call thoroughly Americanized. They took up the Thanksgiving idea the first day, appointed committees for everything, assessed fifty cents around for expenses and collected it. After that, until Thanksgiving, every time I went there they wanted time out from class for the committees to meet to work out details and everybody was all pepped up.

"Over here I thought the idea had died out, but then one day the women asked me to come to celebrate Thanksgiving at the Community Hall with them on a certain night. I asked what to bring but they said they didn't need anything. There was still no talk so I had no idea what they had planned.

"Well, when I got to the party it was in full swing with an orchestra playing and everybody dancing czardas and polkas with all the children in the village looking in the windows. There weren't enough men to go around but the women danced with each other so it didn't matter and I never had a better time in my life.

"There wasn't anything in sight to eat and I didn't know whether there was going to be, but after a while one of the women said, 'Miss Teacher, come now,' and opened the door into the next room. You ought to have seen the mounds of food: fried chicken, *hlupki coregi* (they're sort of like potato chips), pigs in blankets, *kolachi* (a kind of pastry with a tart fruit in it), pumpkin pies, and all kinds of Thanksgiving fruits and nuts.

"But before we ate the women started pint bottles of whiskey around the room, one at a time with a shot glass to drink out of and when the bottle was empty they'd open another. After everybody had had one or two drinks, they passed the plates loaded with food. I started right off to eat mine but most of the women only took a taste and then covered it with a paper napkin to carry home to their families. Then they called in all the children standing outside and gave them all they could eat. What was left they packed in a big box for me."

"And what about the other patch where they had the committees?" asks the visitor.

"They had their party too," says Miss Lessinger, rising to go. "And what did we have for refreshments? Two bologna sandwiches—all nice and sanitary in wax paper, a Dixie cup, and a bottle of pop. The children whose parents didn't belong to the Americanization Class and hadn't paid their fifty cents dues got sent home and they wouldn't even have given any food to the orchestra if I hadn't suggested it. Sometimes I wonder if we want to Americanize them."

The recent crops of prospective citizens have had to worry through their oral examinations before the naturalization examiners the best way they could because during the war the Adult Citizenship Schools ceased. As long as they were available the foreign-born made good use of them.

It is difficult to tell what proportion of the Coke Region population is of recent foreign extraction. In Fayette and Westmoreland Counties with a combined total population of 504,410 the foreign-born of all races is 55,717. Add to these the first and second generation children of immigrants who came during the period of wholesale importation of European labor in the mine wars and expansion period from 1880 to 1920 and the Yankee stock is probably outnumbered.

Of the foreign-born in the two counties, according to the 1940 Census figures, the Slavonic peoples are most numerous, with the Italians in second place. That is, taking the main Slavic groups—Czechoslovaks, Poles, Hungarians, Yugoslavs, and Russians, the total for the two counties is 22,368 with the Czechoslovaks (9,027) and Polish (7,067) in the majority. The Italians number 14,648 foreign-born. Little Greene County is still largely American but with the opening of her coal fields the percentage of foreign population is rising.

There are three steps to being naturalized: The Declaration or First Paper: the Petition for Naturalization, often called the Second Paper; and the Final Hearing before the Court. The total cost is $11 and the whole process takes about five years.

When an applicant appears for the preliminary hearing to file his Petition for Naturalization he may also ask the court to change his name. If the judge rules that the request is a reasonable one, particularly if the name the man wants to part with is so unpronounceable to Americans that it may handicap him and his family, the change is allowed. Sometimes the new citizen chooses to be called by the surname of an American friend, a boss or a neighbor, and so occasionally one encounters men named Brown or Baker who hailed from Lithuania, Serbia, or Poland. Usually however the applicants prefer to keep their own names.

To see how the naturalization process works, suppose that Istvan Szabo, whose alien registration card says that his last place of foreign residence was Hodmezövásárhely in Hungary, wants to become an American citizen. He knows nothing about the United States Government except that its general reputation in Europe was so good that he has gone to a lot of trouble to get here. Now he wants to make sure that he will get all the benefits. Istvan has a job drawing coke at the Mary Ann ovens; his family lives in a company house that doesn't cost too much, and his boss and his neighbors speak his language so he gets along all right without English. Iwan Kulick, who lives in the other half of Istvan's house, is already a citizen so he offers to help the Szabos get their papers. When he was naturalized his wife didn't have to worry about her citizenship because she automatically became a citizen when he did. Now the law is changed so Istvan's wife, Maria, will have to take out papers just the same as he does.

So Istvan and Maria go to the clerk of the court in Uniontown, fill out applications for Declaration of Intention, and send them with two pictures each to the Immigration and Naturalization Office in Pittsburgh. It doesn't matter that neither can speak English yet because the Declaration does not require it, but before they come up for the Second Papers they will have to learn enough to speak for themselves. And they will have to study something of American history and government so they can answer the questions of the naturalization examiner or he won't recommend them for citizenship.

There is no Americanization school to help Istvan and Maria but the deputy prothonotary gives them a booklet in English called *How To Become a Citizen of The United States and Questions for the Prospective Citizen,* by Joseph P. Matuschak. It outlines each step of the naturalization process, explains the status of the children of aliens, and gives the answers to the questions about the Constitution, Washington, and Lincoln that Istvan and Maria will have to learn.

Two years after the Declaration of Intention they may apply for Second Papers and come up for the Preliminary Hearing, but if their English is not good enough yet, or if they do not feel sure of the questions, they may take up to seven years if necessary. After that the First Paper runs out.

Also, now that he wants to be naturalized, Istvan will have to look out about being arrested for fighting, stealing, destroying property or being drunken and disorderly because if he is he will have to explain about it to the immigration authorities and it will not help his reputation as a good moral character.

When the Szabos appear at the clerk of the court's office to apply for their Second Papers they speak English with difficulty but enough so that this time they can do their own talking instead of depending on Kulick to do it for them. The application they must fill out requires detailed information of the circumstances of their coming to this country, what city or village they hailed from, where they bought their steamship tickets, what port they came to, as well as the names of some of their fellow passengers and of Istvan's employers in this country. It wants to know whether they understand the principles of government of the United States and would defend it in time of stress; if they have ever been arrested, and if so, what for? Do they believe in anarchy? Have they ever been confined in an insane asylum?

The completed application finally goes off to Pittsburgh to the Immigration and Naturalization Office along with more photographs, taken within thirty days in the prescribed manner, on thin paper, front view without a hat against a light background, unmounted and signed by the applicant but not on the face or clothing.

After the Immigration Office has had time to check the application, the Szabos receive notices to appear with witnesses to their good character at the Uniontown Court House to meet the examiner for the Preliminary Hearing. Istvan lays off work and they go dressed in their best clothes, Istvan in his dark Sunday suit with a white shirt, Maria in a neat blue coat with a printed silk *babuska* over her head.

The Hearing is held in one of the upstairs courtrooms with two examiners sitting at a long table in front of the judge's rostrum, facing the audience. The applicants and their witnesses sit in a long row by the wall to the left until they are called. Istvan stares at the American flag that stands by the judge's vacant chair, at the man filling out applications on a typewriter in the little room by the jury box, at the two government men questioning two applicants who face them across the table flanked by their witnesses. One of the examiners looks as though he were from southern Europe himself; the other is an American with spectacles, a little bald but young with a fresh complexion.

Benvenuto Cecci, the heavy-set Italian in the chair opposite the American, has his case complicated by the fact that he came to the United States as a stowaway. He would have been deported but for his entry being legalized by a marriage to an American wife. The naturalization seems to have been held up for a long time because the government man with glasses has a stack of documents in his brief case about it.

"Do you believe in killing the officials to change the form of government?" he asks.

The man says no, he does not.

"Have you ever been a member of a Fascist organization?"

"No."

"Ever belong to the Sons of Garibaldi?"

"No. No society at all but the Sons of Italy."

"What is this in the record about your having served in the Italian Army?"

The man said he had to join but he was no Fascist.

"Would you defend the United States against your country?"

The Italian gives him a flashing smile. "This is my country now. I fight for her. You bet!"

He does not know what the Bill of Rights guarantees and is not certain who Abraham Lincoln was but his answers show that he has studied. The two witnesses he has brought along testify that they have known him for five years and are certain that he will make a good citizen.

"It seems everything is in order now," says the examiner and lets him go with an admonition to brush up on the Four Freedoms.

The Szabos are next. Istvan doesn't mind the questions at all but Maria has to be helped a little. She knew all the answers riding in on the trolley but she can't remember them here in front of all the people.

"Take your time," says the young man with the glasses kindly. "You'll think of it. How many states in the United States?"

"Thirteen," says Maria.

"That is how many we had to start with. How many do we have now?"

She looks at Istvan, panic in her eyes. If she fails in the examination she may have to be questioned in open court by the judge when she comes up for the Final Hearing.

"How many stars in the flag?" asks the examiner. "You know that one."

"Forty-eight."

"That's right. What do the stars stand for?"

"Each one for a state."

"Then how many states have we?"

"Forty-eight." Maria is all right after that.

When the immigration official is through with their character witnesses he says they will be notified when to come to court again to finish up.

On the morning of the day when Istvan and Maria's naturalization class appears for the Final Hearing to take the oath of allegiance, the last step in the process by which they become citizens, they meet the federal examiner in one of the small court rooms on the second floor of the courthouse for a final check-up to be sure that their papers are in order. The government man who will see them through this last bit of red tape is the American who questioned Istvan and Maria at the preliminary hearing. He looks over their records, asks a routine question or two and tells them to be in the big courtroom down the hall at one o'clock.

The room empties quickly. The Szabos are signing their papers by the deputy prothonotary's desk when the examiner stands up and calls to an old man with bristling waxed mustaches wearing a wrinkled blue serge coat and cotton trousers, who has been sitting on the edge of his chair by the rear wall all morning. As the others went forward one by one he looked questioningly at the tipstaff. Once or twice he half rose but settled back again until now he is the only one left in the body of the courtroom.

"Have you a letter telling you to come to court?" asks the immigration officer.

The last man fumbles in his pocket, pulls out a paper and hitches up the aisle very slowly, favoring a twisted leg that bows out and will not bend.

The American looks at the paper and takes from his file the documents that relate to it.

"Your name is Janko Latovich?"

The old man nods vigorously.

"And you come from Bitolj?"

Another nod.

"When did you come to this country?"

The answer comes in a Yugo-Slav dialect.

"I only talk English," says the examiner. "Try to tell me in my language when you came to this country."

"Thompson No. 2."

"I know that is *where* you went but *when* was it?"

"No have English."

"You come on boat?" asks the Inspector.

A nod.

"Can you remember the name of the boat?"

"Easter."

"You mean you came to America at Easter?"

A nod.

"Did you have a friend, somebody you knew, when you got to Thompson No. 2?"

The man says he did.

"Who was it? What was his name?

"Me."

"We're not getting anywhere," says the examiner in an aside to the deputy prothonotary. Then he notices Istvan pulling on his coat by the door. "Wait a minute," he calls. "You speak Slovenska. Help me out, will you? Ask him if he has a wife."

So Istvan goes back to the table and repeats the question. He says it two or three ways but it is no use.

"He's some kind of a Croatian that I can't speak his language," he tells the American and goes back to Maria. The deputy says there is no interpreter in the building, so there is nothing to do but worry through with English.

"You catch woman?" begins the examiner patiently.

The old man is all smiles. Yes, sure he did. He holds up two fingers.

Now begins the long-drawn-out business of finding out when he married, whom, and how old he was. The only facts that emerge are that the first wife was a girl named Berta whom he married in this country but she "one week, two week, maybe die." Then he went back to the Old Country for half a year, returned to America and caught another woman.

The data is not checking with the government records but it is obviously a case of the old man's not understanding the questions. It would all be so simple if he had learned English. As it is the investigator tries one avenue of approach and then another, giving the old man all the help he can because he is in bad shape and has made a great effort to come to town. It is no use.

"Get someone to talk for you and I'll squeeze you in later in the day," he says finally, gathering the documents and putting them away.

The old man shuffles off, bewildered. "Don't have English," he says to the tipstaff standing in the doorway. "Must go home?"

At one o'clock the members of the naturalization class take their places in the big courtroom with its carved mahogany panelling, red and white tile floor, and smoke-darkened portraits. The jury box is full of immigrants, so is the double row of chairs on the other side of the judge's ornate rostrum;

another row sits along the rail with their backs to the audience, with four American women a little apart who have lost their citizenship through marriage with aliens but want to be reinstated. The deputy prothonotary takes his place at the desk below the judge's chair; the examiner goes to a small table at the right as the hands of the clock creep to 1:20. A gray-haired tip-staff enters from the right and speaks in a low tone to the immigration officer. Then he goes out. Five minutes later an elderly woman in a dark dress with white collar and cuffs brings a glass of water to the judge's desk and disappears. At 1:30 all heads turn to the right as the judge enters in his black gown and mounts the dais; the spectators rise to their feet and the crier opens court.

When everyone is settled in his seat again the examiner goes forward to present the naturalization class to the judge, calling attention to the fact that fifteen of the thirty-seven petitioners ready for citizenship are technically enemy aliens who have, however, been investigated and found acceptable. Thereupon the prospective citizens file to the open space in front of the judge and listen with upraised hands while he reads slowly and distinctly, so that even those who have trouble understanding English will realize the solemnity of the occasion, the Oath of Allegiance which severs the bond with their home countries:

"You and each of you do swear by ALMIGHTY GOD, the Searcher of all hearts, that you absolutely and entirely renounce and abjure all allegiance and fidelity to any foreign prince, potentate, state or sovereignty of whom or which you have heretofore been a subject or citizen; that you will support and defend the CONSTITUTION and laws of the UNITED STATES OF AMERICA against all enemies, foreign and domestic; that you will bear true faith and allegiance to the same; and that you take this obligation freely, without any mental reservation or purpose of evasion, as you shall each answer to God at the last great day."

The immigrants swear en masse; the judge pronounces them citizens, and it is all over. Sometimes when there is a large class there is a speaker but this is a small group so there is no speech, no welcome from anybody as they filter out the door to the elevator.

If Istvan and Maria remain in the Mary Ann patch her Americanization will not go very much further. She will continue to cook and bake as she did in her home village in Hungary; she will go to her native church of the Byzantine Rite and to the exercises of the Parochial School attended by her children, to the Magyar picnic, to weddings, and funerals, and once in a while to the American movies.

Istvan's contact with Americans will be through his union and more often than not in the way of collision. But Istvan has no idea of drawing coke all his life. He worked on the land in Europe. The money Maria saves for him is going for a house he has his eye on in town where he can turn the front room into a grocery and have a garden and grape arbor out back.

When the Szabos leave the patch their real infiltration into American life begins. Maria has to use her English when American customers come into the store; she wears a hat instead of a scarf to church. Istvan talks to his American neighbors over the fence about taxes and bean beetles. The store and garden pay their running expenses; the older boys have jobs after school; Istvan rides to the mine in a car pool and saves his wages. When a really good piece of property comes on the market, he has the cash to buy it. It is a fine big house where a rich American coal man used to live, three stories high with a bath on every floor, stained-glass windows on the stair-landing and lots of shiny oak woodwork. Istvan does not plan to live there himself. In his spare time he paints the peeling window frames, and he has had the rooms redecorated with durable paper that will stand being cleaned year after year. Then he rents it at a good price and uses the money to send his oldest boy to medical school. Istvan goes by the name of Steve Zabo now because it is easier for Americans to pronounce and the children like it better.

The Zabo girls are determinedly American, patterned on current movie stars. One of them has a Protestant young man calling on her, which dis-quiets her mother but Steve takes it comfortably. After all, this is America and some of the heretics seem to be good people.

One has only to see the list of graduates from Uniontown High School to realize how high the percentage of children of foreign-born parents has become compared to that of the old stock in the Coke Region. Among the new generation, nationality lines break down more rapidly than among adults and although a Slovak or Hungarian child coming into the city school from a company town will probably find his closest friends in his own nationality group, there is good over-all comradery. Where cliques develop there is apt to be a cleavage along schools-of-origin lines, children who knew each other in junior high school voting for others from their particular school for class officers. The students from certain patches, irrespective of nationality, tend to be more cooperative, easier to discipline and to assimilate into the student body than some from others, reflecting the tenor of living in their community.

The children of foreign parentage are often outstanding physical speci-mens, apt to excel in athletics, especially in football and track. The American stock generally outnumber them on the honor roll, although there have been notable exceptions. The generally lower average may be due in part to a foreign language being spoken at home, sometimes to the difficulty of changing from a country or parochial to a city school, or to the parents' lack of interest in the children's marks. Italian and Slovak boys are apt to have a flair for mechanics and machinery in high school; if they go on to college, they often choose engineering or business. When times are good in the Region a large percentage will follow father or brothers into the mines. A good many girls go into nurses' training; only about 2 or 3 percent go to college.

During and following the strike of 1933 there was considerable radical activity in the company villages. When a group of Communists asked permission to parade on May Day in April, 1934, the Uniontown Police Department was faced with a probability of stirring up trouble whether it gave permission or refused it. If the Communists marched, considering the temper of the district, there might be a riot; if the request were denied, there would be a controversy. Four legionnaires of the LaFayette Post: Chief of Police A. W. Davis, Sergeant Smith, Matty Bane, and Allen Park solved the difficulty by offering as an alternative an Americanism Day celebration with speeches and a giant parade that would include everybody, native and foreign.

Five thousand school children marched, along with the Knights Templers in plumes and swords; nationality groups in native costumes, Slovak, Polish, Russian and Italian lodges; the American Fraternal Orders; the Unions and the American Legion. It was a great show, so well received that it has become an annual feature of the Coke Region. Seven years ago the state representatives from Fayette County secured the passage of a joint resolution in the legislature to set aside May first as Americanism Day throughout Pennsylvania by the governor's proclamation.

In 1944, fifteen thousand marched in Uniontown. This year, the twelfth Americanism Parade took in so many organizations that it is a wonder there were any people left to be spectators. Natives and foreigners worked to organize it and marched together behind Joseph Panzera, the Italian Grand Marshal.

It takes time to achieve a blend of the Coke Region mixture but it is brewing.

CHAPTER XIII

COKE REGION SUNDAY

THE EARLIEST SETTLERS OF THE COKE REGION WHO found their way over the mountains by Nemacolin's Trail to grub out clearings in the rich land between the rivers were mostly Virginians and Marylanders, many of whom had been reared in the Church of England. The first Anglican clergyman to conduct service in the district came as chaplain with Captain James Burd in 1754 but went back East when the junket was over. Before the revolution an English divine was preaching near Connellsville, but with the outbreak of hostilities he set sail for England and was lost at sea. By 1780 there was a little group of Anglicans in the vicinity of Dunbar centering around the plantation of Virginia-born Colonel Isaac Meason, who was later to make a name for himself in the iron business. Brownsville had an itinerant minister in 1785 who served several missions in the vicinity but in the reorganization period following the break with England when anything English was out of favor, there was such a dearth of Episcopalian missionary clergy that the chapels stood idle while communicants drifted to other congregations. With the reorganization of the church under American bishops new ministers came to the Region, but it was after 1800 before the parishes gathered momentum again.

The Great Bethel Baptists were the first denomination to get under way with a permanent organized congregation in 1770, six years before Quaker Henry Beeson tacked up his notices announcing the grab-bag sale of lots that was the genesis of Uniontown. The Scotch-Irish settlers who began coming to the district before Cornwallis surrendered set up the Red Stone Presbytery in 1781; the Methodists were on the ground in 1784.

They were a churchly lot, those homesteaders of the Coke Region. First they set up their meeting-houses and after that the distilleries and little iron furnaces that crimsoned the night sky just as the lines of coke ovens do today. They had no idea of letting their faith be watered down just because they were a long way from their parent congregations. When eight members of the Redstone Presbytery fell under suspicion of entertaining religious ideas not in accord with "the plain, obvious and commonsense construction of its doctrines," the ruling members put them out. Communion was by token, little lead discs distributed to members in good standing only, a relic of the days of persecution in Scotland; and when certain modern-minded Covenanters made bold to introduce Watt's hymns into the worship of their congregation, a hundred members rose and walked out to build a stone church across the road where they could sing the Psalms in peace. The Great Bethel Baptists of the new school and old school fought bitterly on the subject of missions, locked the doors and windows against each other and broke them down, and finally petitioned the legislature to settle their differences.

There had been Roman Catholic worship in the district as early as 1800 under the direction of a missionary priest, the Reverend F. X. O'Brien, charged with the care of ten and a half counties in the western part of the state but the Region was overwhelmingly Protestant until Pittsburgh blast furnaces began calling for Connellsville coke after the Civil War. Ever since, the balance of power has been shifting toward the Roman and Eastern Churches of the Latin and Slavic immigrants imported to work the mines and coke plants. This is not surprising considering the magnitude of the migration and the high birth rate and the fact that the old stock tends to decrease rather than increase.

The Coke Region still takes its religion seriously and makes a newcomer conscious of it at once by tripping him up with unexpected regulations. Uniontown retains and enforces an old ordinance against Sunday movies in spite of sporadic efforts to set it aside, and a recent patriotic display of fireworks scheduled for a Sunday evening had to be changed to another night in the face of evangelical opposition.

On Sunday the traditionally English-speaking stock connected with the coal and coke business mostly sort themselves out in Protestant congregations. The rest of the employees assemble in Roman Catholic or Eastern Orthodox Churches.

Although there are Protestant Czechoslovaks, Hungarians, and Italians, the sporadic movements to start missions among them have been short-lived. Nonsectarian social service undertakings have fared better. The

Pencraft Cooperative Community project of the American Friends Service Committee in the crowded Klondike section is solidly established with a long list of applicants waiting for places in a second settlement now being launched.

The community betterment work under the Women's Division of Christian Service Board of the Methodist Episcopal Church has been going on for seventeen years. The three social workers live in the McCrumb Community House near the Federal Housing Project in Uniontown, a high ceilinged Victorian mansion with walnut woodwork, iron lace trimming, and a cupola, that was once the home of a famous Coke Region family whose calamitous history kept the county in a dither back in the eighties.

The Methodist work began as a Training School for Czechoslovak Protestant girls who came to the denominational center direct from Europe to receive missionary and deaconess training before going out to work among their own people in the company towns. Miss Van Scioch, the present director of the McCrumb Center, came to the district seventeen years ago while the training school was still in operation. When it was about to be abandoned she suggested that the house become a nucleus of community work to be carried on in the countryside featuring kindergartens, handicrafts, supervised play, and adult women's study groups. Three staff members conduct classes in three mining communities which had no local church activities and at the Community Center in Uniontown, making no distinction as to creed, nationality, or color. The kindergartens meet daily; the groups of children, up to sixth grade, once a week, and the women's organizations meet once a month with occasional travelogues and movies. In the summertime vacation schools offer nature study and organized games for children.

A newcomer in the Coke Region is confused by what seems to be a large variety of Catholic Churches. He hears about the Italian Catholic, the Slovak Catholic, the Polish, Irish, and Greek Catholics; he sees church steeples with Latin crosses or floriated crosses and lily-bulb domes surmounted by crosses with an extra bar across top and bottom parallel to the main bar and others topped with the "crooked cross" that has the lower bar placed at an. angle.

Actually all of them fall into two fundamental categories, Roman Catholic and Eastern Orthodox,* with the Greek Catholic (which is really a Roman Catholic) a bridge between the two—as much as one can say there is a bridge when one group recognizes the Pope in Rome and the other an Eastern Patriarch. The Italian, Slovak, Polish, and Irish congregations hear Mass in Latin, and draw upon Western religious customs. The Catholic Church of the Byzantine Rite—popularly but inaccurately called the Greek Catholic in that its people are not Greeks but Ruthenian, Czech,

* Officially the Holy Orthodox-Catholic Apostolic Church.

Slovak, Hungarian, Croatian, and Serbian—hears Mass in the Old Slavonic, the language of its great missionaries St. Basil and St. Methodius; it uses the religious liturgy and ceremonial developed under the influence of the Byzantine Empire to interpret a creed essentially the same as that of the Western branch of the church, and it acknowledges the authority of the Pope in Rome.

As for the Slovak, Polish, Irish, and Italian churches, although the Roman hierarchy prefers that congregations be made up along territorial instead of nationality lines, with the communicants in a parish drawn from people in the immediate vicinity that the church building would naturally serve, in a district so thickly settled as the Coke Region, the Central and Southern Europeans have liked to assemble with their own kind, which accounts for the multiplicity of nationality churches. Ninety percent of the Polish people in this country are Roman Catholic and strongly clannish in their worship, just as Americans are apt to be if they stay long in Paris or Berlin or Buenos Aires.

The Eastern Orthodox churches found in the Coke Region are mainly of the Russian variety but made up of the same nationality groups as the Byzantine Rite and springing from the same cultural background. There are many points of similarity in the ceremonial. The different branches of the Eastern Orthodox Church * have intercommunion with each other, the Church of England, and the Protestant Episcopal Church of America, but not with the Roman Catholic Church. Thus the services of the Greek Orthodox people, who have no church of their own in Uniontown, are held in Episcopalian St. Peter's, an arrangement that works well because, with one congregation on the Gregorian calendar and the other on the Julian, special holiday services do not conflict.

A Slavic coal miner or coke-drawer sees so much of darkness and dirt in his day's work that when he goes to church he craves all the beauty money can buy—satin and brocade, velvet and gold fringe, lace and silk ribbon, ikoni (holy pictures) like the ones he remembered in his childhood, and candles, hundreds of them; and he likes the service to last a long time. The simple exterior of the Coke Region's Eastern churches under their mosque-like domes give little hint of the grandeur within.

It is the second of September, the day the Russian Orthodox congregation of the Church of the Holy Trinity is to robe the bishop on his pastoral visit. It is a small church of yellow brick with three latticed minaret-like towers, the two at the front corners of the building a little taller, their double bulges topped each with a crooked cross. A trolley track runs beside it, separated

* The Patriarchates of Russia, Rumania, Serbia, Antioch, Alexandria, Constantinople, Jerusalem and Cyprus, the Church of Sinai, Greece and Bulgaria, the Old Catholics under the Bishop of Utrecht and the National Churches of Poland, Georgia, Albania, Finland, Esthonia, Latvia, Lithuania, and Czechoslovakia.

from the churchyard by an iron fence; behind, facing the track and St. Mary's Church of the Byzantine Rite on the knoll above, stands the priest's home, a prosperous city house set down in the country with a banner over the front door announcing in Slovak the day's festivity. The congregation is gathering but most of them stay on the church steps or go to the manse where the bishop's procession is forming.

Inside the cool church the air is heavy with incense, spicy and very sweet, the light richly colored, filtered through red and blue stained glass. At the front the high altar is separated from the nave by the *Ikonostás* or Image Screen, a solid wall richly decorated with three rows of small religious paintings, three pairs on a side, the Old Testament prophets on top, the apostles in the middle, and incidents in the life of Christ at the bottom, with a picture of the Son as Judge of Judges and "The Last Supper" high up in the center over the entrance to the high altar.

Three arched doorways open through the *Ikonostás,* the one to the left gives a glimpse of the credence table set on an angle against the rear wall of the church next to the priest's robing-room. The leaves of the wide middle door, the *Tzárskiya Vratá,** sometimes called the Paradise or Holy Doors, are closed concealing the high altar, their gilded surfaces resplendent with colorful round medallions. Fastened to each doorjamb part way to the floor is a small exquisite *ikona,* the Birth-giver and the Holy Child to the left, the Son in young manhood to the right. Through the third doorway on the far right the altar boys are visible getting ready for the ceremony, the outside door opening and closing as they go back and forth from the manse running errands.

The middle aisle is wider than in Western churches. In it a few steps in front of the oval platform, the *Amvón* or *tribune,* that extends forward toward the congregation from the Image Screen, stands a low table backed by a metal standard with a row of cream-colored candles. A framed *ikona* lies upon the table, the top edge propped up a little, with a round shiny loaf of Russian bread on one side of it, a basket of salt on the other. Close by stands a shining brass cross on a standard with a pink satin ribbon ornamented with red rosettes wrapped around it fastened at the tips of the main crossbar and upright beam.

To the far left by the *Ikonostás* stands the shrine of the Blessed Mother, the Virgin of Povcanska, with a kneeling bench in front of it facing the *ikona* under an arched canopy of white net over soft blue, the side curtains held back by crimson ribbons, invisibly lighted from above by concealed electric bulbs, from below by a bank of winking candles of wax and olive

---

* So called because through them at Communion (Divine Liturgy) the King of Glory comes to feed his Faithful. No woman may pass beyond them to the sanctity of the altar at any time.

oil which, being pure substances, are the only kind the Church considers worthy to honor Holy Things. They cost a great deal, used in the profusion required by the Orthodox ritual. For an ordinary service in a small church like Holy Trinity the candles cost about $20 but at a special ceremony like the robing of the bishop they will run to at least $150, at Easter more than $180.

The *ikona* is Holy Trinity's most prized possession, brought from Czechoslovakia at a cost of several thousand dollars raised among men who work hard for their money. The painting is in the flat, slightly out of perspective Byzantine style, in palest gold—almost like silver, with faint lines tracing a High Russian mantle and crown with a heart superimposed in high relief, and at the bottom, etched in gold, are the domes of the European church of which Holy Trinity is a replica. The face of the Madonna makes the formalized background come alive—long, delicately colored, and intelligent, caught in an instant of vivid awareness, eyes full of friendly light, and a gentle word about to be spoken.

The shrine to the far right, balancing the *ikona* of Holy Mary of Povcanska, holds a conventional painting of the Crucifixion similarly canopied and draped. In front of each shrine at right angles to the pews and facing the oval dais in front of the Paradise Doors stand the *Kliros,* single raised seats with kneeling benches and high tilted book-rests for two choirs. The congregation of Holy Trinity, however, prefers to do its own singing so the benches are used only for occasional guests.

In front of the choir stall on "the Epistle side" of the church a small table holds a stout three-branched candlestick all in wax, beautifully decorated in deep aqua, rose, and gold, the stem by which it will be carried of wax like the rest, the weight of the thick branches supported by a narrow piece of wood bound across them by a thin waxed rope. At certain points in the service a layman will hold it, facing the dais.

The main body of the temple, which corresponds to the nave in Western churches, is half filled with pews and unpadded kneeling benches, leaving a wide space at the back under the balcony empty except for a chair and table for keeping records and counting out candles. The Russian Church officially recognizes only two attitudes as suitable for divine worship, standing or kneeling. There are parts of the service where it is permissible to sit briefly but only as a concession to weakness. Four oblong velvet banners on carrying staffs, symbolic of Christ's victorious battle with Evil, stand among the pews, ornamented with holy pictures. In a small bay to the right, facing the side door in the left wall, a wooden frame like a narrow canopy bed holds a soft pallet, covered with a white drapery edged with lace, that will become Christ's tomb at Easter.

Worshippers arriving go first to the ikona table in the center aisle to kiss the picture before taking their places, the men on the right, the women on the left. Some of the old women kiss the bread as well.

As the time nears for the coming of the bishop the priest directs the congregation to go to meet him. They leave, taking the banners with them, while he remains behind in the empty church facing the main door in his elegant chasuble of white brocade embroidered with gold, carrying the bread and salt from the ikona table.

Meanwhile the congregation and visiting priests, headed by a cross-bearer and banner-carriers, approach along the side of the church from the manse bringing the bishop—a frail, elderly man, not very tall, with a pointed beard, his head covered by a square-topped black biretta with black monastic drapery hanging down in back. He wears a flowing mantle of dark silk that envelops him completely, symbolic of the rigorous discipline, submission, and piety of the monastic life, with squares of black velvet at neck and foot on either side of the front-opening representing the Tables of the Law, and bands of lighter contrasting ribbon stitched around the robe horizontally representing the *Istóctchniki* or fountains, emblematic of the streams of teaching that issue from his mouth. Around his neck hangs the Panagía, a heavy gold medallion with a holy image.

In the vestibule by the front door the procession halts for the offering of bread and salt; then the parish priest and visiting clergy escort the bishop up the aisle and over the *Amvón* to the high altar, first pausing for him to kiss the small ikoni on either side of the Holy Doors.

Within, the sanctuary is gorgeous with color, the white lilies in the center of the altar flanked by massed bouquets in pink, purple, and red dahlias and asters, the crosses bound about the tips with pink scarves, and on the Fair Linen, the *Sratchítza,* spread over the rose brocade altar cloth that reaches to the floor, is a big golden book with glossy raised medallions.

A good many of the young people climb to the balcony, leaving a place in the middle front by the railing for the cantor with his big song-book; the overflow congregation stands below in the open space behind the pews. Some of the older men look startlingly like Stalin, ruddy and heavy with sandy hair and waxed mustaches; the younger ones would be indistinguishable in a group of Americans anywhere, more fair than dark, but with all the gradations in between. It is the same with the women. Some of the old ones with heavily lined faces, their hair pulled out of sight under *babuskas,* look like Central European peasants; but the middle-aged are conservatively dressed American housewives. A few young girls of exceptional beauty stand out from the worshippers in the pews: a tall girl with brown hair softly waved, slender and pale in a slim black dress and high black hat, a double string of small pearls around her smooth throat, and a gold-edged prayer book in white gloved hands; a blonde girl with gold-tinted skin, built like the goddess of liberty, slow-moving and preoccupied, with somber blue eyes, well turned out in green crepe; a gray-eyed seventeen-year-old in a smart tailored suit, her lustrous corn-yellow hair spilling out around a flame-colored pill-box. Because this is a Russian Orthodox Church a visitor would set them all down as Russians; actually there are only two Russian families; the rest are Ruthenians, Czech, Slovak, and Serb.

The preliminary services at the altar over, the bishop returns with the priests to the center aisle where attendants seat him on a backless velvet stool and bring a table piled with vestments of satin and brocade. Then those acting as deacons remove the striped mantle, cowl, pectoral holy image, and outer cassock, and the robing begins, commencing with a cream-colored under-vestment. Instead of a chasuble a bishop wears a Dalmatic, a robe that slips on over the head inspired by Christ's seamless garment, with a wide stole that hangs down in front and behind over the other vestments. At the last he receives the mitre, a high silver crown ornamented with tiny raised circular paintings.

When the bishop is vested, attendants bring two candlesticks from the sanctuary—the *Trikíri* with three narrow tapers, the *Dikíri* with two that lean toward each other—and he bestows a blessing with them in cross form to the East, West, South, and North while the people sing "Preserve O Lord our Master and Bishop. For Many years, O Master." Altar boys carry a big red velvet book and the Golden Book from the altar to be blessed, and the newly robed bishop puts a pointed black biretta, a *skufyá,* on the head of the parish priest signifying that he honors him with a raise in rank for good work done in his parish. Finally in all his elegance he goes back through the Paradise Doors to the altar.

As the service proceeds the voice of the priest and cantor alternate, chanting, the notes true and clear but with a peculiar penetrating quality. Then the worshippers begin to sing and a wide wave of sound crashes forward from the nave, very deep and tall, with all the interstices filled with medial tones, while floating to the surface now and then is a harsh soprano that loses itself the next instant like a shingle tossed up in a rolling flood only to plunge underneath again. They sing like a congregation of Crusaders, those Fayette County coal miners, sure of their way without looking at their prayer books through the service that goes on hour after hour. In the Russian Church the whole Psalter is gone through once a week, during the Great Fast (Lent), twice a week.

There is great informality throughout the service but no irreverence. The parish priest pauses to send the altar boys on errands; during the first sermon by one of the visiting priests, he hears confessions at the shrine in front of the ikona of the Virgin of Povcanska, with the person confessing kneeling with a square of velvet over her head; then he takes up the collection in person, accompanied by a parishioner with tablet and pencil to write down how much each member gives. Later the list will be displayed in the entry by the front steps. A visitor attending Eastern Orthodox service for the first time will do well not to put all the money he intends to give in the collection plate the first time it comes around because there will be another offering taken later, with a chance to contribute to the repair-fund box after that. In the heat the candles gutter and tip and the big one in the tall brass candlestick that stands by the left door of the *Ikonostás* leans sideways so dangerously that it has to be removed. One man is kept busy going about with a candlebox refilling the holders.

Then a hush falls as the bishop comes forward to address his people. He speaks in Slovak but ends with a brief prayer in English for the American Government and its people, calling upon the worshippers to remember how good God has been to spare them the terrible chastisement that has fallen on other peoples, and at the change of language an American marvels that the voice that sounds so hearty in Slovak becomes so gentle in English.

The Eucharist follows, first for the Bishop and priests at the high altar, then for those who have just been to confession, kneeling in a little group on the edge of the *Amvón*. As they leave each dips a drink with a silver cup from a bowl of wine held by an altar boy. Now it is the congregation's turn. Even the babies in arms are communicated, all but one who pulls back in her mother's arms and refuses. The bishop and two of the priests try to persuade her, talking to her reassuringly, but she will not.

There will be a banquet and dancing in the social hall following the service, the parish priest announces, but "Take what is offered in moderation. I don't want to hear you men running around saying *'polinki! polinki!'* all the time!" But first the congregation must escort the bishop three times around the church and come in for his blessing.

As the procession forms in the center aisle the resident priest looks over the children nearest at hand and chooses a little girl in a starched white dress and pigtails to carry the ikona from the table in the aisle. She receives it reverently as he lays it on her outstretched arms and marches proudly off, eyes wide and happy. The worshippers file out again with the cross and banners and holy water in a bowl for the bishop in his shining crown to sprinkle on his spiritual children, an altar boy carrying the Golden Book at a convenient angle for the bishop to read from as they pause by the church doors, twice at the front, once at the side, as they march around in the sunshine.

Back in the church again the congregation receives the bishop's blessing as they file past him, standing at the front of the dais, and scatter down the hill to the Parish Hall to begin the feasting, the speechmaking, the drinking of toasts, the dancing of czardas and polkas that will outlast the day.

The service has lasted three hours, much of which the congregation has been standing. The second hour seems long to a stranger but after that he is so drugged with music, color, and fragrance from the swinging censer honoring the holy images, that he is out of the world.

Up on the knoll on the opposite side of the road a group of Byzantine Rite parishioners watch the festivities of their neighbor church, so much like their own. They robe their bishop every year at the pilgrimage to Mount St. Macrina with splendid ceremony that pilgrims come from all over the country to see. In Central Europe feeling used to run high between the two groups and a man might be buried several times, first by one church and then by the other before the opposing factions among the relatives were satisfied. Fortunately the bitterness has not carried over to America. In the Coke Region as in other places there may be dissension within a church but on the whole relations between them are amicable.

After the Russian Revolution the Russian Church of America was compelled to set up its own organization when title to its properties was threatened by a schismatic group in Russia, called the Renovated Church, who declared that capitalism was a mortal sin and that a battle with capitalism was holy for Christians. When Metropolitan Sergius of Russia demanded that the American clergy pledge loyalty to the Soviet Government, the American Russians refused, whereupon the Soviet-dominated Russian Church broke off spiritual relations without permitting the American Church to plead its case. In the contention that followed, the American party selected the Most Reverend Theophilus, Archbishop of San Francisco and Metropolitan, as Primate. Moscow ignored the action and sent Metropolitan Benjámin as Patriarchal Exarch of North America and the Aleutian Islands.

He was able to get possession of the Cathedral in New York but Primate Theophilus had the allegiance of nearly all of the clergy. Under his leadership it has been the policy of the American branch of the Church not to touch upon political questions.

The re-establishment of the Russian Church under the tolerance of the Soviet Government brought overtures of reconciliation from the Moscow Patriarchate early in 1945. The American branch received them coldly, calling attention to the fact that only 13 of the clergy recognized Moscow's Metropolitan Benjámin to 358 who accept the authority of the Primate Theophilus and suggesting that the American church did not care for the terms in which the Ukase was couched, characteristic of the high-handed methods of an autocratic bureaucracy.

"The American Church is flourishing in an atmosphere of democratic freedom ..." said the American Primate. "It was no fault of the American Church that the Patriarchate laid a suspension on it because its clergy declined to give a pledge of loyalty to the Soviet power. It is an American church and an American church it must continue to be."

The visit of Archbishop Alexei Sergeyev of Yaroslav and Rostow, emissary of Patriarch Alexei of Moscow, who came to America later in the year to effect a reconciliation, brought about no change in the independent attitude of the American Church. At the December Council of the so-called dissident bishops of Canada and the United States, the American Church declined to make submission to Moscow or to resume relations unless the famous Ukase 94 which requires Russian Orthodox Churchmen to abstain from all political activity against the U.S.S.R. is repealed. Although Archbishop Alexei denied that the Moscow Patriarchate is dominated by the Soviet, the American bishops were not entirely satisfied and asked for a full report of the operation of the church in Russia to be submitted at the next biennial meeting in 1947.

Sitting in his office, the hard-working Czech pastor of an orthodox church in the Coke Region explains it thus:

"I should like to see the matter settled but that is a matter for the Sobor to decide. Meanwhile I have to take care of my people and build up my church. But this I know with great certainty: Metropolitan Sergius asked things that were impossible. My people are Rumanians, Serbs, Czechoslovaks, Syrians and Greeks, all mixed up together with just a few Russians, but they are all Americans now. They would not want a Russian to rule over them. Archbishop Theophilus is an American who knows our ways. Look at this!" He points to a single paragraph in English bedded in columns of Slavonic in a foreign-language newspaper from eastern Pennsylvania. "You see what we have promised to the American Government—so how could we promise loyalty to the Soviet?" The paragraph to which he points is the Oath of Allegiance that made him and most of his parishioners citizens.

"You and each of you do swear by Almighty God, the Searcher of all hearts, that you absolutely and entirely renounce and abjure all allegiance and fidelity to any foreign prince, potentate, state or sovereignty of whom or which you have heretofore been a subject . . . as you shall each answer to God at the last great day."

Over his head hangs a calendar with an American soldier and sailor clasping hands under an Amerian flag. On the opposite wall a banner proclaims GOD BLESS AMERICA. Looking at them and remembering the little service flags in the windows of the company houses down the road, some with five, seven, even nine stars, an American realizes that the slogans we mouth so glibly are a prayer and a loyal affirmation in the hearts of these newcomers.

CHAPTER XIV

WEDDED WIVES

THE CORDOS* HAVE LATELY BOUGHT COMPANY HOUSE No. 310-12 on the third row up the hill of the Columbia Mining Company's Grace No. 2 patch. Until last week it looked exactly like the other 112 double frame houses on the slope above the power house, each with a narrow front porch divided in the middle, set high off the ground because the hill slopes down so rapidly, five rooms on a side and a basement kitchen with a grape-arbor out back.

Pietro and Anita Cordo paid seven dollars a month for it for twenty years and didn't pay much attention to how it looked on the outside as long as it wasn't theirs. When the company painted one house it painted them all and that was all there was to it. Now that the Cordos own No. 310-12 they are giving it individuality with a covering of dark red composition siding painted to look like brick and ever so much richer than the plain ranks of green clapboards.

There are five of them at home now; Anita, widow of Pietro, who used to load coal at Grace No. 2, a fine big woman with a wide mouth, square white teeth and blue-black hair in a thick coil at the back of her head with little wisps of curls ravelling out at the neck line; her son Mike, a gangling seventeen-year-old, who goes to township high school and drives a truck when he gets home; Stella, a year younger, who looks as her mother used

---

* All names and identifying details have been changed purposely so that the characters and places in this chapter may not be interpreted as representing any actual persons and places, and any similarity is unintentional and accidental.

to before she got so heavy; Maria, twelve, with a sober, pointed face too small for her big eyes; and Grandma Savarita, Anita's mother, a short, dark-skinned woman, wiry and quick-moving, with fierce, black eyes and a good many wrinkles. Grandma Savarita came to America from Livorno when Anita, her first child, was a year old. She didn't want to leave her people but when her husband Enrico sent passage money for her, she came like a good wife. Lately she has learned a little English from Anita's children but living in the Grace patch she doesn't need it, and when Enrico was alive and she lived in town with her children growing up, they could do the talking for her.

Nowadays, as soon as the weather is fine, Grandma spends a good deal of time sitting on the front stoop in the sun or under the grape vine in the back yard, depending on the time of day; and whether her fingers are busy shelling peas, or sewing, or telling the beads of her rosary, her thoughts are mostly of Italy. It seems as though her life as she looks back over it was like a road that ran a while through sunshine and bright country and then dipped into a cloudy place full of smoke and strange ways and unfamiliar talk. She bears no resemblance to the black-eyed Elena Andaloro who became the wife of Enrico Savarita in 1902 back in Livorno.

They would probably have been there yet if it had not been for a regrettable occurrence that started off the marriage under the worst possible omen. The Andaloros considered Enrico a splendid match for their daughter. He had a good business of his own in cheese and oil tucked away among the warehouses of the Venezia Nova and was a handsome big fellow to boot, so tall that tiny Elena could have stood under his upraised arm. He was twenty-five to Elena's fourteen but that was as it should be. The only difficulty was that she had already signified a preference for young Vido Turbo; but Enrico knew nothing of this until he came out of the church with his bride on his arm. Just as they appeared under the archway, coming into the sunshine of the piazza, a shot cracked so close on Enrico's left that he involuntarily stepped sideways, bumping Elena; otherwise, when Vido Turbo fell forward with a bullet in his temple he would have landed directly on Enrico's polished wedding boots. Everything about the affair was unfortunate, but nobody seriously blamed the Andaloros for not waiting for Vido to grow up when they could marry the girl to a good, settled man making money every month down at the port with his barrels of oil and big brown cheeses.

Enrico was a kind man and in the months that followed he could see that although Elena was a dutiful wife, she would be happier if he put some distance between her and the mourning Turbos. A new start in a new country seemed like a solution. Enrico had heard of many men who went to America for just a few years and came back rich. His own uncle, Regolo Contadina, was doing well for himself in the produce business in New York. So Enrico wrote to ask how he would like to have his nephew come over to help him sell olive oil.

When the reply came it brought a new suggestion. Uncle Regolo could use his nephew's services, but not in New York. How would Enrico like to start a little store for him in Pennsylvania, near to New York as distances were in America, where he would not be beset by so many other merchants? Much coal was mined in this Pennsylvania and men who worked in it only a short time became wealthy. Great numbers of Italians were going into the mines. It was Uncle Regolo's idea that Enrico should go to the coal country and there provide the money-making Italians with oil and cheese and whatever delicacies the Americans did not have.

So Enrico took a boat for America which delivered him in New York in a July heat wave. He found the little mining town in the Coke Region recommended by Uncle Regolo even hotter and a good deal dirtier; after Livorno it had an unfinished look as though the citizens were soon going away. One could not blame them for that but while one chose to remain there was a chance to make a good deal of money. Enrico found store rents surprisingly high, even for a small building on a side street. There were, however, living quarters on the second floor and if they were a bit dark, what with the smoke cloud that never seemed to lift and the press of other buildings, there were gas lights to dispel the gloom and an indoor toilet the like of which Elena had never seen.

After Enrico sent for her she lingered at her parents' house long enough for the birth of Anita Maria. It was early February when she followed Enrico down the trolley steps on to the station platform in the black little town, shivering in the sharp wind that slid beneath the smoke cloud without parting it. It was only two o'clock in the afternoon but the streets were lighted as at night, every lamp a blurred ball of brilliance full of moving particles.

"It is only for a little while that we must stay here," encouraged Enrico, piloting her through a crowd of men in working clothes with coal on their faces and dinner pails in their hands. "In the summer it is much better with days in a row when you hardly smell the smoke, and all the year business is good."

The Savoritas did well in the Region. Although the time when they would be rich enough to leave remained always a receding point in the future, by 1910 Enrico owned a brick building which housed, beside the business bought from Uncle Regolo, a barbershop and a garage with three flats on top. People said that Enrico and Elena were the handsomest couple who ever came to town. Whenever the Sons of Italy had a parade Enrico was marshal and rode a white horse, and Elena, walking to Mass with the children, was a sight to see. There were five of them now, which was one reason that the date for the Savoritas' departure had to be postponed. After Anita came Primo and Regolo, a year apart; Carlotta followed, and then another son, Sebastian. Elena had the children's picture taken to send back to Livorno with Anita in a white albatross dress, her thick braids tied with satin hair-ribbons, seated in a wicker chair holding little Sebastian in the lace christening dress. Primo, Regolo, and Carlotta—curly-haired and black-eyed— stood in a bashful row beside her against a painted background of columns and draperies. The coming of each new baby was a great event and the children could hardly wait until it got there. Nineteen-twelve was a bad year in the district because a lot of men worked only part time but Domenico came that year and brightened things up for the Savoritas. Gloria was born in 1914, which wasn't very prosperous either, but Henry, named for Enrico, came on the rising tide of prosperity with the coal-drags growing longer and the smoke settling thicker every day.

Elena had gotten used to the smoke and the winter fogs, or maybe she was too busy to think about them. When pictures formed in her mind of the bright harbor in Livorno and the sun-mottled shade of Viale della Stazione she turned resolutely from them. Better to live a day at a time and not look back over the shoulder. Meantime there were the children to think of. When they wanted to eat too much *pasta* and too few vegetables, she grated raw carrots and mixed them in mashed potatoes; or she concocted extra appetizing salads with endive, capers, tomatoes, pickled egg-plant and basilico. How else but with green things, olive oil, and lots of milk to drink, did they hope to keep the handsome white teeth the Good God had given them? For general discipline she leaned heavily on proverbs. "Tell the truth next time, Carlotta. Lies have such short legs almost anybody can over-take them."

Anita Maria had a whole new outfit for Easter the year she was fourteen; new white kid shoes with silk stockings, faintly pink, a white crepe de Chine dress, and a white straw hat with a black velvet streamer hanging down the back. That was the day Pietro Cordo first noticed that the eldest Savorita girl was growing up and promised to be a beauty.

He asked Enrico for her that same week and got "No" for an answer. Anita a wife at fourteen? Not in America. But that wasn't the end of the matter. Pietro would wait a little, he urged. Perhaps until Anita was fifteen. Enrico was a polite man but finally he had to make it plain that he did not want Pietro for a son-in-law any time at all. Not that he had anything against Pietro, but what had he ever done but mine coal? Would he ever do anything else but mine coal? No. Had he any learning? Well, Anita was going to graduate from high school like the American girl she was, now that Enrico was a citizen. Then would be time enough to think of marrying; and didn't it stand to reason that Anita would want a husband with American schooling as good as she had?

Pietro's friends spoke for him after that. It would be a great pity if Enrico were to bring down on himself bad luck by offending a countryman who knew far more of the ways of America than he did. Suppose a great accident were to happen to his building so it tumbled down like a block of coal in a mine when the dynamite goes off? What would Enrico do then with so many children to support? Pietro asked for only one daughter and he would still have one left.

Finally Enrico talked with Elena about it and she asked Anita how she would like to be married. The girl said she would not like it at all; only that didn't end it. But, urged Elena, it had at one time seemed very sad when she had a husband chosen for her at just the same age, and look what a good man he turned out to be!

Everything changed at home. Anita knew that her father and mother were worried about something and that if she married Pietro Cordo, who seemed almost as old as her father, although her mother said he wasn't, it would make everything better. Elena embroidered the top hems of six linen sheets and bought a long linen tablecloth with chrysanthemums woven in it for Anita; she was even going to cut the lace off from the satin dress that she brought from Italy to trim the wedding nightgown, but Anita wouldn't let her.

While all these preparations were going on, Anita went to St. Thomas' every day to pray that the fear which had taken possession of her parents might pass away so that they would excuse her from becoming the wife of Pietro Cordo, but nothing happened. Pietro bought her a beautiful white satin wedding dress with slippers to match, a lace veil, and a bouquet; and when the appointed day came they were married.

Unexpectedly the wedding turned out to be a good deal of fun. Pietro looked his best in a new blue suit, his thick black hair cut short and wet down with pomade and his plump cheeks shaved so close there was only a faint blue shadow of beard. He had supplied five barrels of beer and forty quarts of whiskey for the wedding guests gathered in St. Thomas' Hall so the celebration lasted past the time when the men should have been going into the pits with their dinner-buckets. But before that Pierto took Anita back to the room at the Savaritas' with a new bed and dresser that was to be theirs now that Pietro was going to live with them.

That was the end of the beautiful evening. Pietro at once began being a husband and Anita, who had had no sex instruction whatever, was at first terrified and then furious.

Anita came out of the experience with a hearty dislike of Pietro but under

Elena's watchful eye she treated him civilly enough. Elena reasoned that a husband was a husband whether one wanted him or not, and it was up to Anita to make him a good wife. The girl's hardness of heart was something that came from living in a country where women married today and quit tomorrow. Pietro was a good steady worker who wasn't bad to drink or run after women—and a wonder it was with Anita treating him the way she did.

"Everyone has a cross to bear," she told Anita, watching her send Pietro off to the mine with eyes as hard and shiny as pieces of coal. "I tremble to think of what is in store for you if you were to die full of hate and bad temper." And she told her about Uncle Nicola whom she would be like if she didn't watch out. He had things all his own way and look at the end he came to.

He lived on an olive plantation near Livorno but his father, who was Grandfather Andaloro, had enough money to hire people to run the oil presses so Nicola didn't have to work. No, he was free to play the violin and ride horseback to Livorno or any place else he wanted to go. Pretty soon he was writing music and then he began to go around with fine people in the city. It would have been better to put Nicola at the presses though, because he grew wild and willful and there was a mean streak in him that got worse. When he was composing, if the notes wouldn't come right, sometimes he'd throw down his violin and go out where they were making oil and crack the whip over the horses to make them run so the press would creak around at a great rate. His mother didn't like the way he was mean to animals, taking out his bad temper on them, but she couldn't do anything with him.

Nicola had a rupture that he always had to watch but every time the bunch came out he'd put it back quickly and be all right. Once though he had to go into Livorno with a score and the bunch came out when he was with a lot of important people so he couldn't get a chance to take care of it right away. Finally he excused himself, got his horse and rode home as fast as he could to fix the bunch only he'd waited too long and it wouldn't go back inside.

They called the doctor and the priest but it was too late because he had a stricture. There was nothing the doctor could do but tell him to make his peace with God because he was going to die. Then Nicola began to rage and curse his fate because he wasn't ready to die so young with all the world before him; and when the priest anointed him he tore off his shirt with the Holy Oil on it and threw it on the floor. And that's the way he died, bitter and cursing God. Everybody knew his soul was lost but Grandma Andaloro and she wouldn't give up but that he'd be forgiven because he was in great provocation with pain.

But then, when he'd been buried a little while, all at once the oil-press began to creak in the middle of the night and there was the crack of the whip and Uncle Nicola's voice yelling at the horses the same as ever. Everybody came running out of the tenant houses and his mother came out to see who had taken the horses out in the middle of the night. The workmen swore, every one of them, that they hadn't gone near the press; but there were the horses hitched to it, wet with sweat and shivering. So then Grandmother Andaloro knew that Nicola was damned because his spirit came back, bad and cruel, cracking the whip, and she grieved about it until it killed her.

Anita listened and worried about the state of her soul until she heard Pietro's step on the back porch. Then her heart froze up as hard as ever. She eased her conscience by cooking him extra good meals in the daytime or at night, according to which shift he was on, and there was no man on the gang with better food in his lunch bucket. No children blessed their union.

"Hot and cold iron won't weld," said Elena.

The winter of the great influenza epidemic all the Savoritas were down with it. Her mother and Sebastian were having pneumonia, and Anita hardly realized how sick her father was until he was dead. It was incredible that a big hearty man could go like that and a frail little thing like her mother, worn out with childbearing, should recover. She was too sick to be told about Enrico but as she lay in bed she dreamed that she spread white roses on the ground. Water swelled out of the grass to drown them but she snatched them up and shook the petals dry. Then she laid them down again but they swam in water as before. When Anita told her at last that her father was dead, her mother remembered her dream and asked if he were buried in wet ground.

"The earth was frozen," said Anita. "I don't know. So many were dying and being buried."

As soon as Eleana could go out of doors, Anita took her to the cemetery and, sure enough, Enrico lay in marshy ground where water filled in the tracks of their shoes. Elena wanted to have him moved right away but there was a rule that a body could not be disinterred for a year, so all that time she worried nights, lying in her warm bed, thinking of Enrico rotting in the water.

Elena was thirty years old, unable to speak English, with eight children living at home. Pietro knew nothing of storekeeping and Anita would have to take charge until Primo was old enough.

In 1922 the whole Region foamed up with a mine war. Pietro was working at the Advance Mine close to town and he wanted to go on working but pickets came in from the River so that every time the shift changed, it meant a fight. The company put on a lot of extra deputies to help the men get through the gates, so Pietro said he was going to work if he could get there.

Anita filled his bucket as usual and watched him start down the road with the others in his shift. Then she joined a crowd of women trailing their men to see how they made out.The trouble had already started when they reached the row of houses facing the mine entrance. Anita climbed on a high porch just in time to see a strange woman snatch Pietro's bucket and throw it against the fence so that her good cheese and meat and bread went rolling into the dirt. She jumped into the fray, snatched the woman by the bun of hair on the back of her head and pulled her off her feet. Around her men and women struggled and the air was full of dust and then stinging smoke that made water run out of her eyes. Once there was gunfire. When it was over two men lay in the road but neither was Pietro. He was safe inside with blood running down his face. It was two days before he came out and Anita worried about what he was having to eat, where he was sleeping, and how he was going to get through the mob. When he came up the road at last, she was so glad to see him that he seemed like somebody else, a fine brave man who looked like Pietro but had nothing to do with the unwelcome husband she had grown used to.

Things went very well with the Cordos after that. Their first child came the next summer and they named him Alessandro after Pietro's father back in Calabria. Arturo came next and that was the year they left the crowded Savorita flat to move to house 310 at the Grace patch where Pietro got a job after the Advance pits were exhausted.

Primo, Anita's eldest brother, was old enough to run the store business now, what there was left of it. When the hard times came the company stores carried their people, but Primo and her mother didn't have money enough to do that so customers were scarce. Pietro had no work for months at a time and although Anita and her mother filled a discarded candy case with embroidered pillow slips and camisoles, there were no takers.

Then Pietro fixed up a hotbed with a couple of windows from an abandoned engine house and began raising tomato and cabbage plants to sell in town. Presently their whole back yard was full of makeshift flats and every spring after that the Cordos sold plants. When the strike of 1933 shut the mines down tight, Pietro used the time to build a greenhouse with Primo on the back of the store lot and did so well with it that they bought a truck to deliver plants in the summer and haul coal in the winter.

Then World War II came and the army took all of Anita's brothers but Primo, so the Savorita store had four stars in the window. And after a while the draft board got Anita's Alessandro and Arturo, so there was only Pietro to get off to the mine in the morning. Nearly every day she and her mother went to the church to light candles for them and for Regolo, Sebastian, Dominic—who had had a chance to see his relatives when he was in Livorno, and Henry, who was missing in Germany.

In the spring of 1945 Anita was out in the back yard counting out an order of tomato plants from the old flats Pietro had made so long ago when suddenly it seemed as though a veil came between her and the little green stems so she couldn't see to count, and suddenly everything was very sad. She was going on with her work, folding cornucopias of wet newspaper, when she saw Mike Ganowich, the pit boss, and Tony Scorza, the machine operator, coming around the house. Anita didn't have to more than look at their faces before she began to cry.

Pietro had been caught in a slate fall with two others. There had been no warning so they hadn't had a chance to jump clear. One minute everything was all right and the next there were tons of stone and coal on top of them. Then Anita knew that the sadness had come when the slate fell.

The dead-wagon brought Pietro home in the early evening with the lid on the casket and the undertaker said it was better to leave it on.

Grandma Savorita came to live with Anita after that. Primo had a wife to cook for him and wait on customers in the store so she wasn't needed any more and she felt more at home with Anita. The new daughter-in-law would turn out to be a good wife, no doubt, but she had had an American raising and didn't understand Old Country ways.

The settlement that came to Anita for Pietro's death put her in a position to buy the house and pay for the remodeling with something left over for a nest egg. And the local took up a collection that bought a fine tombstone for Pietro with a little oval picture of him set into the front under glass. Anita often goes out to the cemetery to tell her beads beside it, kneeling among the geraniums.

She is a woman of property now with the other half of the house to rent, a half-interest in the greenhouse, and an undivided share in the store, well able to afford the new steel cabinet-sink and three-piece maroon velvet living-room suite. Grandma Savorita is anxious for fear such good fortune may bring bad luck through the envious eyes of the less fortunate and she was careful to put salt back of the cushions before any of the neighbors saw the new furniture. Alec and Art will hardly know the place when they come back from the Pacific.

II

The bus terminal at eight o'clock on a winter morning with soot sifting through the frozen fog to the snow of the empty platform. Across the street in the Krczma a dim bulb has been left on all night but the other little bars have not begun to light up yet. Inside the station the crowd has surged up against the glass swinging-doors, waiting for the driver to come out of the dispatcher's office so they can make a dash across the windy trolley tracks for seats in the bus parked in the shadow beyond the lights. People are always shouldering their way through, letting in blasts of cold air; trolleys jingle in, spilling out people, siphoning more away, but the permanent residue of sitters in the seats never seems to thin out; sometimes there are substitutions but never an exodus.

Just now there are no miners in sight because the day shift is underground and the night men have gone home to bed. A sleepy, blonde woman, middle-aged and heavy, with spectacles and a kinky permanent, stares into space in the Canteen Corner. The magazine-stand is deserted except for a dark girl making sandwiches at the far end. All the seats are full of people with luggage piled around their feet; women in slacks and high-heeled galoshes with tin dinner buckets in their hands and scarves over their heads; heavily rouged sixteen-year-olds, bareheaded and barelegged with bobby socks and enormous mittens, schoolbooks hugged under their arms; old men with waxed mustaches and coal dust in the wrinkles under their chins; young mothers, harassed and cross, trying to cope with paper sacks of diapers, milk bottles, animal crackers, and assorted babies.

The sulky red-haired girl by the dispatcher's office with the two-year-old stumbling about in front of her and another baby on its way is Orpha Zuric, born Orpha Sanders, who used to work in Reba's Quick Lunch. She is on her way out to see her people. They live in a small slate-colored house on the single street of Beech Bottom, a country village that antedates the coke business but now owes its continued existence to the trade that filters down from the mine patch on the hill behind it. Her father works as black-smith for the coal company when the mine is running; when it is not, he farms the three acres behind his house that end in an unfenced bluff above a strip coal operation.

There was nothing for Orpha to do if she stayed home but keep track of the younger children and help with the housework. She was eighteen, pretty in an unobtrusive way, and reasonably intelligent. What she wanted was money of her own to buy clothes and a place to wear them. So she came up to town and fried hamburgers and hot dogs at Reba's whose barbecue sauce could be smelled two doors down the street.

In the evening she went to the movies with Mary Cornish, the dishwasher, or did her laundry in the two rooms she shared with Mary on the third floor above the restaurant; or maybe they went for a walk around and around the three brightly lighted streets of the downtown section.

That was how she met Mike Zuric. She and Mary stopped in at the Blue

Dove, which was mostly confectionery with dusty cloth geraniums on a trellis partitioning off a dance floor and a juke-box; it also sold beer, oranges, salad oil, bologna, and bread. The girls were sitting on stools at the counter when Mike came in carrying a miner's round dinner bucket with a black leather coat on his arm and his miner's cap pushed back so a triangle of light brown curly hair stood up in front of the visor.

Orpha looked long at Mike. His eyes were blue above wide cheekbones; he had big shoulders like Johnny Weissmuller only he wasn't so tall; and the smears of coal dirt on his face made his even teeth flash white and handsome. When he saw the girls staring at him he went over to the juke-box and put in three nickels. Then he bought a roll of *kolbasy* to take home. Orpha, who had grown up just across the field from a mine patch, instantly set him down as some kind of a Slovak even though he looked exactly like an American. That was the way with so many of those Russians and Hungarians and Czechs. They were dark and fair, sandy, blue-eyed and black-eyed in all the ways Americans were, and a person couldn't tell they were foreign just to look at them.

The two girls had three beers at the Blue Dove that evening, one they bought for themselves and two that Mike got for them. When he left to wait for his trolley, they went with him as far as the corner. After that Mike took to dropping in at Reba's whenever he got to town in the daytime and Orpha went out with him pretty nearly every night in the week when he worked the day shift. Then with Mike's number liable to come up any time in the draft, they decided one night all of a sudden, when they were sitting in the Blue Dove over a couple of beers listening to their favorite song on the juke-box, that they might as well be married right then so as to enjoy what time they had.

Mike was a Greek Catholic but Orpha wasn't anything in particular, although her parents were vaguely Methodist, so it would have meant a lot of red tape to get a priest to perform the ceremony. Instead they rang the door bell at the Methodist parsonage and it was all over in no time.

Orpha kept on working because there was no knowing when the army would get Mike, and when Mary Cornish offered to move out so they could have the two rooms upstairs to themselves, it seemed like a good idea. Mike thought they ought to move out to White Horse No. 3 where he worked but Orpha had lived in the country long enough. Before they were married he had stayed with his mother at White Horse No. 2 up the river but the coal was nearly mined out and the company was taking out the last of it from No. 3 on the other side of town through connecting headings. Mike's job as repairman took him to the lower mine; so just coming in to town was not as much of a trip as he had been making having to go on through to the No. 2 patch. Of course, if they went down to the lower mine he would not have to travel at all; but Mike all to herself in town, was one thing, reasoned Orpha, Mike with a flock of his Czech friends would be something else.

Her one visit to his mother's house was not much of a success although the place was fixed up a lot nicer inside than she thought it would be. Mrs. Zuric had a taupe davenport and two easy chairs—one red and one blue—that were so big they practically filled the little living room so there was hardly space to set the shiny radio cabinet. The rug was handsome, almost like an Oriental, and the curtains as clean as could be. Just the same the room looked sort of plain with no knicknacks lying around and nothing on the walls but a Holy Picture and an oval enlargement in a convex frame of Stefan Zuric, Mike's father, who was burned up in the explosion at Mary Ann Mine. The kitchen had an electric refrigerator and a new white enamel table-top gas range with a vase of red paper flowers sitting on the lid with a doily under it. Steve's mother did her cooking down cellar on a big old coal range and she ate down there too. The walls were whitewashed and it was fixed up handy but Orpha thought it was too dark. Mike said his mother liked it because it was cool in the summer and warm in the winter.

Mike's two unmarried brothers were already in the army, so now that Mike was gone his mother could live with some of the other children, but she didn't want to. She was used to the house and thought she would buy it when the company began selling the patch.

The old woman could not talk much English. The only things she said that Orpha could make out were: "You like cup coffee?" and "O. K." When she and Mike talked Slovak, Orpha felt left out although they sent her reassuring glances and he kept breaking off to translate for her.

"You'll get on to it," he told her. "I'll teach you."

"Sure," said Orpha, without conviction.

Mike's brother's wife Marta came from next door to see her new sister-in-law but, although she could talk English as well as anybody and had graduated from the township high school, she made Orpha feel more uncomfortable than his mother did. She had the feeling that Marta didn't think she and Mike were really married because they hadn't been to the priest. And sure enough, when he suggested a little later on that they get married over again, just to make the folks feel better, she got it out of him that it was Marta's idea.

Orpha had never thought much about religion one way or the other, but now when she found herself married to a Czechoslovak who kept a Crucifix on the wall she remembered almost every day that she was a Protestant. Neither of them went to church. Mike liked to stay out late on Saturday night and Sunday morning was his one chance to catch up on sleep. After she wouldn't go through a second marriage ceremony he dropped the subject, but they had two Christmases. He went to her family's holiday dinner and brought presents on December 25 but then he wanted to celebrate all over again on January 8. In the end she rode out home on the trolley for the week end and he went to White Horse to be with his folks. If she had gone along it would have meant being swamped with a lot of talk she couldn't understand or falling back on Marta whom she didn't like.

They had lived together seven months when Mike had to go in the army. Orpha wasn't too sorry to see him go, although she cried a good deal at the Greyhound Terminal while they were waiting for the driver to open the door so that he could get on the bus. His mother was there too, looking like the Old Country woman she was, with her fat ankles and black cotton stockings, a black crocheted scarf tied over her head. When Mike swung up the steps and appeared a minute later standing in the crowd in the aisle, leaning over a couple of people to tap on the window and wave, his mother's face puckered up and turned spotted in big red patches so she looked like an old wrinkled baby crying. Orpha felt sorry for her and for herself and Mike, so she had her come across the street to Reba's and plied her with coffee and hamburgers and pie. She didn't work there any more because she was expecting a baby soon but she was keeping the rooms upstairs so as to be near the doctor until she went to the hospital. Mike's mother would have liked to have her come home with her, but Orpha didn't want to.

The government paid for her confinement, and when she came out with Mike's son in a white enameled clothesbasket she put him in the back seat of her father's car and went home for a couple of weeks.

She named the baby George, after her father. When she wrote Mike about it, he said that was fine and they could give him Stefan for a middle name for his father. Orpha agreed that it was all right with her, only they'd spell it Stephen.

She had no idea of staying in the country very long. Her father's house was full enough already; there was no place to go, nothing to see, and lots to do. She liked being on her own and the allowance she got from Mike was enough to pay for the two rooms she rented on the third floor of a boardinghouse back in town. It was run by a Mrs. Altana Andrewson, a harried woman of fifty who never got a chance to change out of a house dress.

The house was a rambling brick affair of twenty-five rooms with turrets and stained-glass windows, a crystal chandelier in the front room—now furnished with two iron beds and three boarders; and a basement with a bowling alley, an oversized antique furnace that didn't work very well, and a mountainous pile of ashes that reached almost to the under side of the kitchen floor. It had belonged to a coal baron of the opulent days of the Coke Region and people still called it the Hurst Place even though the bank had owned it for years, and its wide hall and oak stairway smelled perpetually of stew.

It was admirably suited to Mrs. Andrewson's purposes because trailer people could park in the front yard; the music room, library, and drawing-room took care of seven regular boarders and the wide reception hall made an imposing living room without calling for much outlay. The marble fire-place, panelled doors, and carved stairway practically furnished it. There were bathrooms all over and the five bedrooms over the kitchen wing that had formerly been the servants' quarters took care of transients. As for the bedrooms on the second floor of the main wing, they were so big she had made them into housekeeping rooms with a gas plate handy to the marble washbasins.

There were no water connections on the third floor, which was intended for an attic and used as one until Mr. Andrewson cut off three rooms with sheet rock. When Orpha Zuric came to occupy two of them, the other was furnished with a bed, a pair of shoes, and an alarm clock belonging to a brakeman who slept in it when night overtook him on this end of the line. Otherwise Orpha had the top floor to herself with a fine view of the mountains, the single tall building of downtown, and the parallelogram of smoke above the bank of coke ovens across the field.

In the summer it was roasting hot up there but then Orpha took Georgie down under the trees in his basket or sat talking with the other regulars of the place or maybe watched an occasional car of tourists load in or out. Sometimes while the baby took his nap she helped Mrs. Andrewson with the housework and got something off on her rent. Or she did the evening dishes in return for Mrs. Andrewson's listening for Georgie while she went to the movies with Mary Cornish.

When the Zurics out at White Horse heard that Mike's wife was living in town they thought she must have fallen out with her folks, and the old lady sent Marta in to tell her she could come out and stay with her if she wanted to. She had plenty of room with the children married and gone and she had a good garden.

Orpha had gotten in the habit of staying downstairs most of the time. Mrs. Andrewson had furnished her apartment with good enough things: a pedestal table painted ivory and blue, two rockers, a wicker settee, and a hot-plate with a one-burner movable oven, besides a double bed and dresser. Still, it was lonesome upstairs and she'd rather be doing odd jobs than tending baby.

The day that Marta called, Orpha was embarrassed that she didn't have the apartment in better shape. Her living room was picked up and she had the bed made but there was a mop-pail of dishwater standing by her door with lettuce leaves floating in it. Orpha had intended to carry it to the second floor and empty it when she brought up water to do her lunch dishes but she hadn't gotten around to it, and she saw Marta looking at the sticky plate and the half-glass of milk with a fly in it on the shelf where she kept her eatables. When her sister-in-law delivered her invitation, Orpha told her she thought she'd stay where she was but she'd be out to see them all some day soon and bring Georgie.

Mike came home unexpectedly not long after and they had four days together before the M.P.'s picked him up. He'd come off A.W.O.L. because he couldn't wait to see the baby. Every time he had a leave to come something had happened so that it was cancelled, and he came without one. He hardly went downtown and, except for going out to his mother's when his brother came for him in his car, he stayed with her all the time, wiped dishes, and put up a clothes-line between the apple trees so the diapers wouldn't drip on their heads in the living room.

Then Mack Fulmer from out in Beech Bottom called her on the telephone and when Mrs. Andrewson hollered up the stairway, Mike thought it was him she wanted and took the call. He had a fit about it although Orpha made it perfectly clear that it didn't mean a thing. She'd grown up with Mack, who lived across the road, and when he came to town sometimes her mother sent her eggs and butter by him. Well, if it made so much difference, maybe she had gone to the movies with him a couple of times, but what was that?

The M.P.'s came while the unpleasantness was at its height. He hadn't been able to get back since and when she wrote she was going to have another baby he kept on being jealous and suspicious.

Then one day a Red Cross woman called to ask some questions about Mike. He wasn't making a good soldier any more the way he was at first and the army wanted to know if there were anything in his past life to account for it. Had he always been unsocial? Orpha said she thought he liked men a lot, maybe better than he did women. He'd sit up till daylight talking and drinking with them. Everybody seemed to know him around the works and he was always joshing and cutting up. No, he didn't drink to excess, but he was just like most foreign fellows on Saturday nights and pay-days, or when his local called him out, or maybe if he'd get with a bunch of his friends up at the Slovak Club he'd get pretty tight. It didn't do to quarrel with him about it, either. Once when she did he wouldn't get up and go to work the next day. Her father was no drinking man and she didn't like it around the house but Mike always kept a jug of wine in the kitchen cabinet and if anybody came in he'd get a bottle of whiskey. She'd tried making cocoa or coffee for his friends but they didn't seem to care for it.

"Was your home life happy?" pursued the visitor, scribbling in a form.

A tear or two ran through Orpha's fingers. Well, yes and no. Of course

Mike was foreign but her folks were nice to him. It just seemed they couldn't get off on the right foot. Mike was fine when he didn't get with his folks, who didn't like her.

Had there been any shock, any depressing memory from his childhood that could be affecting him now?

Orpha couldn't say. She'd only known him a little while before they were married. Of course his mother would know, but it wouldn't do any good to go out to White Horse to ask her because she couldn't speak English.

When the Red Cross worker stopped at the company store at White Horse No. 2 to inquire for Mrs. Steve Zuric, mother of Private Michael Zuric, the grocer advised her to stop at John Zuric's next door in House No. 101 first and she'd probably be able to get Mike's sister-in-law to go with her to translate.

So when the stranger came up the steps under the grapevine on the elder Mrs. Zuric's back porch she had Marta in tow. The old woman made no attempt to use her scanty English, sitting stolid and quiet while Marta relayed the stranger's questions. It was a cold day and Mike's mother wore an old black sweater, men's shoes, and an ancient boudoir cap that had belonged to one of the girls. Behind the defensive blankness she reserved for foreigners she wondered what the caller meant about Mike's being "emotionally unstable." Marta explained it as "upset in his mind" and Mrs. Zuric told herself that if he was, it was no wonder, what with his wife running out with other men and going to have another baby that belonged to somebody else. She hadn't fooled Mike any, you bet. The other fellow called her up on the telephone when Mike was at home and it didn't take him long to catch on. It was a shame to all of them having Mike's wife talked about in the patch. Nick Turnish had seen her with an American fellow in a beer joint or a show or some such place and of course he told it all over. But then Americans were always marrying and breaking up, so maybe it was just as well she and Mike had never been to the priest. You couldn't tell that to a stranger though.

Now if he'd just have married a nice Slovak girl and had a wedding they could have pretty nearly furnished with the wedding presents and had some money extra from the dancing with the bride. Mike could have had as good a wedding as Paul and Marta's that had lasted three days. The men liked to see if they could throw down their money hard enough to break the plates set out for the dancing-with-the bride collection and they certainly broke them for Marta. And they kept the gypsies primed up fine by throwing dollars on the drum every time the music started to die down. The women had a good time too, sitting out in the wash-house singing. If Mike had married one of his own kind the girl would be there with her now, keeping her company so she wouldn't be afraid in the house alone, and she could have helped take care of the baby. She hated to think of Mike's son up in somebody's attic, maybe without a soul to think about him while his mother was running the street.

"She wants to know was Mike a bad one to drink?" translated Marta. Tears suddenly rolled down Mrs. Zuric's cheeks.

"Naa. Good boy," she said in English. "Saturday night drink sometimes maybe. Then he puts his arms around my neck," the old woman gestured expressively. "And he says, 'Mama, I love you,' and I tell him, 'Go on with you. I fix coffee. Pretty quick you sleep it off.' "

Orpha and Mike may be able to work it out if he doesn't have to stay away too long, particularly if the new baby is lucky enough to look like the Zurics.

CHAPTER XV

COKE PATCH—NEW STYLE

THE OLDER COMPANY PATCHES LOOK MUCH AS THEY used to but they are not the same. For one thing visiting delivery wagons or the travelling public no longer have to ask permission to enter. Many of the inhabitants work at a considerable distance from their homes and go back and forth in cars, stopping to trade where they can make their money go the furthest. The company stores compete in an open market nowadays but through large-scale buying they have been able to hold their own successfully with other chain groups. At the end of 1945 the Union Supply Company of Frick Coke Company, the largest chain, with ninety-five general retail stores and fourteen service stations, was planning to spend between $300,000 and $400,000 for improvement in western Pennsylvania, with a separate expansion program for West Virginia and Alabama. A visitor to the Coke Region will be surprised to see the large stocks of expensive, nationally-known merchandise carried by the patch stores until he realizes that probably no other district in the United States has a larger per capita buying power. Union Supply's Continental No. 1 store in Uniontown offers everything from fancy groceries to Mexican bubble glass, fur coats, and electrical equipment, and draws trade from people who have no business connection with the parent company. Buying in large quantities, they can compete with other chain stores.

When an employee buys at the company store on credit his store bill is deducted from his pay check, and if the ease of charging items tempts him to spend too much so that his check is smaller than he thought it would be, there is complaint; but he depends heavily on the same easy credit to tide him through hard times.

In the old days the patches were policed too much; since the dissolution of the coal police they have not been regulated enough. Usually each patch has a squire who will take charge in small altercations, or perhaps both parties to a dispute may allow the superintendent or a local man of good standing in the community to arbitrate, but, for law enforcement and policing a company town must depend upon the state troopers. That would be all right if there were not so many patches.

Suppose a company town is five miles out in the country. In the evening there is nothing for the growing boys to do but loaf in front of the company store or the beer joint or whatever becomes the favorite hangout. When there is something going on at the schoolhouse, or if there is a movie within reach, they flock to it, but there is no organized program to depend on. A trip to Uniontown, Connellsville, or Brownsville is likely to mean a clubby evening in a pool hall.

What happens is that a lot of bored boys, who feel that the law is a long way off, get into trouble. Perhaps it becomes a game to bait a teacher who has fallen out of favor or to play hide-and-seek with a truant officer or a state cop. Minor property damage that started as a joke becomes more serious as the offenders discover that they can get away with it; or somebody borrows a car for the gang to go for a ride without the owner's permission, planning to get it back before it can be counted stealing, and maybe wrecks it instead. The weakening of the family tie is also a persistent factor in creating conditions that produce lawless children as evidenced by the high percentage of boys on parole who come from broken homes.

Overcrowding is another potent factor. Not long ago when the authorities had to deal with three children from the same family, investigation showed that they came from a home where twelve people lived in four rooms. The thirty-four-year-old mother was trying to keep track of ten children with the eleventh on the way.

The over-all total of delinquency complaints, adding city to country, would be enough to keep a staff of investigators busy; but Fayette County, facing the day when its dwindling coal supply will mean less taxes from coal companies and less money to spend on public service, could not finance the added personnel even if trained workers were available. The salaries for men social workers before the war were too low to attract many into the field and the armed services drained it still further. Fayette County has had to cope with its delinquency problem with one probation officer for boys and one for girls. In the face of the staggering amount of work, it was as much as an officer could do to take care of the interviewing and necessary routine without trying to do home investigations.

The obvious way out of the dilemma was for the probation officer to deal out justice as far as possible and let the rest go. William Gladden, the Fayette County probation officer for boys, was not satisfied to do that. The more he studied the problem, the more he became convinced that the depredations of children are not a state nor a county matter but a local problem which must be dealt with in the home community. It was his idea that delinquent boys should be put under the care of men from their own neighborhoods who liked and understood boys, who would act, not only as advisors to help them through the particular trouble that brought them to his office, but also to find out what was wrong in the individual case so as to prevent further offenses.

Probation Officer Gladden took his problem and a solution which he thought might meet it to the service organizations and found two Exchange Club members, E. E. Burgess and T. A. Barnett, who were willing to help to put it in practice. The Fayette County Delinquency Clinics, as finally worked out under Gladden's direction, are unique in the field, particularly adapted to counties with a large nonurban population, and so successful that J. Edgar Hoover has sent Federal Bureau of Investigation men to observe the work.

Six delinquency clinics serve the county with thirty-five volunteer probation officers, each unit serving in its home district, all bound together in the Fayette County Youth Council, which sponsors a semi-annual forum for discussion of common problems. The personnel of the local board of the clinic is apt to be a pretty good cross section of the community life. Uniontown's delinquency clinic, which meets in St. Peter's Parish House, is often called upon to handle both city and country cases because the city is ringed with patches and handy to the county probation office and county court. The volunteers include the rector of the church, an insurance agent, a clothing merchant, lumber operator, school teacher, postal worker, newspaper circulation manager, and an auto and electrical supply merchant. One member left to become senior psychologist at the Western State Penitentiary.

When a boy is arrested he may be turned over to his local clinic immediately, if his offense is a serious one, because the county has no provision for the detention of youthful ·offenders separate from adults, and wherever possible the probation office prefers to parole minors in experienced custody. In this event, the clinic to which the boy is assigned will discover as much as possible of the causes behind the act, make a report to the officer who has the disposition of the case, and send one of its members to the hearing to give any needed help. If the case comes up in Juvenile Court, it will be heard in the judge's chambers to necessitate as little publicity as possible, but records will be made of the proceeding. Often the hearing will be held informally in Probationer Gladden's office and, to save the boy's being hampered by a criminal record later on, no official record will be made.

If the boy is turned over to one of the delinquency clinics, it is on a voluntary basis. They have no legal status but work under the direction of the probation officer and the court. Boys may be assigned to the clinics by the schools, by the police, or by the probation officer and will remain in their custody as long as they report according to their parole. If a boy fails to put in an appearance, the clinic reports to his parents that the child must go back to Mr. Gladden, sends a copy of the letter to the county probationer's office, and drops the case. It is to the boy's advantage to keep his case with his home clinic because the members work with him as friends and cajolers, not as punishers. If the clinic abandons the business, he must deal directly with the court and the county probation office.

While a boy is on parole to a clinic he will be required to keep a diary that gives his supervisors a check on his particular failing. If he is a night owl, his diary will list the time he came home every night in the week and must be countersigned by his parents. If his family had to put up money to make restitution for his misdemeanor, the boy is expected to work to reimburse them and the diary will record his payments, countersigned by them. A boy who is in trouble for truancy will keep a record of his school attendance and have it vouched for by the principal.

The delinquency clinics have been in operation long enough now, about three years, so that personnel of offenders and types of offenses begin to fall into a pattern. To date, no Jewish child and only two Boy Scouts have had to appear before clinics. Only one-third of the delinquents attend any church. At least 60 percent of the white offenders are aggressive types, leaders in their groups, not of the calibre usually classed by psychologists as incipient delinquents; conversely, the colored boys in trouble are apt to be shy and backward.

Delinquency runs higher in the patches than in the cities. Twenty-five of the last thirty boys to report to the Uniontown clinic were from the surrounding district. City offenders are more apt to be brought in for petty thievery (stealing bicycles, etc.), out-of-town boys, for truancy and the destruction of private property. In cases where restitution must be made it seldom runs above 50 percent, sometimes because the parents are unable to pay; sometimes because they are not willing to cooperate. One of the most common offenses among the fifteen-to-seventeen-year-old group is the operation of a motor vehicle without the owner's permission.

Usually juvenile crimes are group affairs with three, five, or more called to appear. A recent case of housebreaking and property destruction involved twelve children, eight of foreign extraction, four of American. The house of a well-to-do professional man in one of the Region towns had been left furnished with drawn blinds without a caretaker while the owner went in the army. The boys effected an entrance and used it for a clubhouse over a considerable period until someone opened the house to do an errand for the owner. The rooms were in wild disorder, mattresses slit, bureau drawers emptied, mantles and furniture chopped with a hatchet, plaster dug out of the walls, the owner's private business files broken open and the papers strewn and torn, and valuable instruments tampered with. The boys had everything ready to burn the house to destroy the evidence of the damage when they were caught.

The clinics staffed with citizen volunteers have been highly successful in keeping their charges from becoming repeat offenders. "What we need most now is parental education," says Emil Burgess who has worked with the program from the beginning. "The parents who need the Parent-Teacher Association, etc., are the ones who don't go. Bad children, the ones we can't do anything with who have to be sent away, come from bad homes. Once I didn't believe that but now I do. After San Francisco tried compulsory education of the parents of delinquents, no matter who they were, lawyer, banker or ditch-digger, with lectures and motion pictures over a period of six months, there were *no* repeat offenders."

The probation office and the volunteer workers have been learning something of what their program can do for the community as a whole as the public shows an increased awareness of the need to take the responsibility locally for the background that breeds child crimes. In effect, the county has begun thinking of itself as country-and-city instead of over-emphasizing the urban angle where the law enforcement centers. Those interested in the program are working toward a goal of cooperation of all county agencies dealing with children to eliminate the present confusion where a single family may be getting help from several departments at once, each unaware of the other's activities.

As to the present performance of the clinic system worked out by Mr. Gladden, Chief of Police A. W. Davis of Uniontown says that since the clinics began to operate and the city-sponsored recreational program went into effect, delinquency is at the lowest point it has ever been.

When a strike is on, the patches are comparatively peaceful places of late. It has been several years since they have seen pitched battles, tear gas, and firing back and forth between company houses. The men still use a refusal to work or to let others work as a weapon, but the game is played out in labor conferences far from the coal country.

The real test of union strength came in the spring of 1945 when the miners had to choose between backing their union leaders in a strike for a new contract in war time, which would mean stirring up the public's patriotic wrath, or following the recommendations of the War Labor Board.

In World War I they had lean pickings because they held to their agreement with the Administration; and they had a long hungry stretch afterward. Now it looked as though the same thing might happen again. Prices
were going up while their wages remained at a point fixed by the contract,
with the government unwilling to let them have more money even though
the operators would give it to them. When they heard about the big checks
paid by shipyards and airplane factories for work a woman could do, they
felt that they were not getting enough out of dangerous jobs just as necessary to the war effort.

Anyone who saw the service flags in the windows of the company houses,
some with seven, eight, and nine stars, could not doubt the miners' basic
patriotism, but the miners felt they were not getting a square deal. The tie-up
of production in the spring of 1943 to enforce a better wage contract, allowing portal-to-portal pay, ended in the seizure of the mines by the U.S.
Government with a few bewildered miners carted off to jail. Just the same
they got certain concessions.

Then Lewis called them out again. The miners were unhappy, acutely
conscious of public opinion, pulled two ways by conflicting loyalties, but
while they damned the union with one breath, they worried for fear they
would lose it with the next. The result of the patriotic economic conflict was
confusion, but the Union lines held.

As a veteran reporter of Region labor troubles saw it: *

"Back in the good old days ... in 1933 and 1934, and as late as 1941 and
1943, the miners pulled no punches. When they decided it was time for
action on some question in dispute, the boys pulled up at a mine entrance,
jumped out of their cars and yelled: 'All right, you guys! There's a strike
on here and we're pickets and there ain't nobody goin' through this picket
line.' ...

"There would be arguments. A few fist fights. Even a little gun-play, perhaps. Everybody accepted these as part of the situation, even the five-year
olds. . . . Not so today. In this most recent mine trouble this is what we
heard. 'This mine won't work today. It's a work-stoppage—not a strike.
We're observers—not pickets.'

"It was terribly confusing until, boiled down, it was discovered that it
was just a case of dressing up an old situation in brand new 1945 clothes
patterned by the War Labor Board.

"Here's what I mean: On March 28th, the Government asked the miners
to vote on the strike or work issue. The War Labor Board supervised the
voting procedure under a provision of the Smith-Connally Anti-Strike Act.
But the ballots didn't come right out and ask: 'Do you want to work or

* Ruth Love, "Miner and Family Have Many Worries," *Morning Herald*, Thursday,
April 19, 1945.

strike?' Nope. It had to be something fancy such as: 'Do you wish to permit an interruption of War Production in War Time as a result of this dispute?' The miners themselves had a good word to describe the phrasing. It was 'tricky.' So the miners voted and on the day of the voting, the Capital War Labor Board permitted each Union Local to have two men at the voting place. These union representatives were described as 'observers.' And that's how 'observers' were born.

"From that time on the picture changed. The dispute was the same old question between management and labor. The miners were the same old friendly kidding boys of the pre-war days. But a strike now was dressed up and introduced to the public as a 'work-stoppage.' The pickets became 'observers.' And the miners and the reporter had to be re-educated.

"The War Labor Board's March 28th vote started an epidemic. Every other night or so, the boys voted. Even that wouldn't have been so bad if the votes had been decisive. But one night the miners at a certain place would vote to go back to work. The next morning they all stayed home. At the next meeting, they would vote to stay home and believe it or not, they'd be out the next morning, buckets, lamps and all. Even that wouldn't have been so bad if they had worked. But no sireee!... They would swing into their parking places on the mine property, grab their buckets and start for the lamp shanty. The lights would flare up on their pit helmets.

" 'This is it,' I'd think. 'They're going in this time.'

"But with one minute to go the lights would begin to go out; the miners would pick up their buckets; one by one the cars would begin disappearing from the parking lot.

"And when I asked what the trouble was, they'd say: 'Work stoppage!' ...

"None of it made sense. Leisenring mines which had worked through the 1943 strike were the first to call a strike—pardon me, a work-stoppage—this time. Several Leisenring miners were blamed, deserving or not, with picketing the Colonials—only they were 'observers' and not pickets.

"The Colonials, always the hell-raising trouble points in the good old days, were really mad at having to stop work....

"The Clyde mines of Republic Steel went to work this time without giving anybody an argument. And that was one for the books. Back in the Thirties the Clyde miners usually went on strike first and then got up early in the mornings to see that nobody else worked.

"In 1941 at Edenborn when I was caught in a cross-fire with a host of pickets, it was the Greene County boys who jumped from cars and yelled: 'We're the river rats from Bobtown and there ain't nobody gonna work here today. We're takin' over.' And they did. But this time they worked and didn't seem to give two hoots and a holler what anyone else did.

"One District No. 5 Union Official pleaded one afternoon with the Vesta miners to be patriotic and American and go back to work—and the very next morning this same Union Official indirectly pulled the hard-working Clyde miners out on strike to further organization of the bosses.

"Even the miners began to get confused. They wanted a contract. They understood that. But their efforts to get a contract became so involved that they had to keep saying 'contract' over and over so they wouldn't lose sight of their objective.

"As one of the miners told me: 'We sure were gettin' the votin' fever. Once we voted to go back, then we stayed out; then we voted to stay out and the next day we went back. Darned if I can figger that business out yet. I was comin' and goin' until it got so bad I couldn't figure what direction I was headed—whether it was toward home or into the mine.'

"The miners' wives would get up in the middle of the night and pack their husband's buckets and see them off to the mine. Before they were warm again in bed, the husbands were back in the house and ready to sleep until noon. In one hour the husbands would say goodbye and hello.

"I got to thinking I'd take an option on a nice quiet room in the Union-town Hospital where there is sanity and order and things are just what they seem."

The following sample conversations recorded on a survey conducted by the *Morning Herald* of Uniontown give a representative idea of the miners' reaction to striking in war time. The interviews were held at random in different parts of the Region.

"What difference does it make what I think?" asked an inside miner at Republic Steel.* "To the public I'm gonna be one of them damn traitors if a strike is called. 'Cause if a strike does come, I'll probably be sitting around on my fanny waiting for the big boys to say when I can go back again. I have two sons in there fighting. The big boys ain't going to think of that if they decide to call a strike. And what can I do? You tell me—and no matter what you say, I'll still be one of them ——— miners who went on strike during war time because I didn't have no other choice."

"It sure looks bad right now," says an inside miner at one of the Frick plants. "Lewis always runs off at the mouth and then we have to back him up. Some day we'll be running off at the mouth and telling Lewis. But that won't be until we have another depression and we get desperate so we have nerve enough to say what we think. But right now, if a strike comes, I'll be out."

"No matter what comes, we gotta go with the union," declared an outside man at one of the captive mines. "Everybody says the union man should work, not strike. Nobody say the company should sign a contract so we got

* Ruth Love, "Opposed to Coal Strike—Miners Have Their Own Idea," *Morning Herald*, March 3, 1945.

our union for sure. Always the miners get hell. Why? Just because we want our rights. We got union now. We gonna keep union.

"Here's my envelope for last pay. It got 14 days at $6 for $84. Then here I get $6.52 extra added for premium cause I work one hour and 15 minutes extra in day and company pay for an hour and 37 minutes. Now here they take out of my pay $1 for union dues, this for my insurance, this for my old age pension, this for my income tax. See what I got left. Around $85. Now here I show you my wages last year (the annual statement given by the company to each employee). It says I got $2,200 odd dollars and I pay this much for taxes which they check off. Divide this by 12 and you see I got average of over $180 a month last year. I pay store bill and rent and electric and water like everybody else. I give $3 to Salvation Army, $12 to Church, about $8 to Red Cross and $4 to U.S.O. and every month they take out for my War Bonds. Watta I got left? No more'n you or anybody else—and I work damn sight harder.

"Besides, five, six union men die last year. Every time union man die in my local, I gotta pay $1. Every time union man's wife die, I pay 50 cents. Everytime union man's kid die, I pay 25 cents. That ain't check-off. The union collects that and turns it over to family where death is. And on payday, when there is death, the union man is right there to get that before you get home with your pay. And if you don't pay. Zing. They put you on blacklist.

"Oh yeah! We got union, all right. We got blacklist too. But nobody want it. So we pay. Mebbe everything ain't just right. But we gotta have union."

"I don't want to strike," worried an inside miner at Frick. "To lay down my tools and walk out now will make me feel like a damn traitor. I got boys over there and I'm just as much worried about them as the guy who runs a store or works in an office is worried about his sons.

"But until some of the evils of this union business is ironed out and the union is operated to serve the man instead of the man serving the union, the miners are going to go on being the little guys caught in the squeeze plays.

"Miners know what they used to have here in the coal fields. So they built up something they have to have—a union. But the union is controlling us. Down deep in under all this arguing and striking is the fear of every miner that he might lose this union unless John L. Lewis gets something down on paper to prove it's gonna last. Me and a lot of miners don't feel we ought to strike right now. But the big shots who can't seem to be able to do their jobs without us, may call us out.

"I don't mean there'll be a general strike-call. Even John L. Lewis ain't that brave. The word will just go round—like 'no work tomorrow'—and what do you suppose will happen? Well, I'll tell you. Every man that carries a union card will just stay home. He'll sit there cursing John L. Lewis and Billy Hynes and the guys in the headquarters office. But he'll sit. Why? Because if he don't, the very union he helped to build will blacklist him. And every miner is scared of that. That's the biggest weapon they got over us. Let a guy be blacklisted—lose his union card—and there's not a damn person can do anything about it. He's just out. That's where the union runs us.

"Some of us ain't never known anything but working in coal mines. We wouldn't know where to turn if we lost out in the coal mines. That's why we keep our mouths shut even when we don't want to strike and have to. You see, every local has a couple of stooges who report everything on everyone. Why they'd even stool on their own mothers to feel important turning stuff in to headquarters. These stool pigeons carry anything they can—and just imagine how they'd run to report a miner who talked against Lewis and a strike. And them stool pigeons are our own members too, not company men. They're trying to get in good with headquarters.

"Yep. The union is a good thing. But the day is gonna come when the men will have to do something about running the union instead of having it run them. Till then, I guess we'll strike when the word comes—and hope the public won't damn us too much. We got boys in there, too."

In the autumn of 1946, following the victory in the spring strike, Lewis' prestige was at its peak with the miners until the November walkout got them in legal trouble with the government and brought them no gains. They hated to lay off just before the holidays but they obeyed orders; production began hitching to a stop even before the dead line. A miner walking along the road with his bucket toward the pit answered, when asked if he were going to work: "I don't know. It depends on what the boys want to do." The women made the best of it but they had plenty to say about it and it wasn't flattering to the labor boss.

"We can't depend on John L. Lewis to help us," said one housewife, worrying about the bills of last spring that weren't paid yet with new bills adding to them. "I hope the day will come when miners will be able to work with or without Lewis' approval. I'm tired of debts that pile up every time he calls the men out. I'm going to pray for God to end this strike."

The company stores hereabouts extended credit to miners regardless of the work stoppage but although some families had turkey for Thanksgiving, most of the women bought cautiously.

What are the people in the crowded patches going to do when there are no jobs for the union leaders to regulate? The day is close and we have already had a taste of what it will be like when the coal is gone. The river and Greene County mines can absorb only part of the labor available even if they run to capacity. Unless there is to be a repetition of the scenes of the thin thirties, somebody has to figure out what to do with the thousands of people whose means of earning a living has been whisked away, leaving them no other trade to turn to, without savings or enough land to grow what they eat.

At the moment the only agency at grips with the problem is the American Friends Service Committee. They don't pretend to know the answer but from a long period of acquaintance with coal country problems they have worked out a project that may serve as a model for later large-scale development. Meanwhile the experiment grows quietly with no more flourish than a tomato plant preparing to bear fruit.

The Friends began feeding hungry school children in communities where need seemed most desperate as far back as 1922; by 1931 the situation had become so serious that at President Hoover's request they undertook an ambitious program of child-feeding under the United States Children's Bureau; in addition they gave out clothing and did what they could for babies and nursing mothers.

The better they came to know the coal country the more they realized that, necessary as the emergency relief was, the real problem that must be met was how to prevent a similar collapse when the next boom cycle rolled around. They didn't have a theory yet but the facts were there from which a workable solution could be formulated. To initiate a down-to-earth study of the situation the Friends Service Committee sent two workers, Errol Peckham and Levinius K. Painter, to live in the Coke Region under the same conditions as the miners to try to find what those facts were.

Peckham took his family to Republic; Painter went to the mine patch at Brier Hill. By 1937 the Philadelphia office was armed with enough information to be sure that the solution lay along the line of teaching the miners other skills to fall back on when a shifting coal demand put them on part-time. It might probably mean large-scale resettlement when the coal fields were exhausted, but so large a project would require government financing. The thing the Quakers wanted to do was to relocate a group of miners to plots of land big enough for gardening and chicken-raising that would supply food to get along on in a pinch and at the same time be near enough to the mines so the men could go to their familiar jobs when the mines were in operation.

So they bought a two-hundred acre farm in the midst of the thickly settled Klondike Region where the homesteaders would be near the ovens and coal galleries of Thompson No. 2, Filbert, Buffington, Gates, Ronco, Tower Hill No. 2, and Isabella. David Day, a specialist in community management, came to take charge of the settlement, building program, farm work, and homestead organization; Mr. Peckham moved over from Republic, where he had been fostering interest in gardens, to take charge of the case work. The gabled brick farmhouse with its long double parlor facing the road housed the staff and became the community center.

First they chose forty or fifty key people—miners, labor union leaders, mine operators, doctors, lawyers, teachers, and ministers to act as an interpretation committee so that the district in which the homestead settlement was about to be launched would understand what they were trying to do. Some of the steel companies and local industries helped with money to launch the experiment. From the first it attracted wide interest.

"We have on all occasions commended the character of work upon which your Committee is engaged in this field for several years past, so far as we are acquainted with it," said Myron C. Taylor, chairman of the Board of the United States Steel Corporation at the time the project was being started, "and we believe that the proposed experiment will be well worth the making. I earnestly hope that from it some plan of far-reaching importance will be evolved."

Herbert Hoover, who had had a part in securing the American Friends Service Committee to initiate the work of rehabilitation in the coal areas, Andrew Mellon, Thomas S. Baker, president emeritus of Carnegie Institute of Technology, A. E. Holbrook, dean of the Schools of Mining and Engineering of the University of Pittsburgh, Ernest T. Weir, president of National Steel, and Governor George H. Earle endorsed the project and were watching it closely.

"The problem of whole communities desolated by the obsolescence of an industry upon which they have depended is beginning to become a familiar phenomenon in the United States," wrote Newton D. Baker. "Exhausted mineral veins and the discontinuance of local units of industries make it necessary either to remove the population in order that it may follow its vocation elsewhere, or to provide new means of livelihood. The complications of this problem are many and the solution of it varies, of course, with the local conditions. I am delighted to know that the American Friends Service Committee has undertaken to make a concerted attack upon the problem. From this sort of voluntary activity, the length and breadth of the problem can be learned and experiments with solutions undertaken which will have a high social value as well as minister in a humanitarian way to many stricken people."

It was one activity in which capital and labor could join without friction.

"I have learned with a great deal of pleasure of the intention of the American Friends Service Commitee to raise a fund with which to rehabilitate groups of stranded miners, victims of the machine age," wrote Thomas Kennedy, secretary-treasurer of the United Mine Workers of America. "This rehabilitation plan in my judgment is not only excellent, but timely. I highly endorse the contemplated plan and express the hope that it will be properly and adequately financed. I trust, too, that there shall be cooperation between all of those who are interested in the rehabilitation of the stranded groups of workers so that the foundation may be laid for a satisfactory solution of their most difficult problem."

When there began to be talk up and down the coke patches that the new people who had bought the Craft place proposed to break it up into fifty pieces, help people to build houses on them and then let them have land, house, and all the improvements for only a little more per month than they were paying to live in the patches, they didn't believe it. Men who hadn't worked for months told each other bitterly that they had enough trouble getting coffee, bread, and bologna for the children without worrying with gyp real estate promotions. Wasn't it just like the Americans, who acted so happy-go-lucky but were sharp when it came to business, to figure out something like that? The bitter laughter in the company settlements was so loud it took a brave miner to come to inquire what a man had to do to get one of the fine stone houses that were going to be built.

Nevertheless 250 applications came in and Errol Peckham looked up their references to sort out the best prospects. Nobody but miners, wholly or partially unemployed, were eligible and those who were chosen worked on probation for a while, laying water lines, building roads, clearing thorn brush out of the fields. The candidates finally selected were a fair representation of the nationalities who make up the Coke Region population, mostly Central Europeans, a few Latins, and four Negroes, the heads of families, with an average age from thirty-five to forty-five, and able to do the hard work entailed by housebuilding. They received their pay in credits of man-hours toward the outlay for their own farmsteads and no money changed hands in the transaction. If a man proved undesirable, he was paid off in money, however, and someone else took his place.

The success of the homestead settlement depended on the committee's ability to assemble industrious, responsible families who would live and work together well when the building program was over. The Quakers were taking a tremendous risk in guaranteeing to prospective homesteaders that they might withdraw and cash their equity if they decided they wanted to leave. If factional disagreements arose and there should be a wholesale withdrawal, it would swamp the fund that made the farmsteads possible. David Day used to lose sleep thinking about the chance they were taking, but there seemed no other way to convince the community that the Friends weren't trying to put over a deal.

After the prospective homesteader had passed his probationary period and a satisfactory physical examination, he entered into a simple contract with the Friends Service Committee outlining the rights and duties of each.

If he were working at the mines two or three days a week he reported to David Day for as much more time as he wanted to put in. The faster his man-hour record added up, the sooner he would have his home. More than half of the homesteaders were entirely unemployed so their labor credits mounted fast, especially if they had sons from sixteen to nineteen who would get three-fourths man-hour credits if they helped out. The homesteaders settled the problem themselves of whose house would be built first: those of the men who had put in the most time. Usually there were about ten houses in process of construction.

As it worked out, a completed house meant about 2,750 hours traded labor with 1,250 hours of the homesteader's own time added for the finishing.

When the crew reported to Day's office in the morning, he dispatched them to quarrying, plowing, mixing concrete, sawing lumber for forms or whatever was most pressing, and if the man didn't know the job he learned it. It was this very acquiring of new skills, farming, masonry, carpentry, road-building, grading, electric wiring that would give a man several strings to his bow. If coal mining slowed up, he need not be reduced to desperation next time.

It would have been easier for the management to let a man who had learned to install electric wiring keep on piling up man-hours as an electrician past the amount required for his homestead but that would have thrown the labor-credit system out of joint. Some men would be busy all the time on work that others should be permitted to do if they were to learn practical crafts while they built their homes. As a result the staff trained ten electricians and fifteen plumbers before the building program was finished.

The details of the hour-credit system developed as the work progressed. If a man worked in the quarry, his time was credited to the inventory account; later when he wanted stone for his house he had a credit there to get it with. If he worked on another homesteader's house, he had that much time coming for men to help him, trading even whatever the job to be done. Each settler kept his own time but when he worked on his own house he took no credit-hours for himself.

That first summer saw the biggest turnover among the homesteaders. One colored family fell by the wayside during their probation period but they had only accumulated fifty hours credit. Then two Italian families got to quarreling and dropped out. Two more homesteaders had a chance to take permanent jobs out of the district and withdrew before they moved to the settlement but that was practically the end of the change in personnel. There have been no voluntary withdrawals since the families moved to Penncraft; two have died and one was asked to leave.

The idea of temporary homes came from the workers themselves. Sometimes men on part-time work at the mines had three or four hours they could have used to advantage working on their own plots at Penncraft, but it took so much time going back and forth that they could not use odds and ends of days as they would after they moved to their new homes. If the Penncraft Community was going to have them build chicken coops later anyway, why couldn't they build them first and live in them while they built the permanent houses? The Service Committee was glad to encourage initiative among the homesteaders so fifty temporary houses went up in 1937-38. They proved so satisfactory that a good many of them are rented now when the first occupants have moved to their stone houses.

Meanwhile the staff was worrying about the question of laying stone for the permanent houses. They wanted to use the stone from their own quarry and from near-by abandoned coke ovens because the houses would be substantial and require little upkeep. But how, working with untrained crews of constantly shifting personnel, could they keep the walls plumb and level, especially when the amateur masons were working with weathered stone that broke in unexpected places? The Quaker leaders, Day and Peckham, struggling with the problem, were faced with four alternatives: they could call in outside stone masons for the work at a price the budget could not afford; they could go on with the present set-up and build walls that would probably fall down; they might abandon the idea of using stone; or possibly they could figure out a way of laying it that untrained men could do.

David Day, experimenting with the latter, finally devised a form system similar to one that had been used at the Brookwood Labor College in New York State. The basement walls were to be 16 inches thick; the first and second floors, 14 inches. He faced the stone against wooden forms to fit and backed it up with spall, poured in grout to stick them together and did the pointing up after the form was taken away. The result was a wall as true and handsome as though it had been laid in the traditional way.

At first the men worked in two gangs, one headed by an experienced mason foreman, the only cash man on the job, the other under a foreman homesteader. Later both sections worked without outside supervision. Using the form system the men were able to lay twenty inches around a house in a day and cut the cash cost of the basements from an estimated $140 to $60, about $210 on the whole building. The cost of the stone itself was only about $6 a house.

By turning a hay shed into a wood-working shop equipped with $500 worth of machinery, David Day cut the cost of individual houses another hundred dollars through giving the men a chance to make their own window frames and interior trim out of lumber bought in quantity. They saved another $61 per house by using extra narrow flooring. It took more time to lay it but it kept the budget down.

It would have cost three dollars a ton for sand but the householders made their own for fifty cents a ton out of the spalls from the stone, using a stone crusher and tractor picked up for a community outlay of $675. That saved another $187.50 per house.

Homesteaders had a choice of five fundamental house plans with plenty of leeway to satisfy individual needs. Some families wanted to use the downstairs bedroom for a dining room; more preferred to eat in the kitchen or a corner of the living room; fireplaces were not popular because the company houses had them. But whether he intended to use stoves, a furnace, or fireplaces, every man built his own chimney and even though it strained the budget, his house included a bathroom. Often there was a shower in the basement so the man coming in dirty from the mine could clean up before he went upstairs.

David Day and Earl Peckham were building their houses along with the others and when they offered suggestions in the community council, it was as homesteaders sharing the common lot of their Polish, German, Croatian, Bohemian, Negro, Italian, and Russian neighbors.

The finished houses cost about $2,000 apiece, including the land. One of the most attractive, that looks like a five thousand dollar property, cost its owner $1,720.11, plus $297.50 for the two-acre lot it sits on, the road that leads to it, and water connection. The men pay only a little more for their tidy stone homes and big gardens than they did for the patch houses—that is, $10.00 a month to retire the loan from the Friends Service Committee and $3.00 for taxes and insurance as against the usual rate of $7.50 for a company house with a strip of cinders for a garden and a johnny on the alley instead of a bathroom.

A little over two years elapsed from the digging of the first basement in August, 1937, to the time when the first family moved in in November, 1939; a year later twenty more homesteaders were in their houses, all fifty were ready by the summer of 1943.

The fifty homesteads use about ninety acres of the two hundred bought by the Service Committee; the staff operates the other hundred and ten as a commercial farm where the miners learn to care for stock, use modern machinery and do practical farming. The community tractor plows the homestead gardens at cost and a cooperative store sells the butter, milk, eggs, stock feed, and meat raised on the undivided land available to the community at wholesale prices. Thus until the O.P.A. regulations Penncraft people bought choice pork at prices from seven to ten cents less than it would cost in a market, milk at nine cents instead of fifteen and other things in proportion. The store started in a converted cowshed with a nest egg of $25; now it has a monthly turnover of $1,300 and handles stock feed, clothing, and groceries in addition to homegrown produce. It has moved to a modern stone building with a frozen-food locker plant big enough to take care of meat, poultry, and garden truck for the countryside on a rental basis. It averages about $25,000 worth of business and pays back in dividends approximately $1,400.

In 1939 the homesteaders contributed a thousand man-hours of labor toward the construction of a knitting mill to develop an extra source of cash income. It supplied training and employment to twenty-five men and women for three years when they needed it most but it was not always easy going to get the cooperative idea across. On one occasion the workers went on strike against themselves. Then the war brought the coal boom, the men went back to the mines and the government shut down on the source of raw material. The mill has been idle most of the time since. Nevertheless in 1945 the factory turned out 6,000 dozen sweaters that sold for $230,000. The sixty-five employees are able to live inexpensively at home besides averaging seventy-five cents an hour with free hospitalization, insurance, and $500 worth of life insurance thrown in. In addition the miners add to their incomes by raising small fruits, calves, and poultry.

Because Penncraft is an experiment, as soon as one problem is settled a new one comes up. Now that the building program is done the staff has to find a way to tie the community together with a common interest. Religion won't do it because their faiths are too diverse. The 40 percent who are Catholic, either Roman or Eastern, go to church more regularly than the Protestants, but their affiliations are outside the community. David Day says that while the families were building their homes they were all extroverts and community spirit flourished; afterward they were introverts, going their own way, splitting up into cliques along nationality lines just as they had in the patches. About the only common denominator is the labor union. The Boy Scouts languished for a while for want of leadership then began to flourish under their own momentum. The same thing has been true of the Young People's Council.

When gasoline rationing kept people home more, community interest picked up again. The Mothers' Club has been successful all along. It sponsors a Well-Baby Clinic at the Community Center in the farmhouse once a month and a Maternal Health Clinic by appointment. Then there is the vital Community Council with representatives of all the groups and the Board of Directors of the Cooperative Association. The shared responsibility and pride in the expanding cooperative store and locker plant make for added group solidarity.

A new development of the same type is under way on the Krepps Farm, adjoining Penncraft. The new project, looking forward to the time when mine work will be increasingly intermittent, is made up of sixteen 10-acre plots—large enough to feed a family if tilled carefully—that can be operated as pasture when the owner has another job. This summer a Quaker-sponsored work-camp at Penncraft brought twenty-two boys of high school age who dug the water line for the new development. By winter it was completed, a $10,000 job recently taken over for operation by a near-by water company. Three basements for new houses have been excavated. During the cold weather, homesteaders will be busy in the Krepps Farm barn, making cement blocks and dressing lumber so that building can move rapidly in the spring.

Recently three coal companies have been in conference with representatives of the American Friends Service Committee, asking advice from their experience for setting up the frameworks of similar self-help housing units.

"When you deal with top management," says A. Hurford Crosman of Friends Service, Incorporated, "you find men concerned with the treatment of their employees and what can be done for them. The point in question with them is how best to do it."

Last autumn Cleo Blackburn, the young superintendent of Flanner House, Negro rehabilitation center in Indianapolis, visited Penncraft with Paul Jewel, a chemical engineer, staff director of vocational training, and Fred Reeves of the American Friends Service Committee, who are planning a similar housing project for their district.

The Quakers are a religious society interested in demonstrating, not talking, Christianity. Their special concern is for areas where there is misery caused by people not having learned the art of living together, for districts in the wake of war and industrial tension areas. They do not try to undertake disaster work or projects that belong particularly to the Red Cross. The Penncraft project put the American Friends Service Committee temporarily in the real estate business. How well they have succeeded may be judged by the new tidy settlement of stone houses set down among the smoky patches of the Klondike and the fact that after a group of steel company officials with large coal holdings, who had contributed one third of the cost of the first project, visited the first completed housing unit, they offered to underwrite a proportional amount for the second.

CHAPTER XVI

OLD KING COAL

APRIL 1, 1946, THE TRADITIONAL MITCHELL DAY FOR THE miners, honoring the United Mine Workers' president under whom they won the eight-hour day, was the first to be celebrated since the war. And like so many other years, this Mitchell Day of 1946 was to usher in a new spring strike that was getting to be a pretty regular thing—like Easter and Memorial Day.

For a week the bars along Peter and Penn Streets in Uniontown had been courting favor with a display of placards announcing WE CONTRIBUTED TO THE U.M.W. APRIL FIRST FUND, while the local press pumped up enthusiasm.

The morning began warm and lowery with the sun dodging in and out of gray clouds that fluttered across the luminous April sky like fluffs of dust in a draft. By nine-thirty the patches had taken over the streets along the line of march and the only familiar faces downtown were those of the clerks behind the counters. Women with babies in arms and queues of children too young to march with school deputations lined Main Street five and six deep. Their men were down Gallatin Avenue with their locals getting ready to march. Spectators sat on handkerchiefs spread on sooty ledges of buildings and stood in the upstairs windows of the smoky brick Y.M.C.A., the furniture store on the corner, and the law offices overlooking the courthouse. It was a good-natured crowd ready to cheer anything, a pair of ponies arriving, the decorated truck of a river local, a miner in a cream-colored shako. Balloon venders circulated briefly but pin pricks and lighted cigarettes took such a heavy toll of their wares that they retired in disgust.

The parade began at ten o'clock, orderly and well spaced, each sector under the tutelage of a corps of sergeants. It began with a long column of shining automobiles; brightly uniformed high school bands with gay felt banners; high-stepping majorettes, with nodding plumes and glistening boots, whose coquetry would turn to the fixed smile of weary endurance before they had pranced their way around town; and the long files of miners, grouped in their locals, marching with eyes straight ahead like soldiers—miners in shirt sleeves and slacks, in business suits, miners in white hats, miners bareheaded, keeping time to the music with only an occasional straggler weaving uncertainly on the end of a line while the crowd ribbed him for starting his celebration too soon. They were all there above ground in the pale morning light, locals from LaBelle, Maxwell, Bridgeport, Isabella, Crucible, Kyle, Palmer, Mather, Taylor, the Clydes, Colonials, and Ronco, while photographers and press men from out of town jockeyed for position, and a man with a movie camera, strategically placed in an intersection, cranked steadily, surrounded by an admiring audience of children who had elbowed their way through the crowd.

Through an error in orders the line of march broke up on Beeson Avenue and swarmed in the welcoming bars and hot-dog stands while only a few of the faithful trudged on to Reagan's Field to hear Billy Hynes' speech. By that time the clouds had gotten the best of the intermittent sun and rain began to fall while the speakers at the field waited for the arrival of an audience.

Finally the district president began with what listeners he had, telling them what to expect in the days ahead. William J. Hynes has made a good president in District No. 4; he is respected by the operators, courteous, efficient, and sincere in routine union business, and a fiery orator on occasion, who tells the miners what they want to hear.

"While the miners are idle, you'll hear editorials criticising John L. Lewis; you'll see vicious cartoons showing Lewis as the head of a rattlesnake; you'll read all kinds of propaganda," he told them. "But remember this—the coal miners are Americans. They are loyal and patriotic, strong muscled, strong hearted and clearheaded.... And they're not going to be bulldozed by anybody.

"Royalty! Oh yes, you're going to hear a lot about royalty ... that ten cents-a-ton that John Lewis is asking to rebuild broken backs, to help men who lost arms and legs. The operators are alarmed about that. Royalties! Why Great God, everyone lives on royalties—the men who write books; the people who produce anything at all. And for years, in the Southern industries, 15 cents a ton was set aside to hire detectives, to bribe governments, to buy judges and elections, to take care of those industries. They used that royalty for a standing underground army in this country until Roosevelt was elected and broke that up.

"The history of coal mining in this country is as black on the pages of that history as the coal you mine. . . .

"And as far as Winchell, Gabriel Heatter and all the rest are concerned, if the nation had to wait for any coal they could produce, it would be a long cold wait. . . .

"But the men will stay at home to rest their weary bones until a contract is negotiated that will take care of them on hours, wages, welfare and safety.

"The United Mine Workers Union is more clear of Communism than any union in America. The United Mine Workers won't stand for Communism, Socialism or any other *ism* except Americanism.

"We are not antagonistic towards the owners of these mines here in our district. We have had good friendly relations with them. We have accomplished much together. But the men will stay home until a contract is signed that will give the coal miners justice.

"This whole nation has been on strike. But you'll hear more criticism just because the miners are out a few days than you ever heard in connection with the other strikes. Don't let it alarm you.

"We want an orderly stoppage of work. We won't need picketing—unless some scab wants to go to work. And we are organized. We'll let Walter Winchell produce the coal in the meantime. . . ."

A deluge of rain finally drowned out the speech so the other speakers had to content themselves with telling the newspaper reporters what they were going to have said.

As the day advanced there was a near riot in Peter Street but the police, veterans of other April Firsts, broke it up; two men seriously injured in street brawls went to the hospital; magistrates dealt out $12.25 fines right and left for unruly behavior; and by night there was quite a sizable congregation in the bull-pen in the big gray stone jail back of the courthouse, but no more than had been entertained there by the city in other years.

On the surface the strike had started off like a spring recess from school. The next day, the women of the patches did the washings they hadn't been able to do on Monday on account of the holiday, while the older men tinkered their cars, worked in the gardens, nailed wire on their chicken coops, and a few shamefacedly had to help with the housework. The young bloods rode around with their girls, went to the movies, or loitered on the porches of favorite beer joints. They had more enthusiasm for the strike than the older men, who had worried and fought their way through twelve work-stoppages, long and short, since World War I and had seen the union beaten in 1927 so thoroughly that their leaders told them to sign contracts with any companies they could. Not that anything like that was liable to happen with John L. Lewis running things down in Washington. He had the whip hand now and the operators had to beg him to tell them what kind of contract he wanted. But wasn't he getting just a little too high and mighty, tossing away an offer of an 18½ cents an hour increase, the same as the steel and auto workers got, that the miners could start enjoying right away, so he could get his hands on a big Welfare Fund to spend any way he wanted to? And wasn't Lewis running these strikes a little too close together? In the bars along the river and in the thickly populated rolling plain below the mountains, men with time hanging heavy on their hands talked it over.

"What do the miners care about a Welfare Fund?" asked a pessimist with his chair tipped back against his house wall, his eyes on the idle ovens in the hollow below where the smoke had all blown away.* "We'll never get any of that, anyway. Lewis and the rest of 'em will use it to buy elections and play politics. So I say to hell with the Welfare Fund. Most of the miners I talk to would take the 18½ cents the operators offer and let it go at that. That's the same raise the other industries got. And if Lewis wasn't playin' politics, he'd take it, too, and let us get back to work. Welfare Fund! Hell!"

A number of other miners, while voicing the same sentiments, thought that if a Welfare Fund could be established it might mean added advantages for the men in the pits.

Where state compensation was lacking or inadequate the Fund filled a real need and was a good talking point, but Coke Region miners were lukewarm because Pennsylvania provides $20 a week to the widow for five hundred weeks if an injury results in death, the payments to be extended until the youngest child is sixteen years old, if there is a family. Thus sometimes state compensation for a widow with young children may run as high as $10,000 to $20,000. If a miner is injured he gets compensation for five hundred weeks, after which, if he is still in difficulty, another state agency takes over.

"When we get the union, we think we get something," worried one of the old men killing time at the grocery.† "We get it all right—strike, strike, strike. The union leaders keep the miners as poor as the coal companies used to. But in the old days, the companies left us live in the houses and we bought at the company stores. The union gets us a small raise now and again—but it takes it all to pay the bills we run up when we're on strike. In the long run, we ain't much better off. If this strike lasts as long as the automobile, the miner will be in the same spot as the automobile workers— broke. It's like this: in Detroit, the automobile workers got big war wages,

---

* For a full discussion of this see "District Mine Workers Active During Layoff," by Ruth Love, Uniontown *Morning Herald,* April 3, 1946.
† *Ibid.*

saved money, and bought bonds. Then the union called a big strike and the automobile workers had to use their savings and their bonds to live. Right now, they ain't got nothin' to show for the big war wages they got. If Lewis pulls the same thing on us, we'll be in the same box—with nothin' to show for the long hours and big pays we got during the War. So it's beginning to look like the union leaders want to keep the union members ground down as bad as the companies did. That's one way to keep the union leaders in power. If there were laws for unions, like companies, maybe the union members would get a break. Something has to be done—or the unions will run themselves out of business. That's all I got to say."

The women were unanimously against the work-stoppage and didn't hesitate to say so.

"There's only one good thing about it ... there's no war on," says a miner's wife, sluicing water on the back steps and putting the pail away with a clatter. "It was awful when Mike was on strike and Miljus and John and Steve were in Italy. Now all we have to worry about is whether we'll have to go without pay for the rest of the summer. A lot John Lewis cares; he don't have to worry about money. We never get out of debt, thanks to the union. We no more than get the bills paid from one strike than we're facing more in another. I think it's a damn shame that the union leaders whose big salaries go on, can't settle this business without dragging out the poor miners whose pay is shut off when work stops."

"Not a new stick of furniture have I had since long before the War," agrees her neighbor on the other half of the porch. "Every time I think we'll be able to buy, along comes a strike. You'd think Lewis would be able to settle something once in a while without the miners paying the bill. I'm getting sick of this union business."

The operators had been having plenty to worry about ever since Lewis filed his strike notice early in March. The captive mine owners' troubles began earlier than that. During the C.I.O. United Steel Workers' strike in January, the steel mills down-river which consumed their coal couldn't take it, so they had to run on part time and sell what they could to the railroads. Now with the steel industry just recovering from its knockout in January, it was about to get another; United States Steel was banking 2,800 beehives in Fayette County and 20 of its 32 blast furnaces around Pittsburgh.

No matter how they figured it, even with a short strike, operators were bound to lose heavily. The mines had to be pumped whether the men worked or not and if they didn't keep the complicated ventilation systems going, enough gas would collect to blow their roofs off, if a spark landed in the right place. But they couldn't give the men a new contract and prevent a walkout when Lewis wouldn't say what he wanted. Give him a Welfare Fund first, he said, and then he'd tell them the rest. He didn't have to bargain collectively under the Wagner Act, but they did. The figure he mentioned last year for his Welfare Fund was ten cents a ton royalty. But ten cents a ton, an estimated $60,000,000 a year for Lewis to juggle with in power politics, would call for an increase in the selling price of coal. Ten cents a ton was as much royalty as many coal land owners were originally paid for their coal in the ground. A higher price for coal meant that competing fuels would make serious inroads, and business once lost had a way of not coming home. Pennsylvania had never been able to coax back the volume of business she lost to West Virginia in the long strike of 1933. In that case the loss was to another area; the loss to another fuel was just as menacing.* And if Lewis were able to jam through his royalty on coal and set up the principle that a union leader had a right to levy on the public a private tax for the benefit of his union, where would it end? Why not a private tax for union benefits on every radio, automobile, and washing machine? If the taxing power were granted to one labor leader, the others would have to have it too.

The operators, however, were willing to consider a plan "to create by joint contribution a reasonable fund to be used to mitigate unusual hardships arising directly from mine accidents, the fund to be administered by an independent agency (possibly the Red Cross) with the advice of both mine workers and operators." They were willing to turn over to representatives of the mine workers all funds collected from mine workers for payment of doctors, burial funds, etc., where union locals were dissatisfied with existing arrangements, to accept workmen's compensation laws in any states where acceptance is optional; and to set up a committee of three operators and three miners to study safety seriously. Most important of all to the miners' pay check, they offered to increase the day and tonnage rates to meet the requirements of the government's wage-price policies already worked out in other big national industries—steel, oil, and automotive.

But John L. Lewis was not willing to talk about anything until he had his Welfare Fund, nor would he discuss an extension of contract, retroactive or otherwise, while they worked out details. The men would be called out on April first.

As March drew to a close the United States Government tardily began building up a stock pile of coal to be parcelled out by priorities. The coke operators put in a final charge of ninety-six hour "damper" coke, wet so that the ovens would burn at low heat for a couple of weeks, hoping that the strike would be settled by then. If it were not, the men had agreed to

---

* Pennsylvania bituminous operators have good reasons to worry about competing fuels. Whereas in 1909 soft coal supplied 70.2 percent of the country's energy, it had dropped to 53.2 percent in 1928, and to 47 percent in 1946. See *Trends in Bituminous Coal Industry* (Dept. of Commerce, Commonwealth of Pa., 1940), II, 10. Also *New York Times,* Nov. 24, 1946, Editorial Section.

draw one charge after the strike was called. Even if they kept their promise, such a long burn would mean a loss. Suppose they were using coal that produced six tons of coke from nine tons of coal in the small ovens; eight tons of coke from ten to twelve tons of coal in the big ones. Striking an average, if an operator charged 300 ovens with 8 tons of coal each, he would have 2,400 tons in the burn and 1,600 tons of coke at stake. At $7.50 a ton, that meant $10,500; but under the "damper" system, even if the men rescued it before it smoldered to ashes, the operator stood to lose one-third of the coke. Still it was better to risk it than to let the ovens cool off.

The general public was taking the coal strike casually. Just another labor wrangle in a long annoying series of work-stoppages that were slowing up reconversion. Householders who didn't have to worry about their furnaces until fall, women cooking with electricity and gas who had not seen a piece of coal in years, gave the matter little thought. The American people didn't know the part that coal played in their lives but now John L. Lewis proposed to teach them. For his purpose it was as well that they didn't realize what was going on, because it was near-strangulation of industry that would show them what would happen if his union declined to produce coal, and it would take a little time to bring this about. For some time he had been the most powerful single figure in American public life but there had been no time up to now when it was politic to call attention to it.

The Coke Region was peaceful—no marching, no speeches, no pickets. At some plants the locals had called out the maintenance crews who usually took care of plant repairs during strikes, the prohibition against their working inspired not so much by animosity against the company as by fear of stirring up jealousy within the ranks. "If we can't work, why should they?" The empty plant yards looked as though the clocks had stopped on a dull Sunday and never got going again. In the patches there was grumbling because Harrisburg had decreed that Pennsylvania's 92,000 striking soft coal miners would not be eligible for compensation until a five weeks' penalty period had elapsed because they were involved in a voluntary suspension of work. That meant that strikers could not sign up for their $20-a-week compensation until May 4 and there would be a waiting-week after that.

An angry deputation from locals in Cambria, Indiana, and Somerset Counties went to Harrisburg to point out to Secretary of Labor William H. Chestnut that they were not really striking, just not working. "From time immemorial it has been the policy of the union 'no contract, no work.'" they urged, but the ruling stood.

On the diplomatic front in Washington, John L. Lewis still would not talk until he had his Welfare Fund assured and negotiations had broken down.

Meanwhile relief agencies abroad were being hindered in the distribution of food inland because, with U. S. coal shipments cut off, they had no fuel to run the trains in France and Belgium. To take care of the emergency, Fiorello La Guardia, as head of UNRRA, made an urgent appeal that operators and miners lay aside their quarrel to the extent of producing 500,000 tons of coal a month for the relief-trains overseas, UNRRA to pay any additional costs resulting from adjustments coming out of the eventual coal settlement.

But John L. Lewis was making no concessions. As the paralysis slowly crept over the country, he observed coolly, like a scientist who has innoculated a rabbit with fever to demonstrate a theory, "Our economy is being gradually stagnated. As the days progress, tonnage will go off the railroads, factories will close and distress will come to the American people."

By May first the strike had really begun to pinch. Class One railroads still had coal for twenty-six or twenty-seven days but five smaller carriers reported only ten days' supply in their stock piles. The Elkins Division of the Western Maryland Railroad, which depended on coal for approximately half of the system's normal freight, furloughed between 650 and 750 employees indefinitely. The Delaware, Lackawanna, and Western Railroad announced curtailment of freight service between Buffalo and Elmira. There were 23,000 idle in the Pittsburgh district steel mills. In Wheeling, Block Brothers Tobacco Company closed. Only four or five of a winter fleet of sixty ships in New York Harbor had sailed.

In Washington, Lewis and the operators picked up where they left off when negotiations mired in April but were getting nowhere. They were meeting temporarily in a rococo green and gold room back of the stage in a government auditorium building where a troop of employees from the Interstate Commerce Commission were busy rehearsing for their annual play to the tune of Spanish dances, enlivened with castanets—but the dour futility of the coal parleys was not enlivened.

The public was begining to be annoyed but up to now no great volume of mail had been coming to Washington protesting the inconvenience. Then as the country's coal supply dwindled to a matter of days, the distress that Lewis had foreseen came with a rush. Americans suddenly discovered that it is coal which makes the electricity that runs trollies and elevators, lights stores and houses, freezes food; coal that fuels most of the trains, coal that makes the steel for sorely needed new refrigerators and automobiles that were farther off than ever.

Chicago plants, hardest hit by the coal famine, cut operation to twenty-four hours a week and inaugurated more severe power restrictions than during the war. Department stores were allowed only enough electricity to stay open four hours a day; candles guttered on the tables in night clubs where a single spotlight briefly illuminated the floor show; apartment dwellers toiled up thousands of stairs because there was no power for the elevators; housewives rediscovered sad-irons and kerosene lamps. In Washington, the dome of the Capitol was dark as in the war years, sharing a brown-out with Chicago, Philadelphia, Detroit, and New York. Subway service in Manhattan was ordered cut 10 to 35 percent to be effective the following week.

The South complained that unless coal came from somewhere its textile mills would have to close down; Minnesota creameries were suspending; canneries wailed for tin cans to save food spoiling on their hands; the National Fertilizer Company announced that the output of ammonium sulphate made from coking coal, a basic fertilizer ingredient, had been so reduced that the farmers would have to go short on fertilizer.

The press gloomily estimated that a million people were out of work. Besides the country's four hundred thousand coal miners and the auto workers, harder hit by the coal strike that cut off steel than by their own strike, men were being laid off by the thousand in Chicago and Pittsburgh steel plants. Carnegie-Illinois Steel Company was down to 9 percent capacity now, less than at any time during the depression. The great Clairton and Duquesne works were being shut down along with Vandergrift; McKeesport's National Tube Company was banking its fires.

Acutely responsive to steel, the Pittsburgh Steamship Company, operating the biggest inland fleet in the world, tied up its ore boats; every day more trains went off the road and more goods piled up in warehouses, with the prospect of worse to come.

By May 9, John L. Lewis's patient had a very bad fever. The newspapers reported twelve hours' coal supply left in the United States emergency coal stocks. The railroads, three-fourths of which burned coal, had orders to cut their passenger service 25 percent on May 10, 50 percent on May 15. The freight and express embargo, belatedly ordered by the government, would go into effect the next day along with the passenger service cut, and after that nothing could move but food, fuel, and absolute necessities. And, lest the parcel post service become gorged with diverted merchandise, post offices must refuse shipments in excess of eleven pounds, with some exceptions. Trucks must hold themselves in readiness to convey perishables and essentials according to priorities. It looked as if the country were headed for complete paralysis when plants were not able to get raw materials or ship what they made.

The center of the disturbance from which ripples of disruption widened across the nation remained peaceful. On the thirty-eighth day of the strike there was a brief flare of violence in Harlan County, Kentucky, where one man was killed and six were wounded in a U.M.W. picket party heading for a mine being worked by nonstriking members of the Independent

Miners Union, but it was only a flicker that ignited no further violence. In the Coke Region the miners waited with lessening patience while John L. Lewis did their talking for them.

The labor-management meetings convened in one place and another in Washington with nothing to report. Recently they had been occupying a sound-proof projection room in the Patent Office. Sometimes Lewis came; sometimes not. As one observer remarked, "They moved so often maybe he lost track of where they were."

Tension in the country was growing dangerously high but Lewis didn't seem worried. When the cry rose, "Why doesn't the President do something? Isn't he going to seize the mines?" it was just what he wanted to hear. Let Truman take over the mines if he wanted to. He wouldn't produce any coal. The men wouldn't work without a contract so it would be up to the government to make one and an agreement worked out with government conciliators, promising other people's money, would probably contain more concessions than he could get from operators trying to protect their own interests.

The worst feature was the threat that Congress, jealous of sharing the taxing power with a union-block leader, would pass legislation outlawing the royalty levy on coal before Lewis had a chance to negotiate it on higher levels. There had been serious talk about legislation to curb the royalty demand for more than a week, and, with the taboo that had checkmated labor restriction laws for more than a decade temporarily inoperative under the wrath engendered by the mass paralysis of industry, an angry Congress might rush through something that would spoil the strike. Lewis had no intention of letting that happen. For the moment the British Loan was in the way of any legislation menacing his program but the Senate had voted to take up the Case Bill curtailing labor's privileges, and there was no knowing what drastic riders they might tack on to it. Lewis would have to act soon.

In the midst of the tension of May 9 the White House summoned the U.M.W. head and Mr. Charles O'Neill, spokesman for the Northern Division Coal operators. It was none too soon for the union president. And as once he spoiled Franklin D. Roosevelt's build-up by settling a strike fifteen minutes before the President was going on the air to give him a public scolding, now three hours before he went to call on President Truman, Lewis ordered his miners back to work for a ten-day truce, with any wage increase later agreed upon to be retroactive. It was no settlement but it would let off dangerous steam and give the utilities and common carriers coal for the moment, while he did his trading, without relieving the pressure he needed for leverage. According to his press statement, he was permitting the truce as a contribution "to our nation's economy which is being

Photo by Philadelphia Inquirer

PENNCRAFT—A GENERAL VIEW—These homes at Penncraft were built cooperatively by coal miners from native materials in Fayette County, Penn.

TEMPORARY HOUSE—Some temporary homes are turned into chicken coops; others are used as rentable homes for new couples in the community

Photo by Wurts Brothers, N. Y.

HOUSE UNDER CONSTRUCTION—Note concrete, rocks, wood, and other materials and skills that go into these homes. Boys work with their fathers

A HOME—This house was built for $2,000 and about 4,000 hours of labor

MODERN KITCHEN—This kitchen has been lived in for five years

A LIVING-DINING ROOM AT PENNCRAFT

A LIVING-DINING ROOM IN A SIX-ROOM HOUSE IN PENNCRAFT

Photo by Wurts Brothers, N. Y.

PENNCRAFT COMMUNITY LIBRARY

KNITTING MILL—The mill provides new skills and a source of income for miners' families in an area of shrinking coal supply

Photo by Philadelphia Inquirer

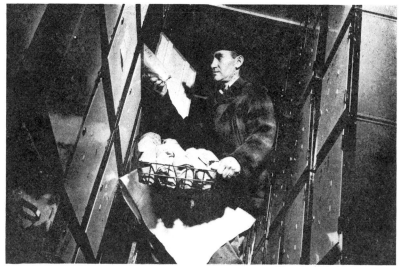

FROZEN-FOOD LOCKERS—This plant is part of Penncraft's subsistence program for preserving food raised in the homestead gardens

PENNCRAFT CO-OP ASSOCIATION—Penncraft homesteaders built and own the cooperative store which sells groceries, meat, and feed, and operates the frozen-food plant of five hundred lockers

BISHOP OF THE RUSSIAN ORTHODOX CHURCH—Bishop Benjámin Basiliga of Pittsburgh visits Holy Trinity Church in New Salem

MOUNT ST. MACRINA PROCESSION—Procession of the Eucharistic King in front of the Mother House at Mount St. Macrina during the pilgrimage

MORNING WORSHIP AT MOUNT ST. MACRINA—Morning worship during the pilgrimage on the front terrace at the Mother House

MOUNT ST. MACRINA PILGRIMS—A crowd of pilgrims starts the Way of the Cross

OUTDOOR SHRINE—An outdoor shrine at Mount St. Macrina. The *ikona* is that of Our Lady of Perpetual Help, patroness of the shrine

imperiled by the stupidity and selfish greed of the coal operators and associated financial interests and by demagogues who have tried to lash the
public mind into a state of hysteria."

The Coke Region miners were stunned at first and then bitterness and
doubt ran riot. Had John L. let them down after all? And were all the days
of idleness without pay checks going to come to nothing? Now, the very
day before they would have started to draw their twenty dollars a week
compensation, and with no contract in sight, he told them to go back to their
shovels. Never in the history of the district had the union been so unpopular.
On top of the general confusion and disappointment came the State Bureau
of Compensation's ruling that payments to miners would be automatically
cut off by their return to work.

"Why the hell should I go back to the mine, lose my unemployment
compensation, and then get jerked out again in two weeks because Lewis
wants to be big stuff?" a miner sitting on his doorstep asked grumpily.*
"No, I'm not going back. And you can print my opinion of Lewis, while
you're at it." (The opinion was unprintable.)

"To hell with Lewis and any ——— ——— truce," said another. "I'm
getting so I like to loaf. I'll just start collecting my unemployment compensation—and Lewis can rest his damned bones for a while. Listen to me—
the miners as a whole didn't want no strike in the first place. But Lewis
made us come out. Most of us have used up what little we saved. Most of
us are down to our last war bond—if it isn't cashed already. You tell me
something—what the hell are the union leaders doing? Are they trying to
smash the men to keep the unions going? Or do they think they can handle
us better by keeping us broke? I'd like John Lewis to answer a few of those
questions since he's so damned smart."

"If you want to know what I think," said another miner with quiet deliberation, "I think this country is so damned close to a revolution that it
ain't funny. We can lick the Germans in two wars; we can lick the Japs.
But we ain't got anybody big enough to put these union guys—and I mean
Lewis, too—in their place. When any man gets bigger than the Government
of the United States, it means he's a real big guy, or the men we got in
Washington ain't nothing but a bunch of yellow-bellies."

Most of the miners felt that Lewis had called the Truce to head off
Congress but that he ought not to have carried things so far in the first
place.

"If there is any legislation against the unions, Lewis would have to take
the blame for it from every union," said one. "He ain't got the guts to face
that. All he can do is run us into debt while he horses around down there

* For a full discussion of this see "District Miners Denounce Action by Union
Leader," Uniontown *Morning Herald*, May 11, 1946.

in Washington. We want to get back to work. I know I do, and so do most of my buddies. We got to keep families. Lewis eats fancy meals in fancy hotels. His salary goes on. But we pay his bills when we can't even pay our own."

"John Lewis is beginning to find out that he ain't bigger than the United States Government," declared one miner, pausing to heave a spit over the near-by curb before continuing, "But he's just stalling for time. He's trying to stop legislation. And them damn fools in Washington are dumb enough to play suckers for him."

Many of the miners frankly stated their belief that proper legislation was the solution to their problem of strike after strike in the coal field and voiced fear that Lewis's present tactics would prevent that legislation.

"When they cut out the gravy at the expense of the union men, the racketeers will get out and let the unions operate for the men," said another miner. "I don't believe in no truce. Every miner that's honest would like to see unions governed by law instead of guys like Lewis and Petrillo and other fellows who want to be dictators."

The U.M.W. headquarters of District No. 4 in the Second National Bank building remained hopeful that the men would go back to work on Monday, but angry locals voted otherwise.

Over the week end it seemed unlikely that western Pennsylvania's miners were going to return to work but probable that West Virginia's 104,000 would. By government order all coal to be mined (possibly with good luck some 20,000,000 to 25,000,000 tons) was ticketed for priority users only, with public utilities, railroads, laundries, hospitals, food processing plants (including milk plants, dairies, commercial bakeries) in first place, allotted enough coal for their daily burn plus twenty days more for reserve; industrial users, in second place, were to get enough for their daily needs, with domestic consumers in actual distress after them. The freight embargo and parcel post restrictions were cancelled just in time to head off a shutdown of the General Motors plants. The railroads' 25 percent passenger cut would continue along with dim-outs where necessity dictated.

In the coal fields, the operators were getting the mines ready to run without knowing whether the miners would come to work or not, or whether the coal from the steel-owned captives would find its way to the parent mills. It was hardly worth while to fire the big open hearths for twelve days of borrowed time when it would take a month's production to give them a margin of safety. Nevertheless the fifteen huge captives of Carnegie Steel, Jones and Laughlin's Greene and Washington County operations, Republic's Clyde mines, and Weirton's Isabella were getting ready.

In Washington, Government Conciliator Paul W. Fuller submitted two questions to the coal parley.

1. Would the operators be willing to pay the miners for $3,000,000 overtime holiday pay they claim is due?

2. If this sum is paid, would the miners state specifically what demands they had?

The miners' claim for back pay covered Labor Day, Thanksgiving, Christmas, and New Years', arguing that those who worked the full week ought to have overtime pay for the sixth day, although they had only worked five. During the war, pay checks were figured on this basis but operators discontinued giving overtime in such cases after August of 1945, when President Truman revoked the Executive order authorizing pay for six major holidays, including the four in dispute.

To break the impasse the operators agreed to allow the fund, whereupon Lewis finally stated his price for a contract: a pay roll charge in an amount equal to 7 percent of the gross earnings of the men, paid by the operators for a Health Fund to be administered by the Union and used for medical service, hospitalization, rehabilitation, and training of disabled men, financial aid in hardship cases, and cultural and educational work. There was still no word of what wage increases he wanted but he was reported to be seeking a foremen's union, the demand that created the brief, unsuccessful "bosses" union strike the autumn before.* It looked as though something were wrong with the nation's labor-management legislation when, under the law, a union leader could withold his demands until a strike affecting the country's fundamental economy was in its sixth week, while if the other parties to the dispute had refused to state their position they would have been punished.

President Truman had asked Lewis and O'Neill to bring him a settlement on Wednesday, the fifteenth of May, but with those demands there was little hope that they would be able to do so. Neither was Mr. Lewis's truce going to give the country much coal. In the Coke Region, Frick's Palmer mine went back to work on Monday along with Weirton's Isabella, Republic Steel's Clyde mines Nos. 1 and 3, Jones and Laughlin's Vesta plants and the Shannopin mine at Bobtown, but United States Steel's captives had 10,000 men idle. Only 93 of western Pennsylvania's 677 mines were open, not a single one in Somerset or Indiana Counties. The miners at Homer City voted to return to work but pickets from other mines stopped them.

Harrisburg sent out a clarification of its compensation insurance ruling, hoping that if the miners were assured that no further penalty period were added in the event of their going back to work and then being called out again, it would speed up the opening of the mines. Some of the miners

---

* The Bosses Union plan favored by Lewis would allow an irreducible minimum of five employees on each shift to represent the company; one superintendent, one mine manager underground, one foreman, two assistant foremen.

wanted to go back, realizing that if the strike were settled before the truce ended they would have a pay check coming equal to many weeks of government compensation, but if the radical element forced an adverse vote in the local, they had to stay home along with the others. And where locals voted to return to the pits, they were waited on by pickets. At Robena-Ralph they even went into the small building by the lamp house and tried to bring the men out.

"At a time like this," grumbled one of the older men, "the radicals always come to the top.... Most of the pickets were just young squirts who were wearing diapers when we older men were shedding blood in this coal field. We fought for them then and we're still able to teach them a few tricks about being good union men."

It was hard to keep track of the Pennsylvania mines, they opened and closed so fast. Production dropped to 178,000 tons with only about 42,000 men working.

On the fifteenth the President did not get the settlement he had asked for, Thereupon he suggested that both sides submit to binding arbitration. The operators were willing in the matter of wages and hours but balked at the Welfare Fund. Lewis cagily took the position that his union negotiating committee was not authorized to arbitrate anything at all. Frayed by the long deadlock, Production Administrator John D. Small, speaking unofficially, denounced Lewis as "a breeder of industrial chaos" who by withholding details of his demands "has made a travesty of collective bargaining. . . ."

Negotiations between Lewis and the operators bogged down again and to further harry the President and the citizenry, it looked as though the rail strike were a sure thing if the union leaders Johnson and Whitney pursued the high-handed tactics already working so well for Lewis. The public was like an angry lion being held at bay by a trainer with a chair and unable for the moment to tell which leg to bite.

Meanwhile the days during which Lewis had agreed to allow the men to work slipped quietly away with production thinned to a trickle. In western Pennsylvania, where coal production was hardest hit, only 130 of 677 sizable mines were operating with 51,720 out of 56,000 miners idle.

The public faced a recurrence of the coal famine at the week's end while Lewis's position strengthened hourly as the rail controversy focussed the growing storm. Unless his hand had lost its cunning, Mr. Whitney and Mr. Johnson of the Railroad Brotherhood were going to draw the thunderbolts, not he. The A.F. of L. had gone on record that its 7,000,000 members were ready to back him to the limit, Welfare Fund and all. His triumphal return to the fold last January was paying dividends now when he was almost ready to begin serious trading.

The country had been looking for President Truman to seize the mines ever since his mild warning earlier in the month that unless the parties to the dispute settled their differences soon, the miners might find themselves striking against the government. As another work-stoppage came nearer with the truce drawing to a close, the cry from the states, "Why doesn't the President do something?" swelled loud enough to be heard in Washington.

At one minute after midnight on Tuesday, May 21, the United States Government technically took over the soft coal mines and put Secretary of the Interior J. A. Krug in charge with power to negotiate a contract with Mr. Lewis. Thereupon Secretary Krug appointed Vice Admiral Ben Morell, last year's Federal Administrator of the oil industry under seizure, to be in direct charge and tried to assure him man power for production by an appeal to the miners to go back to work. They had done it for President Roosevelt, but that was in war time. Washington observers were not very hopeful that they would do it now.

"All we can do at the moment," admitted Secretary Krug, "is to urge the workers to go back ... I am quite confident that if the leaders of the miners won't support a movement however, the Government will find it unlikely that it can persuade the miners to go back."

In the beginning "seize the mines" had been looked forward to as the formula solution for the coal impasse. Now that it was a fact, all that had happened was that a few more mines joined the idle list. The dead line of the truce's end was so near that there was little hope that more than broad principles of settlement could be agreed upon before Saturday (if such an agreement could be reached). John L. Lewis was being just as noncommittal with the government negotiators as he had been with the operators. Would the miners work for the United States Government? Lewis couldn't say. That was up to the Union Policy Committee.

Meanwhile 243 more mines shut down, bringing the total of idle mines to 2,100 out of a total of 4,500. With the government in the saddle, the Frick Company's Coke Region mines showed only 2 percent production. The company's Alabama mines had worked every day under the truce, but the day after the government took over nobody reported for work.

In the Coke Region there was dead quiet. The Smith-Connally Law, created to deal with miners striking against the government during the war, was still operative and the district had a lively memory of thirty-one miners arraigned after the F.B.I. moved in back in 1943 and subsequently put on probation under a thousand-dollar bond each, some of them reclassified by their draft boards and whisked off to the armed forces for inciting others to strike against the government. But picketing and making incendiary speeches was one thing; choosing to do nothing was another. A man could not be prosecuted because he decided to dig in his garden instead of in a coal seam. Under the Constitution a man could not be forced to work.

The government was being made ridiculous at a time when Mr. Whitney and Mr. Johnson of the railroad unions were already challenging its authority. What about this mass refusal to work in spite of the Smith-Connally bill? It was inconceivable that miners all over the country from Pennsylvania to Alabama suddenly of their own accord decided to stay home; that 243 mines shut down as soon as Secretary Krug took over without instructions by some kind of grapevine communication. If the government really wanted to know who was to blame, it could probably find out through the F.B.I.; or did Washington prefer not to notice a situation it did not know how to handle? And if, armed with the power specifically given for such an emergency by the Smith-Conally Act, the government decided to overlook a case where the law needed to be applied, what good would it do to pass more labor laws?

In the union halls, in stores, on the streets of the company towns, wherever miners gathered in the Coke Region, John L. Lewis's stock was going up. After all, this was America, not like the Old Country. It didn't make sense to work less hours for more pay, year after year, but if John Lewis could get it for the miners, it was a fine thing and probably the American way. If the President of the United States put Lewis in jail for acting like he was a king, it was no more than was coming to him; but if he could get away with it, he was a big man. Anyway, it was a good idea to be on his side.

Something had to break soon. The coal truce had been a fizzle as far as the public was concerned; they wouldn't stand a repetition of the scenes of the first week in May after so short an interval. Luckily the threatened railroad tie-up was diverting the radio commentators and crowding coal into fine print, to the relief of the Coke Region growing sensitive about attracting so much unfavorable attention.

On Thursday the storm broke—and not on John L. Lewis. The Coke Region listened sympathetically to the stories of families marooned in railroad terminals because of the railway impasse; of hotels setting up cots in lounges for stranded travellers; of freight tie-ups; of spoiling food and baby chicks that had to be drowned; but it was an impersonal interest—like long range sympathy for the European famine. In the days before the bus lines were established, when most people travelled by train, the coal business centered around Scottdale and Connellsville with the B. & O. Railroad to take care of them. But as production moved to the Monongahela, the railroads that laced the busy Klondike and the new districts in Greene and Washington Counties were freight spurs, catering to coal drags. Travellers rode the trolley and bus lines or went in their own cars. The rail strike tied up the coal gondolas, but what of it? The mines weren't running.

And then the miners sitting by their radios to hear the President denounce the rail leaders heard him tell the country, "The miners are working." Men who had not worked during the truce or under U. S. seizure either, could hardly believe their ears. Whoever told the President that? Didn't he know what was going on after all? Anyway, he couldn't be very mad at Lewis. If he got his law to put strikers into the army, it would be hard luck, but Lewis would see that his people didn't get hurt very much. He must have gotten on the good side of the President.

The next day there was talk as though the government really meant to run the mines when the truce expired. Anyway the War Department designated Brigadier General Blackshear M. Bryan to take charge of any protective measures needed in the coal fields, but there was nothing to be protective about. The Coke Region was as quiet as a graveyard. President Truman had not yet gotten the power he wanted to make people work when they didn't want to and the miners didn't believe he'd get it, not with the big men in labor shouting him down all over the country. His bill passed the House because everybody was excited over the railroad business but the Senate was not going to be so easy. Congressmen would think twice about pushing it if it meant they lost their seats in the next election. Alexander Whitney of the Railroad Brotherhood was saying he was ready to spend $2,-500,000 to defeat the ones who voted for the President's bill; his union would spend the whole $47,000,000 in their treasury to defeat Truman.

There was still the Case Bill hanging over labor but maybe if Lewis settled on a contract soon, the furor would die down and they could head it off. The long range labor legislation the President wanted was not to come up until after election and all that studying and investigation was nothing to worry about. Congress was always studying labor conditions and what had the operators and Lewis been doing all spring but studying labor conditions?

Lewis was being as adamant with the government conciliators as he had been with the operators. Last minute efforts to get him to accept the government's proposition for a general settlement and order the men back to work flattened out. Saturday brought an end to the truce without changing the picture.

On Monday the conferences still went on between Secretary Krug and Lewis but things looked bright for an early settlement. At least both parties had sent for their lawyers and they did not usually do that until they were getting down to details. In Congress labor members tried desperately to stave off a decisive vote on the menacing labor laws until the miners were back at work when the public pressure would diminish. At last on Wednesday, May 29, on the fifty-ninth day of the strike counting the truce, the settlement came—not with the operators but between the government and the U.M.W. chief.

Lewis had won again.

It was not a contract the mine owners would have signed, but when the government turned the mines back to them it would be hard to invalidate the concessions. The public would have to pay more for its coal but Lewis had gotten his royalty principle established before Congress outlawed it, and put across his Welfare demand.

According to the agreement, the new fund would be in two parts, the Welfare and Retirement Division paid for by the operators and financed by a five-cents-a-ton royalty on production, the fund to be managed by three trustees, one named by the union, one by the government and one by both. The other part—the medical and hospital fund—would be financed by deductions from the miners' pay turned over by the operators to trustees named by Lewis.

To the miners' pay checks the settlement meant that if a man had been taking home $10.00 a day, now he would have $11.85. Whereas the base pay had been $1.00 an hour, from now on it would be $1.18 plus time-and-a-half for overtime to be paid for work in excess of seven hours a day. The new work week would consist of five nine-hour days instead of six as before, but the men might work six days if they wanted to, with time-and-a-half for the sixth day, making a total of $75.25.

In the Coke Region, miners began jumping the gun back to work in the wake of the big Isabella and Colonial locals, the Leisenrings Nos. 1, 2 and 3, Gates, and Kyle.

"The new contract is a victory for the United Mine Workers," exulted Michael J. Honus, secretary and treasurer of District No. 4, "and they're tickled skinny with what they now get. They're behind John L. Lewis 100 percent."

There was still the dispute over compensation insurance payments for the men who refused to work under government seizure but there was nothing serious for the rank and file to worry about, especially after the public indignation cooled and President Truman vetoed the Case Bill. John L. Lewis had not actually put over his Bosses' Union but that would come next.

On July 17, Vice Admiral Ben Morrell quietly announced a government-union agreement covering pay and working conditions for mine supervisory employees (bosses), the first such agreement in the history of the soft coal industry. To be sure, it applied only to 136 supervisory employees at four soft coal mines of Jones and Laughlin between the government as operator under seizure and John L. Lewis's "catch-all" United Clerical Technical and Supervisory Workers of District No. 50 Branch of the U.M.W., but it was a test case and showed which way the wind was blowing.

Now that it was all over, the country could sit back and total up its losses. The miners, whose augmented pay checks would not make up for the weeks of idleness; the thousands of persons laid off in allied industries; the operators, who in addition to their losses due to maintenance without production had to submit to government seizure of their property and its subsequent operation under a contract made without their having anything to say about it; the public who, with scarce articles farther off than ever, faced an increasing danger of inflation because production would be retarded by lack of steel already behind schedule because of the coal strike coming so close on the heels of its own. All the discomforts of reduced railroad schedules and brown-outs, the anxiety of plants closing down because coal piles had melted away, would have counted for something if some kind of legislation had come out of it to prevent its happening again. And it would happen again, because when it was not raining the Washington politicians were in no hurry to fix the roof.

It looked as if nobody had won but John L. Lewis, Old King Coal, solidly on his throne in the coal fields, more powerful than he had ever been.

With pay checks coming twice a month again Coke Region miners began catching up on the bills from the fifty-day lay-off with the uneasy certainty that there would be more fireworks when the government tried to turn back the mines to the operators. The thing the forecasters had not expected was that the peace would be so short-lived or that John L. would try conclusions with the government itself, with whom he had just negotiated a contract heralded as the best the miners ever won.

The public anger at the repetition of the scenes of April and May in November and December, the injunction proceedings culminating in severe fines, the pending Supreme Court appeal which would materially affect all organized labor, and the threat of unfavorable legislation by the new Congress necessitated a surprise capitulation by Lewis on December 7. Then the miners were back at work again, with a slim Christmas in the offing, wondering what it was all about.

A *Morning Herald* editorial for December 9, the day the miners started back to the pits, gives a slant on how the people who live in the Coke Region felt about it.

"... John L. Lewis—always the dictator—has ordered his soft coal diggers back to the pits.

"He couched his cancellation of the mine walkout in language characteristically flowery ...

"But let no one be deluded by the Lewis play-acting. This time the power-obsessed labor boss has suffered a major defeat. This time he has come up against a force, the wrath of the outraged people of the United States, which was too much for him. Therefore, the miners have been shown he is not more powerful than our Democracy....

"Few persons who are not a part and parcel of the coal mining regions can appreciate the fear that is the controlling factor in the coal fields. Few realize that fear—not coal companies nor wage issues nor union contracts—determines whether a mine is open or closed. . . .

"The basic fear of the miner had its inception in the non-union coal fields under company abuses still vividly remembered, grew to terror proportions in the battle to unionize the coal fields, and continues to dominate the life of a miner as the closed shop 'strong arms' obedience to union edicts. . . .

"However, in the last days before Lewis' action ending the strike, there was a growing group of miners anxious to return to their jobs—not from a sense of disloyalty to their union leader but in loyalty to higher obligations.

"One such is Norman Scott of Penncraft, employed at Frick's Ralph plant, father of eleven children of whom the oldest was eighteen, the youngest, one year. In a letter to the *Morning Herald,* he sets forth:

" 'I do not believe the fining or imprisonment of John L. Lewis will make the present situation worse, although it would not help. I do believe it would serve to reduce future strikes and bring about a greater respect from all labor leaders to the government of which they, too, are citizens.

" 'Speaking of loyalty, the majority of miners are religiously inclined and should realize these facts: loyalty to the church and God, next our immediate family and the government, then, and only then, our union. Some seem to have got the cart ahead of the horse . . .'

"Another miner, employed at the Robena plant, had this to say when queried as to the effect of the proposed presidential appeal to have been broadcast last night:

" 'We miners listen to President Truman. He's our president the same as he is the president of others. But we'll sit at home. Why? Because we ain't got the guts to go against the union. Because we don't, everybody in the country will be wanting to nail us to the cross as traitors. How do you think we feel? We had sons who fought in the war. We're Americans. We bought bonds and gave scrap and did everything they asked us in the war. But don't let anybody kid you. No man is going back to the mines for the president of the United States or the United States Marines. No, we gotta wait for that telegram from John L. Lewis. Everybody's a free citizen except the coal miner. I don't listen to the radio any more. Those guys ranting and raving about us coal miners make me sick. If they want to know what they're talking about, let them come down here and get a union card and go to work in the mines for a few months. Would they get a surprise?'

"Another miner, employed at the Colonial plant, gave his views:

" 'I'm afraid Truman would have just wasted his wind. Not because the miners don't want to work. They can't. It's gonna take Lewis to put us back. Some of the miners are yelling about shorter hours and some of them are yelling about a contract. If Lewis orders us back—not one of them is gonna ask if we got shorter hours or if we got a contract. But we'll go. But if Lewis went on the radio and ordered us back, we wouldn't go—unless we was askin' for trouble. We gotta wait for a telegram signed by Lewis before we know he really means it. What he says on the radio or in the newspapers —that's just for the government or the public. The telegram's for the miners.'

"No army ever could boast such discipline. No slave ever could gripe so justifiably."

CHAPTER XVII

KALEIDOSCOPE

THE COKE REGION HAS ONLY A MILD INTEREST IN ITS past. The little group of old families are proud of the history of the Region but there are not enough of them, and their concern is not sustained enough to preserve the vanishing landmarks. Isaac Meason's mansion at Mount Braddock on Route 119 still receives the honor that is its due in books dealing with fine examples of early Pennsylvania architecture, but it has fallen into untidy old age.

The Frick Coke Company owned it for a while and when they were through operating in the vicinity offered it to the county to be preserved as a landmark. The county declined the responsibility and a foreign family bought it. The walnut trees are gone now, killed by smoke, and the fine old house stands on a bare knoll, eerie and lonesome under a flattened umbrella of black smoke fuming up from the Eureka brick kilns. At least the integrity of the architecture is inviolate: the columned doorway beautifully proportioned as ever; the interesting repetition of the round arch in the fan-light over the front door, a second fan-light above the central window directly above and the round window in the pediment accented with a delicate rinceau and leaf motif. And down in the yard a woman washes a plucked chicken in a coal scuttle under a network of clotheslines that bisect the dusty yard.

The wing toward Uniontown and part of the main building is rented out to a lodger. Inside, the drawing-room is gloomy with dark wallpaper, furnished with a pair of modern beds, the floor bare, the raised decoration of the mantel broken and defaced; the music room behind it is dusty and echoing, with old hats and rubbish on the floor.

Somehow the old house manages to rise above its present. It could be restored to an approximation of its former magnificence but it is not likely to be because the present owner has an exalted idea of its value, stimulated by the visits of the historically minded who are willing to pay fifty cents apiece to look at the staircase in the main hall.

A good many of the original furnishings have been rescued by antique hunters; the three-piece banquet table that would seat twenty-four; the great iron-master's coffeepot and Chippendale arm chair; a few silver spoons; a big silver ladle, and General Henry Butler's giant punch bowl that came into the Meason family when the son married the General's daughter. The tall grandfather clock turned up in a stable back of a Negro cabin, the magnificent inlay covered with green paint.

Friendship Hill, Albert Gallatin's old home on Route 166 near Point Marion, has fared well, due mostly to its situation out of the direct path of the coke and coal business but also because the romance of the old place, proud on its bluff between the forest and the river with its lone grave in the woods, its French mantelpieces, and memories of LaFayette, happens to appeal to Fayette County's fancy. The ownership of the estate is clouded by doubt such as clings to most of the properties that once belonged to J. V. Thompson, but for the present it operates as an historical show place under the direction of the Friendship Hill Association, organized in 1927 for the purpose of making it a national shrine. It is always just about to be sold or to have the timber cut from the woodland between the house and the road, but in the meantime the house and grounds are well cared for. A good many of the original furnishings remain and there are more scattered about the Region that might be brought back if its future were secure. As it is, there is a question how long the present collection will remain unbroken.

Since 1860 when Congressman John Dawson of Uniontown rescued the house from neglect and set out to restore its beauty, the furniture of the successive owners has been superimposed upon the authentic Gallatin pieces with the result that the beautifully appointed rooms open to the public reflect the personalities of several people, interpreting their feeling of how to fill the empty spaces left by the years. The result is surprisingly good; one feels Gallatin's presence most in the little panelled dining room looking out on the shady gallery of the old wing and in the delicate formality of the double parlors. The library reflects John Dawson with a strong Gallatin flavor; the sunny bedrooms of the rear of the original building are reminiscent of Charles Spears, the Pittsburgh owner of the estate before Thompson bought it; and Honey Thompson dominates the state dining room with its heavy mahogany candelabra, the more elegant of the upstairs bedrooms and the pretentious carriage house stored with horse-gear.

Abraham Overholt's homestead at West Overton, a mile from the Greensburg-Scottdale Highway where Henry Clay Frick spent his boyhood, is owned by Mr. Frick's daughter now. Beautifully kept with lawns and flower gardens, the three-story farmhouse is in the best Pennsylvania tradition with kitchen and work-rooms in the stone basement handy to the garden, the living rooms well off the ground and reached by a stairway that climbs to a narrow gallery that shades the front windows. The stone and stucco spring-house, where Frick was born, stands to the left of the big house within the white fenced yard, balanced by a brick summer kitchen on the opposite side. Part of the house and the ground-floor rooms of the old distillery across the road are open to the public as a museum.

The downtown section of Uniontown that used to bristle with banks has only one now, the Second National, one of the Mellon group. The old First National Building on the Round Corner goes by the name of Fayette Title and Trust but the banking rooms house the O.P.A., and the Frick Coke Company and Republic Steel occupy the offices that were once the stronghold of J. V. Thompson and the independent operators.

In Oak Grove Cemetery, out West Main Street almost at the edge of town, Jasper Thompson's raised stone sarcophagus dominates a well-kept area at mid-center with his family around him. A stranger will look in vain for the headstone of J. V. Thompson.

"There isn't any," says the elderly man who mows the graves, "but I'll tell you he was a good man and I got no word to say against him. There was those that set out to break him and take what we had here and they did it, but if he could have won out I would have fifty thousand dollars now instead of spending my days down at the courthouse."

Hated or loved, the spirit of J. V. Thompson is much alive in the Coke Region; the plunder from his auction is scattered in its houses; his shaving-cup marked with the lucky number eleven still stands on the shelf in the barbershop in the bank building. And there are durable memories of unobtrusive kindnesses still bearing fruit.

One of the teachers remembers: "I hadn't thought I would get to college but somebody said to me: 'Go tell Mr. Thompson you want to go and he'll see you get there.' When I asked him about it, he said in his slow way, 'I guess we've got money enough for that. Where do you want to go?' I told him and he explained how to deposit the initial check and said if I needed more to go to the president of the bank at the college. When I got to the school the first thing I heard was that the bank was calling to find out if I had arrived yet. Mr. Thompson had written ahead telling them that I was on my way and asking them to help me get settled and see that I had everything I needed. He was always interested in books and studying and I was just one of many students he helped that way. I guess you know he gave all the money he inherited from his father, something over a hundred thousand dollars, to Washington and Jefferson College."

The Mother House of the Sisters of St. Basil the Great in J. V. Thompson's old house is becoming an important link in the international religious life of the foreign community. It reaches its apotheosis in the August pilgrimage that began nine years ago. There were only three hundred worshippers that first season but interest has grown until in 1946, the peak year, 192 chartered busses and several thousand automobiles brought 60,000 people to the Mount.

On Sunday, services at ten pavilions throughout the grounds serve the crowd—some in Slavonic, others in Latin for the Roman congregations who share the festival with increasing interest. The pilgrimage lasts a week or more and ends on the afternoon of Labor Day in the series of devotions of the Eucharistic King following a night of worship when pilgrims stay in the lighted grounds all night, singing and visiting the chapels.

The Sisters have found a permanent home in Uniontown after many wanderings. Priests of the Catholic Church of the Byzantine Rite began to migrate to this country in the 1880's and 1890's but although they kept up the Eastern Ceremonial for their compatriots as well as they could, they had to work under Latin bishops because they had no regular diocese.

When there were 150 churches of the Eastern Rite, the priests petitioned Rome for an Episcopate. In 1907 Pope Pius X appointed the Reverend Stephen Soter Ortynsky, a monk from the Order of St. Basil the Great, as the first Greek Catholic Bishop for the Galicians and Pod-Carpathians in America.

After he was settled in Philadelphia he asked the Metropolitan Bishop of Lemberg to encourage some of the Sisters of St. Basil to immigrate to help with the work. The first three arrived in 1911 and opened a parochial school and orphanage for a hundred children. Between 1912 and 1913 five more nuns came, among them Reverend Mother Macrina, the present head of the Mother House in Uniontown.

Before long the Basilian Community was strong enough to start a *Ruzncia* where religious vestments are made, a printing-house and bookstore. Then Bishop Ortynsky died and the diocese separated into two territories, one for the Uhro-Rusins centering around Pittsburgh, one for the Galicians in the Philadelphia district.

Reverend Mother Macrina became Mother Superior of the Order in 1916 and on the petition of the Uhro-Rusins transferred to the Pittsburgh Diocese. They lived for a while in Cleveland, then in Elmhurst and Factoryville,

Pennsylvania, but the living quarters proved too small for the growing novitiate and the site too far removed from the members of their faith. They would have to look still farther for a settled home.

Just then the Sisters lost all their savings, $20,000, in the failure of two banks. So when they had a chance to buy Oak Hill, which was just what they wanted, it looked like an impossibility. The Union Trust Company of Pittsburgh asked $60,000. They had only three days to decide but in the end they managed to get a reduction to $50,000; Bishop Takach of the Uhro-Rusin Diocese, the Very Reverend Nickolas Chopey of Wilkesbarre, and certain Supreme Officers of the Sojedinenije (Greek Catholic Union) came to their rescue to raise the down payment of ten thousand dollars, and the deal was made. All that summer J. V. Thompson lay blind and sick in his dilapidated palace. After he died in the autumn, it passed to the Sisters.

The Mother House looks down on the busy National Pike from a smooth knoll at the western edge of Uniontown. With the coming of the last week in August a banner marked WELCOME PILGRIMS TO MOUNT SAINT MACRINA appears over Route 40 opposite the iron entrance-gates; the sloping lawns receive an extra trimming; the pasture lying on the other side of the drive toward town becomes a parking lot; wooden refreshment booths spring up along the walk to the retreat-houses, and a long pavilion rises on the old race track. The convent bell rings at intervals all day long, joyous and insistent now, very different from the solemn notes borne on the sulphur-laden fogs of early morning the rest of the year.

The congregation of St. John the Baptist in Uniontown opens the celebration with the first march of pilgrims up the hill. Inside the iron gates they crowd around their crucifer and an elderly bareheaded man with waxed mustaches carrying a spotless white satin banner edged with gold fringe and surmounted by a cross. The marchers are young and old, dark and fair; miners, clerks, business men, housewives, stenographers, and school girls; a few show their European origin but they are in the minority. Behind, cars are turning into the big parking lot. The sun is dazzling but the morning air is cool with a clean wind from the blue mountains blowing the smoke away.

The convent bell begins to ring, the crucifer and the banner-carrier start up the hill and the procession moves forward chanting in Slavonic the Pilgrim Song of their congregation. Other *otpusti* are standing farther along the drive by the ruined conservatory where Honey Thompson's guests used to while away the hot afternoons in the famous pool banked with tropical plants under the big glass roof. The two brick ends of the building still stand and the oval white-tiled pool has two or three feet of cloudy water in it but the glass dome that arched above it has disappeared.

As the procession passes the men and women by the roadside, they bow to the cross and fall in behind, singing. Many of the women carry bouquets of zinnias, gladioli, fox-glove, and asters bound with string and wrapped in wet newspaper. The morning wind flutters the gold fringe of the banner glancing in the sunlight and the chant swells louder.

When the pilgrims reach the half-moon drive that runs under the portico, a priest comes out to meet them from the Mother House; the banner dips three times, and he leads them through the cool reception hall to the Chapel of Our Lady of Perpetual Help that was once the Thompson French Room. A hot sweet breath blows out of it from the hundreds of votive lights in tiers on both sides of the *ikona* of the Mother and Child with the long sharp angles and flat treatment characteristic of Byzantine art, gorgeous with blue and gold and lighted by a circle of blue rosettes, each holding a tiny electric bulb.

Beyond in the shadowy main chapel, where Honey's roulette wheel used to spin, a nun noiselessly prepares the altar while the wind rustles through the open window into the twilight spiced with incense and flowers. In the pews kneel Ruthenian, Serbian, Galician, and Slovak mothers offering prayers of thanksgiving for sons who fought for America and came back safely, asking help to bear the grief for those who did not. Native-born Americans who take what we have here for granted do not realize the possessive love America's adopted children have for her. When they felt that the American Way was threatened they supported her loyally. Even though they miss their relatives in Europe, these Central European and Balkan peoples have no idea of going back to live. Their concern is how to get their kin-folks over here.

In the reception hall two nuns register the names and "Special Intentions" of pilgrims after they visit the chapels and assign sleeping quarters to those who come from a distance. The service of Renunciation when five sisters will take their final vows is about to begin and the big room is full of activity. The pilgrims with votive offerings lay them on tables in front of the statue of Christ with arms outstretched in blessing that stands on the left wall facing the grand staircase. By the door to the porch a woman is confessing with the long end of the priest's stole over her head while he leans over her to catch the words. A group of five little flower girls in organdy with flat rosettes of green maleen pinned to their hair, carrying baskets of asters in two shades of pink, appear from the Refectory wing and are shepherded by a nun into the small shrine with the *ikona*. Through the archway in the library hang the heavily embroidered vestments of satin and fine wool that the priests will wear during the week, some of them gifts of the Basilian Sisters in Europe, sumptuous with gold thread and crimson and ornamented with medallions in infinitesimal stitches.

Under the lofty columns of the front porch, facing the deep lawns that run down to the stone wall by the highway, there is a white and gold altar beneath the marquee with nuns taking their places in chairs to the left. The Host is carried through the reception hall to the altar on the porch and everyone sinks to his knees. Then the crowd goes out into the sunshine, filling the chairs to the right, crowding the steps in front of the marquee and perching on the balustrade.

The celebrant priest comes to the altar, a young man, fair-skinned and pale with black hair, chiselled profile and deep blue eyes, wearing a white brocade chasuble edged with embroidery in gold and flame color. The five flower girls reappear with the five Sisters about to take their Perpetual Vows carrying unlighted wax tapers, the five nuns who will assist with the ceremony, then Reverend Mother Macrina herself, middle-aged, with a wide mouth and keen intelligent eyes, a short figure of great dignity reminiscent of Queen Victoria. This summer she celebrated her twenty-fifth anniversary of service in the Sisterhood.

The five nuns about to make their final renunciation of the world kneel on the carpet facing the altar, their faces pale but tranquil. Two of them are exceptionally beautiful with the perfection that depends on structure rather than coloring. Their attendants take their places a little way behind them and the service begins. The candidates have already received their habit but now it is blessed, first the robe and then the scapular. Then the Reverend Mother Macrina gives each a plain gold wedding ring, a crucifix, rosary, a copy of the Rule of St. Basil, a black mantle, a veil with a black velvet cross, and a lighted candle. As the nuns receive each article they press it to their lips.

Now comes the high point of the service, the figurative death to the flesh, as the five prostrate themselves and are covered by a pall of black wool, edged with white and centered with a white cross. The sweet high voices of the nuns standing in ranks to the left rise in an ancient Slavonic chant, the five little girls strew flowers, and the sun beats down fiercely on the heavily shrouded figures under the square of black. One wonders when the pall is rolled back if all will be able to rise. When it is taken away each nun swears on the Bible that she renounces the world voluntarily and presents the priest with a signed statement confirming it.

Before taking this final step each nun will have been connected with the Order approximately eight years during which she was free to leave at any time. First she was a candidate for two months, then a postulant for six. If, after nearly two years acquaintance with the discipline she still wants to become a nun and if the Sisters of St. Basil think she is adapted to fit into their community, she enters the novitiate, dressed as a bride, wearing a bridal crown of green leaves and carrying the crown that would have been her husband's to hang upon the cross. She will remain a year and six weeks in the noviate, then take Simple Vows for three years and again for three years. All the way through, her remaining in the convent has been a two-way proposition depending on her willingness to stay and the Sisters' acceptance of her. Finally she is ready for the Vows that join her to the Order.

When the last nun has presented her signed statement the priest welcomes the group to their new status and celebrates Holy Communion, first for them and later for the congregation. There will be a sermon after that in Slovak with a general reassembling of the audience as some of the crowd leaves to walk around the grounds before lunch.

The benches near the statue of Our Lady of Victory in a little pool ringed with cannas and ageratum fill with elderly women in clean starched cottons and wrap-around turbans with blue satin *otpusti* ribbons pinned on their bosoms, knitting, telling their beads, singing the chants of their home villages. They have their own spontaneous service of worship all day long. Somebody starts a chant or the rosary any time and the others take it up, the song swelling in volume as it travels over the lawns. Many of the pilgrims have saved their money a whole year to get here and will stay the week.

Over the brow of the hill on a shady path stands a glassed-in kiosk housing a startlingly realistic figure of Christ on a blood-spattered cross, a conception more Eastern than Western, the knees horribly abraded, forearms gashed, with cuts on the chest, and an inhumanly beautiful face sagging under a crown of thorns.

To the right, beyond a little grove, nuns with checkered aprons over their habits serve plates of steaming goulash, hamburgers, and coffee in an open-air cafeteria by the brick academy that was once the stable where the Thompson thoroughbreds used to stamp and nibble their feedboxes. Now it houses a religious-articles store, a laundry which has to take care of the sheets and spreads from some five hundred beds during the pilgrimage, a restaurant and needlework shop with a dormitory for pilgrims above, lined with smooth single beds separated by screens.

A Sister stands at the entrance to the tiled courtyard in front of the building offering chances on a handsome crocheted bedspread. Within the enclosure along the wall of the yard, black-robed nuns sell postal cards, booklets, and *makovniki*—honey cakes with pink icing and holy pictures on top. In Europe where pilgrims went to their shrines on foot, travelling sometimes many days, often sleeping in the fields, they wanted to bring back something from the Holy Place for those of their families and friends who could not make the trip. And so it became the custom to buy the little ornamented *makovniki* because they were inexpensive and easy to carry as well as being mixed stiffly enough to last all year long without breaking. The custom has carried over to America.

Farther down the walk a pale young Sister sits by the door of a grotto with big green glass crystals on the pediment and banks of votive candles in red glass holders winking within. The porches of the Retreat Houses are crowded with pilgrims and day-guests, with nuns acting as hostesses, gentle and remote in their long robes with swinging crucifixes. The greenhouses lie below with beds of salvia, petunias, asters, gladioli, and zinnias. Close by five little boys crowd up to a wire enclosure where black and white goats sit thinking in the tall grass.

Below on the old race track a row of men stand along the counter of an open pavilion drinking beer in the sunshine while behind them young couples stroll around the grassy course. It is surprising to see how much there is left of it after nearly forty years. Some of the roadway has gone back to the turf but the fine grading of the stretch is still good.

To the right lie the vegetable gardens with their grapevines, beans and cabbages. J. V. Thompson must be pleased that the devout, thrifty people who live at Oak Hill have made it beautiful again. And he would like the crowds who come from all over the Coke Region and beyond to walk in his sunny lawns and woods.

New busloads arrive all times of day. The pilgrims from a distance organize for the journey in their home parish and on the morning of their departure assemble at the church for the priest's blessing for themselves and the bus they have chartered to take them. They spend much of the time they are on the road in private prayer, reciting the rosary antiphonally, and singing hymns, but there are intervals of talk and laughter.

When they drive down to the oval of the race track reserved for chartered busses they form in line behind their banner-carrier and the crucifer with his tall cross wreathed in flowers, the convent bell rings in welcome and, singing, they start for the Mother House without waiting to eat or freshen up.

In the shrine after lowering the banner three times in reverence to the Holy Picture, one of the pilgrims chosen for the office gives the greeting, which translated runs something like this: "We have come a long way, Blessed Mother. Some of us are very tired and hungry and we hope you will accept our slight discomfort as a little offering given in love and intercede for us with your Divine Son."

A visitor to the pilgrimage comes away with a store of colorful memories he would be sorry to lose; the passionate wordless prayers of a middle-aged woman in white with a thin haggard face and lean tanned arms and how she kissed each picture in the Prayer Book before she turned the page as she went through the Devotions of the Stations of the Cross; the little old woman, fat and brown, in a long black coat buttoned tightly to the throat, her hair concealed by a black silk scarf with the ends tucked in, wearing felt bedroom-slippers with pompons and carrying a paper market bag, and how she put her hand on the glass of each picture at the Stations and then on her forehead, crossing herself not once but many times, always lagging behind the other worshippers because she kept stopping to look back at the last Holy Picture after the procession had passed to the next; the serene beauty of the young nun at the cash register in the outdoor pavilion; and the look on the face of a tall soldier with a deep purple scar cleaving one cheek as he paused to look in the open door of the dim shrine beyond the Chapel to the peace of the white altar with its angels with spread wings, candles, and pink flowers.

The future of the Coke Region is uncertain, apparently about to go into a reverse curve, but whatever comes, the people are conditioned to change. When Hamilton's Excise Tax spoiled the whiskey business they turned to iron manufacture. When the charcoal-fired cold-blast furnaces used up the forests, they made a good living from the travellers on the Cumberland Road. The railroads took away the customers but by that time the coal business was on its way in, due for a long stay.

Now with the Nine-foot coal almost exhausted we need another miracle, and because America is still young and the people flexible it won't fail us.

APPENDIX A

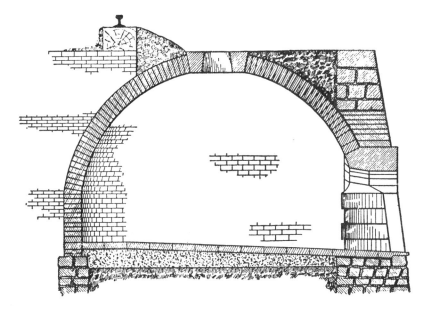

FIGURE 1.—Section of a standard beehive oven.

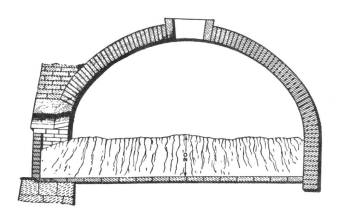

FIGURE 2.—Section of a standard beehive oven with a charge of coke in place.

Reprinted from BUREAU OF MINES INVESTIGATIONS 3738

APPENDIX B

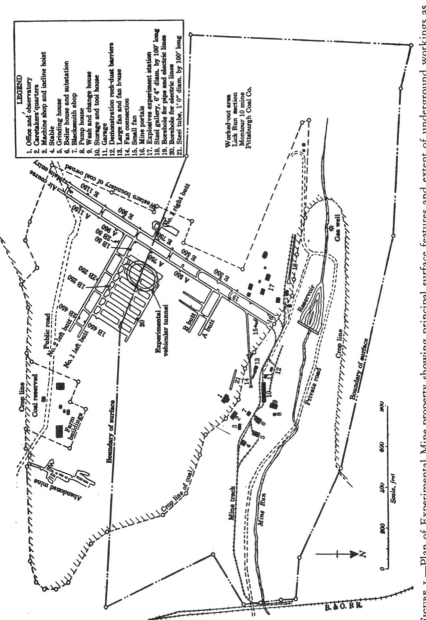

FIGURE 1.—Plan of Experimental Mine property showing principal surface features and extent of underground workings as of June 1933.

"*Reprinted from* U. S. BUREAU OF MINES CIRCULAR 6755"

LEGEND

1. Office and observatory
2. Caretakers' quarters
3. Machine shop and incline hoist
4. Stable
5. Grinding house
6. Boiler house and substation
7. Blacksmith shop
8. Pump house
9. Wash and change house
10. Storage and tool house
11. Garage
12. Demonstration rock-dust barriers
13. Large fan and fan house
14. Fan connection
15. Small fan
16. Mine portals
17. Explosives experiment station
18. Steel gallery, 6'4" diam. by 100' long
19. Borehole for pipe and electric lines
20. Borehole for electric lines
21. Steel tube, 1'0" diam. by 100' long

Worked-out area
Lick Run section
Montour 10 mine
Pittsburgh Coal Co.

SELECTED BIBLIOGRAPHY

Ashmead, Dever C., *Modern Rectangular Coke Oven Plant*. Tarrytown, N. Y. Pamphlet. n.p., n.d.

Atwater, R. M., *The Effect of Coke Oven Construction on Coke*. Proceedings of the Engineers Society of Western Pennsylvania, 1896. Vol. XII.

"Beehive and By-Product Coke," *Coal Age*, Vol. XV, No. 2, p. 619.

Bining, Arthur Cecil, *Pennsylvania Iron Manufacture in the Eighteenth Century*. Publications of Pennsylvania Historical Commission. Harrisburg, 1938. Vol. IV.

Campbell, Alton G., "The Pioneer Iron Industry," an historical paper published in a collection entitled *Fort Necessity and Historic Shrines of the Redstone Country*. Privately printed, Uniontown, Pa.

Carr, Charlotte E., Secretary, *Labor and Industry in the Depression*, Commonwealth of Pennsylvania Department of Labor and Industry Bulletin No. 39. Harrisburg, 1934.

Catlett, Charles, "Coking in Beehive Ovens with Reference to Yield." New Haven Meeting, October, 1902. *American Institute of Mining Engineers' Transactions*, XXXIII, 272-81. Staunton, Virginia.

Conditions in the Coal Fields of Pennsylvania, West Virginia and Ohio. Hearings before the Committee on Interstate Commerce, United States Senate. Washington: Government Printing Office, 1928. 2 vols.

"Connellsville Coke in 1917," *Coal Age*, Vol. XIII, No. 3.

Connellsville Courier (newspaper). November 25, 1915; December 23, 1915; July 20, 1916; November 16, 1916; December 14, 1916; May 17, 1917; June 7, 1917; June 23, 1917; November 15, 1917.

Cook, Robert A., "The Newton Chambers System of Saving the By-Products of Coke Manufacture in Beehive Coke Ovens." Pittsburgh Meeting, February, 1896. *American Institute of Mining Engineers' Transactions*, Vol. XXVI. New Brunswick, New Jersey.

D'Invilliers, Edward V., "Estimated Costs of Mining and Coking and Relative Commercial Returns from Operating in the Connellsville and Walston-

Reynoldsville District, Pennsylvania," *American Institute of Mining Engineers' Transactions,* Vol. XXXV. Philadelphia, 1905.

Eavenson, Howard N., *The First Century and a Quarter of American Coal Industry.* Pittsburgh: Koppers Building, 1942.

Ellis, Franklin, *History of Fayette County.* Philadelphia: J. B. Lippincott and Co., 1882.

Evening Genius (Uniontown newspaper). March 15–September 10, 1894; January 18, 1915; June 30, 1917; October 13, 1917.

Evening Genius Supplement, Illustrated Industrial Edition. Uniontown and vicinity, October, 1901.

Evening Standard (Uniontown newspaper). June 8–10, 1944.

Forbes, J. J. and Humphry, H. B., *Explosions in Pennsylvania Coal Mines,* 1870–1932. U. S. Bureau of Mines Information Circular No. 6710. Department of Commerce: May, 1933.

Fulton, John, *Coke: A Treatise on the Manufacture of Coke and Other Prepared Fuels and the Saving of By-Products.* Scranton, Pa.: International Textbook Co., 1906.

Gans, John L., *Beehive Oven Supremacy Passing But Not Yet Passed. Coal Age,* Vol. XV, No. 14, p. 618-20. Attached Table Comparative Coke Production in the U. S., 1893–1918.

Gazette Times (Pittsburgh newspaper). January 24, 1915; April 9, 1915; December 20, 1916.

Genius of Liberty (Uniontown newspaper). March 15–September 10, 1894; week of November 9, 1904; January 5, 1905.

Greenwald, H. P., *What Do We Know about the Explosibility of Coal Dust in Mines?* U. S. Bureau of Mines Information Circular No. 6112. Department of Commerce: April, 1929.

Hadden, James, *A History of Uniontown, Pennsylvania.* Privately printed, 1913.

Harris, George W., "Changes in Beehive Coke Oven Construction Due to Mechanical Operation," *Coal Age,* Vol. XV, No. 2.

Harvey George, *Henry Clay Frick—The Man.* Scribner's, New York, 1928.

Hoon, Rev. C. D., "Albert Gallatin and Friendship Hill," an historical paper published in a collection entitled *Fort Necessity and Historic Shrines of the Redstone Country.* Privately printed: Uniontown, Pa.

Hustead, James E., "Christopher Gist and His Settlement," an historical paper published in a collection entitled *Fort Necessity and Historic Shrines of the Redstone Country.* Privately printed, Uniontown, Pa.

"Jameson's Oven," *American Institute of Mining Engineers' Transactions,* Vol. XXI.

Joiner, Fred, "Agreements of Gas Coke and Chemical Workers," (District No. 50 U.M.W.). Prepared under the direction of the Bureau's Industrial Relations' Division. *Monthly Labor Review,* April, 1939. No. R 927 U. S. Department of Labor.

Kelley, S. J., *W. J. Rainey.* A reminiscence in manuscript form loaned by Mrs. H. D. Hutchinson of the Uniontown Public Library.

King, C. D., *The Washing of Pittsburgh Coking Coals and Results Obtained* on *Blast Furnaces*. American Institute of Mining Engineers' publication No. 1618.

Kirk, W. F., *Wages and Hours of Labor in Bituminous Coal Mining* (1933). Bureau of Labor Statistics Bulletin No. 61.

Luty, B. E. V., "Connellsville and the By-Product Coke Industries in 1919," *Coal Age*, Vol. XVII, No. 3.

Matuschak, Joseph P., *How to Become a Citizen of the United States and Questions for the Prospective Citizen*. Uniontown, Pa.: Acme Press, . Pamphlet.

Mercer, Henry C., *The Bible in Iron*. Bucks County Historical Society. Doylestown, 1914.

Mine Safety Board, *Mine Safety Board Decision 32: Prevention of Coal Dust Explosions by Rock Dusting*. U. S. Bureau of Mines Information Circular No. 7109. Department of the Interior: March, 1940.

Morning Herald (Uniontown newspaper). January 18–December 31, 1915; files for years 1916–17; May 20–June 4, 1928; August 27–September 2, 1943; July 23–November 22, 1933; June 9, 1944, March 15–June 15, 1946; October 15–December 15, 1946.

Morris, Homer L., *The Plight of the Bituminous Coal Miner*. Philadelphia: University of Pennsylvania Press, 1934.

Nebesnaja Manna. A Practical Prayer Book of Devotions for Greek Catholics. Published by the Order of the Sisters of St. Basil, 1941.

New York Times (newspaper). August 6, 1933; November 24, 1946.

News Standard (Uniontown newspaper). July 26–November 22, 1933.

News Standard Supplement. "The Coal and Coke Industrial Review," October 21, 1913.

O'Connor, Harvey, *Mellon's Millions—The Life and Times of Andrew W. Mellon*. New York: The John Day Co., 1933.

Peterson, Florence, *Strikes in the United States, 1880–1936*. Bureau of Labor Statistics Bulletin No. 651. Department of Labor, August, 1937.

Philadelphia Ledger (newspaper). January 7, 1917.

Pittsburgh Dispatch (newspaper). January 20–21, 1913; November 20, 1915; February 19, 1916.

Pittsburgh Leader (newspaper). December 30, 1915; December 26–27, 1916.

Pittsburgh Press (newspaper). January 21, 1913; December 30–31, 1930; January 2, 1931.

Report of the United States Coal Commission (1923). Washington: Government Printing Office, 1925. Part I.

Report of the United States Immigration Bureau, 1911–12. Chart I.

Report of the United States Immigration Bureau, 1912–13. Chart II.

"Report on the Mather Explosion," *Coal Age*, Vol. XXXIII, No. 6.

Republican Standard (Uniontown newspaper). December, 1882–June, 1883.

Rice, G. S., and others, *The Experimental Mine of the United States Bureau of Mines*. U. S. Bureau of Mines Information Circular No. 6755. Department of Commerce: November, 1933.

Robie, Edward H., "Not Enough Coal," *Mining and Metallurgy*, XXV (1944), 554.

Scott, G. S., and others, *Modern Beehive Coke Oven Practice*. Preliminary Report. U. S. Bureau of Mines Report of Investigation No. R 13738. December, 1943.

Searight, Thomas B., *The Old Pike*, Uniontown, Pa., 1894.

Senate Report 76th Congress, *Violations of Free Speech and Rights of Labor*. Subcommittee on Senate Resolution 266 of 74th Congress, Robert M. La Follette, Jr., Chairman, "Strike Breaking Services," Report No. 6. Washington: Government Printing Office, 1939.

Service Book of the Russian Orthodox Church (English Translation).

Shalloo, J. P., *Private Police—With Special Reference to Pennsylvania*. The American Academy of Political and Social Science, Philadelphia, 1933.

Shoemaker, H. W., *The Man Pinchot*. A pamphlet reprint from *Altoona Tribune*.

A Short History of the Sisters of Saint Basil the Great in the United States of North America. Souvenir Book of Dedication of the Mother House. McKeesport, Pa.: Printing plant of United Societies of Greek Catholic Religion, 1934.

Standard (Uniontown newspaper). March 15–September 10, 1894.

Sun Telegraph (Pittsburgh newspaper). March 23, 1932; July 26–November 22, 1933.

Time Magazine. File for March, April, May, June, October, November, and December, 1946.

Trends in the Bituminous Coal Industry in Pennsylvania. Department of Commerce, Commonwealth of Pennsylvania. State Planning Board, Harrisburgh, Pa., VII (September, 1940), No. 2.

Truesdell, Leon E., *Population Second Series Pennsylvania*. Sixteenth Census of the United States. Department of Commerce, Bureau of the Census. Washington: Government Printing Office, 1942.

Veech, James, *The Monongahela of Old*. Privately distributed, 1892.

Wiley, Richard T., *Monongahela: The River and Its Region*. Butler, Pa.: The Ziegler Press, 1937.

Weeks, Joseph S., "The Elk Garden and Upper Potomac Coal Fields of West Virginia." Virginia Beach Meeting. *American Institute of Mining Engineers' Transactions*, XXIV, 351-64.

Zernov, Nickolas, *The Church of the Eastern Christians*. Society for Promoting Christian Knowledge. London, 1942.

———, *Explanatory Notes to a Manual of Eastern Orthodox Prayers*. Society for the Fellowship of SS Alban and Sergius. London, 1945.